DEVELOPMENT AND THE ARTS:
Critical Perspectives

Drawing by Leonard Baskin.

DEVELOPMENT AND THE ARTS:
Critical Perspectives

Edited by

Margery B. Franklin
Sarah Lawrence College

Bernard Kaplan
Clark University

Routledge
Taylor & Francis Group

LONDON AND NEW YORK

First published 1994 by Lawrence Erlbaum Associates, Inc.

Published 2018 by Routledge
2 Park Square, Milton Park, Abingdon, Oxon OX14 4RN
52 Vanderbilt Avenue, New York, NY 10017

First issued in paperback 2018

Routledge is an imprint of the Taylor & Francis Group, an informa business

Cover design by Gabriela Goldschmidt

Michelangelo, *The Rome Pietà*. St. Peter's Basilica, Vatican State. Detail. Alinari/Art Resource, New York.

Leonard Baskin, Remembered Portrait of Eakins, 1981. Pen and ink with watercolor, $15\frac{1}{2} \times 11$". Photograph courtesy of Kennedy Galleries, Inc., New York.

Library of Congress Cataloging-in-Publication Data

Development and the arts : critical perspectives / edited by Margery
  B. Franklin & Bernard Kaplan.
    p.   cm.
  Includes bibliographical references and indexes.
  ISBN-0-8058-0487-0
  1. Artists—Psychology.   2. Aesthetics.   I. Franklin, Margery B.
II. Kaplan, Bernard.
N71.D495   1994
701'.15—dc20   93-33565
                                                       CIP

ISBN 13: 978-1-138-87607-1 (pbk)
ISBN 13: 978-0-8058-0487-4 (hbk)

Contents

Contributors

Leonard Baskin
Northampton, Massachusetts

Sidney J. Blatt
Department of Psychiatry
School of Medicine
Yale University
New Haven, Connecticut

Bernard Kaplan
Department of Psychology
& Heinz Werner Institute
Clark University
Worcester, Massachusetts

Margery B. Franklin
Psychology Faculty
Sarah Lawrence College
Bronxville, New York

Mark Freeman
Department of Psychology
College of the Holy Cross
Worcester, Massachusetts

Gabriela Goldschmidt
Faculty of Architecture and
Town Planning
Technion—Israel Institute of
Technology
Haifa, Israel

Hilde S. Hein
Department of Philosophy
College of the Holy Cross
Worcester, Massachusetts

Robert S. Liebert, M.D. (deceased)
Columbia University
Psychoanalytic Center for
Training & Research
New York, New York

Louis A. Sass
Department of Clinical
Psychology
Rutgers University
Piscataway, New Jersey

Marx W. Wartofsky
Department of Philosophy
Bernard Baruch College,
City University of New York
New York, New York

Dennis Palmer Wolf
Graduate School of Education
Harvard University
Cambridge, Massachusetts

Preface

The chapters in this volume are, with two exceptions, based on presentations at the conference, "Development and the Arts," which was convened at Clark University in October 1987, under the auspices of the Heinz Werner Institute for Developmental Analysis. The presenters at the conference included psychologists, philosophers, a psychiatrist, an architect, and an artist. The selection of participants reflects one of the aims of the Heinz Werner Institute: to promote dissemination of ideas among scholars and practitioners from different disciplines. The program was designed to realize another principal aim of the Institute: to promote critical consideration of the concept of development—in this case, in relation to the arts: in theoretical/critical discourse, in analyses of the child's work and the adult artist's, and in the discussion of art history.

Unfortunately, two papers presented at the conference could not be included in the present volume. These were "Computers and the Art of Children: The Research of Joachim F. Wohlwill, 1984–1987," by Susan D. Wills, Maryellen Degnan, and Michael J. Rovine, and "Development in the Visual Arts: Basic Skills, Visual Schemas and Creativity" by Ellen Winner. We take this occasion to acknowledge the value of these contributions to the program. Two chapters have been prepared for this publication: "Narratives of Change and Continuity: Women Artists Reflect on their Work" by Margery B. Franklin, and "A Response to Wartofsky" by Sidney J. Blatt. The 12 chapters are arranged under four headings: *Concepts of Development in the Arts, Artistic Processes in*

Ontogenesis, Development of the Artist, and *Development in the History of Art.*

A number of years have elapsed between the conference and the publication of this volume. Interestingly, the issues raised concerning the concept of development, and its use in relation to domains such as the arts, are at least as timely now as they were then.

The idea for holding a conference on development and the arts under the auspices of the Heinz Warner Institute first occurred in a conversation among Jack Wohlwill, Seymour Wapner, and Margery Franklin. Jack Wohlwill and Margery Franklin became members of the planning committee headed by the Executive Committee of the Heinz Werner Institute: Seymour Wapner, Bernard Kaplan, and Leonard Cirillo. We take this occasion to acknowledge Jack's contribution not only to the planning of the program but to our scholarly lives. His untimely death deprived us of his presence at the conference, and in the years since. Another contributor to the program, Robert Liebert, died about a year after the conference. Colleague and friend, he is sorely missed.

We wish to express our appreciation to a number of people who have contributed to work on this book. During the conference, and throughout the first phases of preparing the manuscript for publication, Florence Resnik provided generous assistance. Hollis Heimbouch, our editor at Lawrence Erlbaum Associates, was helpful and forebearing throughout the seemingly endless process of bringing the project to conclusion. Teresa Faella, the production editor for this volume, has been a resourceful guide in the final phases. Jim Dillon undertook the difficult task of preparing the indexes. Finally, we wish to express our continuing appreciation to Seymour Wapner and Leonard Cirillo.

Margery B. Franklin
Bernard Kaplan

Introduction

In recent years, the concept of development, so often taken for granted as to its direction and telos, has become increasingly problematic. In some quarters, the very application of *development*, with its connotations of unilinearity and progress, has been severely questioned. In other quarters, the idea of development has not itself been contested but the particular goals or teloi of development assumed or posited by one or another developmental theorist have been challenged. Although most psychologists are familiar with and utilize certain canonical theories or approaches to development (viz., those of Freud, Piaget, Vygotsky, Werner), it is important to recognize that these theoretical perspectives are typically specifications of a more generic developmental orientation toward phenomena of mind. Among the domains in which theorists and their followers have sought to apply one or another of the canonical theories is that of Art. To be sure, a number of scholars (e.g., Suzanne Langer) have concerned themselves with the entire range of what is usually called *art*: dance, music, drama, literature, painting, and sculpture. The chapters in this volume are addressed solely to the pertinence of concepts of development to the visual and plastic arts.

Chapters are arranged under four headings, with the inevitable overlap that marks any such grouping.

Of the three chapters in the first section, *Concepts of Development in the Domain of the Arts*, the two chapters by Bernard Kaplan and Hilde Hein are focally concerned with the meanings of *development*, with special reference to artistic phenomena. The third, by Louis Sass, critically explores the pertinence of one of the canonical theories to distinctive aspects of 20th-century art.

The second section, *Artistic Processes in Ontogenesis*, was originally designed to emphasize changes in artistic production over the course of ontogenesis. As noted in the preface, we regret that two of the proposed contributions to this section unfortunately had to be omitted from this volume. The two chapters included, by Dennis Wolf and Gabriela Gold-schmidt, approach ontogenesis of artistic production in quite different ways. Wolf infuses her examination of changes in drawing with close consideration of theoretical issues in developmental psychology. Gold-schmidt uses her study of children and students of architecture to recon-ceptualize the design process in developmental terms without tying her inquiry to any traditional developmental theory.

Our third section, *Development of the Artist*, is devoted to individual artists, looked at from the inside and the outside. The first chapter, by the world-renowned graphic artist and sculptor, Leonard Baskin, highlights the importance for himself (and, implicitly, for other artists) of working in several media, of resisting cultural and professional pressures toward restrictive specialization. He urges us to immerse ourselves in, and to try to master, as many media as we can manage. Robert Liebert, in the second chapter, exploits propositions and concepts of classical psychoanalytic theory to illuminate Michelangelo's selection of medium and motifs in the evolution of his artistic work. In the third chapter, Mark Freeman, drawing on interviews with a certain type of postmodern artist, argues against the pertinence of canonical developmental theories for understanding the factors that shape an artistic career; stressing the role of sociocultural and market factors influencing media, mode, and subject matter, Freeman challenges certain notions of self-propelled artistic change, the artist simply following his or her own drummer. In the final chapter of this section, Margery Franklin, drawing on intensive interviews with seven women artists, examines artists' views of change and continuity in their work and explores the consonance of these views with certain tenets advanced by canonical developmental theory.

The fourth and final section of this volume, *On Development in the History of Art*, is devoted to the pertinence and relevance of developmental theory to the history of art. In the initial chapter, Sidney Blatt seeks to demonstrate the value of Piaget's work on the development of spatial thought to an appreciation of transformations in visual art from prehistoric to modern times. In the next chapter, Marx Wartofsky not only critically examines Blatt's use of Piagetian theory for an understanding of a history of art but also raises a number of fundamental questions concerning the application of *any* developmental theory to the *history* of art. In the final chapter, Blatt takes the opportunity to respond to Wartofsky's critique.

One of the principal issues, as we see it, is the one raised by Kaplan in the initial chapter of this volume: Is a concept of development relevant to art? This question may be paraphrased as addressing the issue of the "fit" or consonance of one or another canonical developmental scheme to phenomena of artistic activity—whether in ontogenesis, in the individual artist, or the history of art.

At one extreme, we have some who appropriate either the generic schema of development or propositions within a specific developmental approach and seek to apply that schema or those concepts either to choices of medium and motif of particular artists, or to historical changes in artistic styles. Thus, neither Liebert nor Blatt question the developmental framework they use but rather exploit that framework for the interpretation of the phenomena they seek to encompass.

At the other extreme, some theorists—such as Hein, in this volume— seem to maintain that any concept of development, insofar as it connotes hierarchy, progress, differential and invidious evaluation, is a masculinist or phallocentric project and, as applied to the domain of art or elsewhere, invariably serves to stigmatize or deprecate the activities and productions of women. There is even some suggestion that any current concept of development is antagonistic to the activity of women—that is, construes the activity of women in terms of the values of men.

The majority of the other chapters fall between these extremes. Thus Sass, while perhaps acknowledging the relevance of psychoanalytic notions of motivation and thought to 19th-century artistic movements, rejects the adequacy of such concepts for an understanding of modernism and postmodernism. Specifically, he strongly contests the invocation of primitive processes as the wellspring of creative activity. Wolf, apparently rejecting any canonical theory that proposes a unilinear sequence of stages, does not reject developmental conceptualization *in toto*. Rather, drawing on Werner, Darwin, and other sources, she seeks to construct a new kind of developmental approach that respects diversity and multilinearity. Freeman, restive with universalistic schemes of development, and seriously questioning the autonomy of the artist, foregrounds cultural and economic contingencies that may facilitate or preclude the artist's construction of his or her professional telos. Franklin senses a lack of fit between any of the canonical theories and the self-understanding of their own development among the seven women artists she studied; rather than describing their work in terms of a unilinear, progressive sequence, these artists used metaphors of gathering, of wheels, matrices, and paths that return to their starting point. One might consider here Leonard Baskin's eloquent reflections on his own artistic development in relation to the reflections of the women artists in Franklin's study.

Finally, we may mention both Kaplan's and Wartofsky's chapters that touch on the same theme in somewhat different ways. Whereas Kaplan raises the question of the relevance of a concept of development to art, Wartofsky cogently demonstrates the typical inapplicability of such developmental concepts to the history of art.

This collection of essays does not bring us to a definitive conclusion about the relevance of developmental concepts to artistic experience and artistic production, but moves the study of art and human development away from a circumscribed concern with ontogenesis and opens the way for further consideration of development with respect to many domains of artistic endeavor.

Concepts of Development
in the Domain of the Arts

1

Is a Concept of Development Applicable to Art?

Bernard Kaplan
Clark University

At the beginning of his classic work, *The Elementary Forms of Religious Life*, Emile Durkheim (1915) remarks:

> If we are going to look for the most primitive and simple religion which we can observe, it is necessary to begin by defining what is meant by a religion for without this, we would run the risk of giving the name to a system of ideas which has nothing at all religious about it, or else of leaving to one side many religious facts, without perceiving their true nature. That this is not an imaginary danger, and that nothing is thus sacrificed to a vain formalism of method, is well shown by the fact that owing to his not having taken this precaution, a certain scholar to whom the science of comparative religion owes a great deal, Professor Frazer, has not been able to recognize the profoundly religious character of the beliefs and rites which will be studied below, where according to our view, the initial germ of the religious life of humanity is to be found. So this is a prejudicial question, which must be treated before all others. It is not that we dream of arriving at once at the profound characteristics which really explain religion; these can be determined only at the end of our study. But that which is necessary and possible, is to indicate a certain number of external and easily recognizable signs, which will enable us to recognize religious phenomena wherever they are met with, and which will deter us from confounding them with others. (pp. 37–38)

It should be obvious, mutatis mutandis, that the point that Durkheim makes with regard to the circumscription of the domain of religion applies as well to what one would take as *Art*. Before one can undertake to discuss the application of developmental concepts to Art, one must establish, provisionally, what falls within and what outside the domain of Art, and give at least tentative reasons for such a definition.

My second quotation comes from an editorial by John Fisher (1986) in *The Journal of Aesthetics and Art Criticism*:

There once was a pleasant kingdom by the sea, secure from enemies within and without, and governed by a beloved and benevolent despot. What was most remarkable about the place was that everyone in the kingdom was an artist—not only a painter, but a poet, composer and performer as well. True, few earned their livelihood by the arts, but every citizen was encouraged to be creative. From the earliest age children threw paint on paper, and expressed themselves with fervor by chanting original and profound lyrics, while pounding on or blowing through inexpensive instruments which the kingdom provided. When they became adults they threw pigments on canvases and expressed themselves with fervor by pounding on or blowing through expensive instruments purchased from the gate receipts from their concerts. Others wore berets and painted realistically with brushes and palette knives, and played the lute and the lyre, the rebec, the viol, the psaltry, and the tambor. All of the visual works were displayed quite democratically in travelling shows throughout the kingdom, and all of the music was performed at one time or another in the castle concert hall.

Few ever talked about the works in the kingdom by the sea because it was not permitted that anyone should make critical judgments about the works of the artists. Not that one would be fined or imprisoned for making appraisals or comparisons. The punishment was simply widespread ridicule, for it was well known that grading or comparing artworks was rooted in an ancient and discredited mythology. Art is expressing oneself, everyone knew, and no one but the artist knows when that is taking place.

One evening some friends were relaxing in a cellar by the castle wall. One chap, Walthur was his name, sipped from a bowl of fermented honey, then spat it out in disgust, saying, 'That's just awful! It's really bad. The worst mead I ever tasted!' Now performing in the cellar that night was a very popular group called The Cagey Bees, which played music in a raucous two chord style which was destined to become the precursor of all future cellar music. The lead singer of the group . . . stopped in mid-consonant and sternly (for The Cagey Bees felt very strongly about art and society) rebuked the speaker. 'No, no,' he remonstrated. 'What you mean is that it doesn't please you. No mead is good or bad. In fact mead doesn't exist until it is tasted. Up until then it is just stuff in a bowl. The brewer makes the stuff, the drinker makes the mead when he drinks it.'

Of course, his interest was in something much more important than mead. Interrupting a set in the cellar had to be occasioned by a grave concern for what all this could mean for the arts. Unless this threat were nipped in the bud

one could soon expect all sorts of judgments being made about music and poetry,
sculpture and needlework, with dire consequences for the serenity of the kingdom.
What we don't need, he muttered to himself, is this irresponsible objectivism
which insists that mead or anything else can be good or bad. (italics added,
pp. 115–116)

I've given you enough of Fisher's contemporary fairy tale to highlight
his point and to provide the occasion for me to make mine. Just as the
concept of Art requires some circumscription, so too does the concept of
Development.

I have several times elsewhere, and not a few would say ad nauseum,
insisted that development be distinguished from *change, history,* and
evolution; that it be recognized as a *normative* concept, in terms of which
one discriminates between more primitive and more advanced, lower
and higher, worse and better; that is, I take it that the concept of
development ought to be, as it has typically been in the past, intimately
linked with the idea of *progress* (Kaplan, 1983, 1986). A caveat! It is not
that I think the notion of progress itself to be unproblematic, or
impervious to contestation. Not at all! Progress, development, in my view
is always relative to some actual or as yet unrealized state of affairs or
condition taken as *telos* or *goal,* and different teloi will entail different
kinds of progress, different kinds of development. Thus, Freud's development is different from Piaget's, Gilligan's (1982) is different from
Kohlberg's (1981), and the telos of those who have taken mimesis as the
goal of art is different from those who have opted for expression of
emotions, or from those who have altogether rejected art as representation, whether of the outside or inside world. But even while
recognizing that progress or development is recurrently subject to
dispute, I see no point or value in collapsing the idea of development
into that of mere change over time, whether in the sociocosmos or in the
microcosmos, in collective history or individual history. Although it
was once widely believed that an *immanent law of progress* informed
change, history, and evolution—and this belief still seems to operate in
some quarters—we should realize, I urge, that neither progress nor
development can be read off from the mere facts of change over time,
either in the actual social order or in the individual member of a social
order.

It should now be apparent that the issues I want to raise here are
straightforward. As a specification of my general concern with what it is
that is being referred to when one speaks of the development of this or
that, I would like to understand what it is that people are talking about
when they refer to development taking place either in the sphere of Art
in general or in any one of the Arts.

With regard to the sphere of Art, I begin with the conviction that we have to at least know what we are talking about when we refer to Art, whether in the productions of children and older beings in the course of a life span, or in the changing productions of those who have assumed the *vocation* of artist, whether in a single medium or in diverse media, or in the changes that have occurred in history whether the history of architecture, painting, sculpture, music, dance, drama, poetry, or whatever.

Now, I have already alluded to the fact that I hold a certain view of development or attribute a certain meaning to the term *development*. Development, I take it, in perhaps a neo-Aristotelian fashion, is movement toward *perfection* and characteristically entails what Werner and I (Werner & Kaplan, 1963/1983) have called *the orthogenetic principle*, increasing differentiation and hierarchic integration. But, although I have a brief for that view, I should stress that I have no axe to grind here nor do I explicitly attempt to impose that conception of development on others. Or, perhaps, it would be more honest to say that I merely grind my axe under the cover of night, presupposing it in part in the questions I direct to others when they speak of the development of Art or one of another of the Arts, whether in ontogenesis, in the careers of those who have baptized themselves or been baptized as artists, or those who speak of development in the history of Art or one of the specific Arts.

I am genuinely trying to find out what it is that those who study "artful scribbles" or architectural design mean when they refer to the development of children's drawings or to children's plans for constructions. I would like to know what one means when one refers to the development of painting in the history of the art of painting. I repeat, neither Project Zero aficionados nor psychoanalytically oriented investigators need to take on my conception of development, but I would like to know to what conception of development they subscribe, and what it is they discern when they speak of development as distinct from mere change or continuities and discontinuities in historical sequences.

Allow me to expand upon this issue briefly. In his *Grammar of Motives*, in the section on Antinomies of Substance, Kenneth Burke (1945) makes the point that, despite the seeming elimination of the term *substance* from the categories of all of science and some philosophy, the function of the concept of substance continues to persist in our thought and discourse. In speaking of the development of anything, including Art, do we not presuppose an ongoing substance or a One that, furthermore, undergoes change? Do we not typically talk of and think about development as a process where one deals with more and other than merely a multiplicity of different forms or manifestations? Thus, if we refer to the development of, let us say, painting, it does not suffice, conceptually, to take a series of paintings by different individuals and speak either of development or change (as contrasted with difference) unless we articulate what is the one or unity that presumably undergoes either development or change in the course of time. *Ex hypothesi*, the one is not the painter or the artist, as might be the case, for example, in the instance of Picasso, whose different versions of *Guernica* Rudolf Arnheim (1962) has explored; or with respect to musical compositions, a Beethoven or Mozart, whose symphonies may all be related to a single composer, however problematic such a presumed unity of the artist may be. What I am asking for here is some clarification from those who speak of development, as to the nature of the *substance* of which development, or even change, is predicated, whether that substance be taken as a "fiction," propelled into the arena of discourse by the interests of reason or some kind of ontological entity.

My second point, assuming that such a substance has been decided on, pertains to the distinction between change per se and development. What are the criteria that one invokes in characterizing certain changes, in art or elsewhere, when one speaks of a development from Occasion A to Occasion B, where B is later in time than A, or throughout a time series?

* * *

I assume that when we speak of the development of Art, whether in general or with respect to a specific realm, we presuppose the *autonomy of art*. Not that works of art have to be considered, as some of the New Critics insisted or are taken to have insisted, as independent of socioeconomic determinants or biographical determinants, but that one does not look at artistic productions from what Northrop Frye (1957) has characterized as a *documentary point of view*; that is, we do not refer to the development of art in a *pars-pro-toto* way to refer to the development of society, the development of cognition, or the development of morality, and so forth. I do not mean to suggest, in the slightest, that there is anything amiss in examining artistic productions or manifestations in relation to socioeconomic conditions operative at their birth, or as indicative of the cognitive status of either producers or "consumers," or as having some moral relevance. But, unless we presuppose counterfactually, I believe that, in Kenneth Burke's terminology, one can collapse artistic Acts into such Scenic or Purposive factors we are not engaged, I submit, in discussing the *development of art* but are discussing something else under the guise of talking about *art and its development*.

Cassirer (1944) observes, with respect to the subordination of art to cognition or morality:

If art was regarded as the offspring of theoretical activity it became necessary to analyze the logical rules to which this particular activity conforms. But in this case logic itself was no longer a homogeneous whole. It has to be divided into separate and comparatively independent parts. The logic of the imagination had to be distinguished from the logic of rational and scientific thought . . . [T]he logic of the imagination could never command the same dignity as the logic of the pure intellect. If there was a theory of art, then it could only be a *gnoseologia inferior*, an analysis of the "lower," sensuous part of human knowledge. Art could, on the other hand, be described as an emblem of moral truth. It was conceived as an allegory, a figurative expression which under its sensuous form concealed an ethical sense. *But in both cases, in its moral as well as in its theoretical interpretation, art possessed no independent value of its own. In the hierarchy of human knowledge and of human life art was only a preparatory stage, a subordinate and subservient means pointing to some higher end.* (italics added, p. 137)

Proleptically, Cassirer here gives grounds, it seems to me, for ruling out as examinations of the development of Art such works as Herbert Read's *Icon to Idea* (1955), Silvano Arieti's *Creativity* (1976), or Suzi Gablik's *Progress in Art* (1977), although Gablik, in my view, presents a better argument than either of her predecessors.

All this is not to say that, in talking about the relative autonomy of art, one need treat Art, in general, or any one of the Arts, as occurring in a vacuum. It is surely intelligible to make an assessment of the development of art that would entail a consideration of the social matrix in which works of art are produced. But there does not appear to be any way to consider the relations of art and society unless one uses some organizing theory to deal with the wide range of materials with respect to both art and society in which certain normative views about both art and society are held by the inquirer. One, perhaps, finds this kind of approach in Nicholas Pevsner's (1968) examination of the relations of architecture and society, and again in Joseph Kupfer's (1983) *Experience as Art*. Kupfer, beginning with a Deweyan perspective, shows how *quality* (high-level, advanced) performances in everyday activities require (see Dyke, 1984) "The development of just those sensibilities required for the [creation and] appreciation of art: attention to form, composition, unity, rhythm and the like" (p. 350).

Kupfer's treatment of the nature of experience underlying the production and appreciation of works of Art, his focus on Agent's operations or activities, may prompt one to consider other possibilities for inquiring into development in the domain of the Arts. In this respect, one may use Aristotle's schema of the four aitias, the material cause, the efficient cause, the formal cause, and the final cause. Or, adopting a modern variant, Burke's *Grammar of Motives* ask here what it is that constitutes the development of the *Act* or *Product* (the work per se); what it is that constitutes the development of the *Agent as Artist* (i.e., development with respect to the sphere of creative activity); what it is that constitutes the development of the *Agencies, Instrumentalities,* or *Means* for the production and appreciation of Art (in general or with regard to specific domains), here focusing on the means of executing or realizing, in the public domain, intuitions or visions; what it is that constitutes development with respect to the *Scenes of Artistic* production and appreciation; and, finally, what it is that constitutes development with regard to the *Purposes* or *Ends of Art.*

If we gloss development as progress, these kinds of considerations translate into the following questions:

1. In what way, if at all, can one speak of progress in artistic productions or works, whether in general or in particular realms?
2. In what way, if at all, can one speak of progress in the creative process, prescinding here from all those putative factors that may contingently affect the creative process, and focusing only on those aspects of the creative process that are directly relevant to the production of the works of art?
3. In what way, if at all, can one speak of progress with regard to the instrumentalities or means used to realize or embody a creative vision?
4. In what way, if at all, can one speak of progress with regard to the scenes in which works of art (in general or specifically) are (a) produced, (b) appreciated?
5. In what way, if at all, can one speak of progress with respect to the purposes or ends that works of art serve?

REFERENCES

Arieti, S. (1976). *Creativity: The magic synthesis.* New York: Basic.

Arnheim, R. (1962). *Picasso's Guernica: The genesis of a painting.* Berkeley: University of California Press.

Burke, K. (1945). *A grammar of motives.* Englewood, NJ: Prentice-Hall.

Cassirer, E. (1944). *An essay on man.* New Haven, CT: Yale University Press.

Durkheim, E. (1915). *The elementary forms of religious life* (J. W. Swain, Trans.). New York: Macmillan.

Dyke, C. (1984). Review of John Manfredi's *The social limits of art. Journal of Aesthetics and Art Criticism, 43,* 350–351.

Fisher, J. (1986). Editorial. *The Journal of Aesthetics and Art Criticism, 45,* 115–116.

Frye, N. (1957). *Anatomy of criticism: Four essays.* Princeton, NJ: Princeton University Press.

Gablik, S. (1977). *Progress in art.* New York: Rizzoli.

Gilligan, C. (1982). *In a different voice.* Cambridge, MA: Harvard University Press.

Kaplan, B. (1983). Genetic dramatism: Old wine in new bottles. In S. Wapner & B. Kaplan (Eds.), *Toward a holistic developmental psychology* (pp. 53–74). Hillsdale, NJ: Lawrence Erlbaum Associates.

Kaplan, B. (1986). Value presuppositions in theories of human development. In L. Cirillo & S. Wapner (Eds.), *Value presuppositions in theories of human development* (pp. 89–111). Hillsdale, NJ: Lawrence Erlbaum Associates.

Kohlberg, L. (1981). *Essays on moral development, Vol. I: The philosophy of moral development.* San Francisco: Harper & Row.

Kupfer, J. (1983). *Experience as art.* Albany: State University of New York Press.

Pevsner, N. (1968). *The sources of modern architecture and design.* New York: Praeger.

Read, H. (1955). *Icon to idea.* Cambridge, MA: Harvard University Press.

Werner, H., & Kaplan, B. (1983). *Symbol formation.* Hillsdale, NJ: Lawrence Erlbaum Associates. (Original work published 1963)

2

Is Feminist Art Aesthetically Regressive?

Hilde S. Hein
College of the Holy Cross

The question posed by my title is deliberately provocative. Its intent is not to antagonize the feminists, among whom I count myself, but to cast some dubious glances at developmental theory and the concept of development. I argue that to designate an event a *development* is to say that it is not merely a process or a temporal change but an advance (albeit an advance that may be toward an end that is unpleasant from some point of view; e.g., death). I argue that the standard that defines advance is normally established from a male-centered perspective, and, furthermore, that the concept of development itself is phallocratic. Because movements that do not follow the standard pattern are perceived to be nondevelopmental, aberrant, or even regressive, it follows that the paradigm of development dictates a phallocratic ideal that excludes any alternative.

Some feminists have endeavored to articulate an alternative model that does incorporate nonphallocratic values and retains the basic structure of classic developmentalism. I briefly sketch the general features of such an alternative standard, referring in particular to the ethical developmental model of Carol Gilligan (1982). However, my chief contention is that the inescapable logic of development commits us to a pattern of analysis and to existential expectations that have a phallocratic bias. Concluding with an examination of recent feminist art, I describe it as having passed through a series of phases that represent successive changes in feminist consciousness. I do, however, refrain from identifying these shifts or the

11

representations that arise from them as developmental, because I mean to avoid just those hierarchical and progressivist associations that are attached to developmentalism. My hope is to elicit new ways of asking questions that will promote new patterns for understanding the complex universe of which we are a very small part.

THE NORMATIVE MEANING OF DEVELOPMENT

This volume celebrates one of the great synthesizers of developmental theory, Heinz Werner. The department of psychology he shaped established a reputation during the 1940s and 1950s defending a holistic and organicist philosophical approach against the positivistic reductionism that continues to prevail over the hearts and minds of many Americans. Some concessions have been made to environmentalism and pluralistic relativism, and so it may seem ungracious on my part to express skepticism with regard to developmental theory. In fact, I am drawn to many of its principles, in particular the commitment to holism without sacrifice of attention to concrete detail. I admire its refusal to succumb to the seduction of oversimplification for the sake of efficiency, and for that reason I offer my criticism, which I hope is taken in a spirit of friendly disagreement.

The Heinz Werner Institute, founded in 1960, is described not only as dedicated to the study of human development but also as designed "to articulate and develop means both for facilitating development and for overcoming obstacles and impediments to development" (Heinz Werner Institute Conference Program, 1987). Obviously, the Institute regards development with approval. Its concern is openly normative and even promotional. However, the rhetoric of objective, value-free science is so persuasive that some self-proclaimed developmentalists profess to perform a purely descriptive task that includes no evaluative content whatsoever. The most meticulous of analysts, although acknowledging that *development* is a term reserved for change that is temporally irreversible, oriented toward an "end state," and innovative, nevertheless shy away from declaring that it is incremental axiologically (Nagel, 1957). No one wants to own up to teleology, even where the stages through which an organism passes are described as its achievement of biological or mental or cognitive or moral maturity.

Developmentalists agree that there is a significant difference between the series of motions exhibited, on the one hand, by a ball rolling down a hill or a sand dune eroding into the ocean, and, on the other, by an acorn becoming an oak tree or a local dispute ripening into a revolutionary social movement. Developmentalists retain an organismic language to refer to the latter changes and stand firm against those reductionists who hold that it is simply a matter of time and fancy cognitive footwork before all types of process can be understood under the same unifying laws. I resonate with those who remain in doubt that all phenomena will soon be absorbed under the umbrella of Chaos or Catastrophe Theory.

The qualitative difference between types of change was clearly recognized by Aristotle, who demarcated them as processes that do or do not have an indwelling telos or entelechy. Those things, he says, have a nature (or are natural) "which, by a continuous movement originated from an internal principle, arrive at some completion . . . if there is no impediment." I do not mean to suggest that modern developmentalists believe, as Aristotle did, that developmental change is necessarily the realization of an immanent form, although some theorists would still defend that claim. Aristotle differentiates between this kind of change and externally induced alterations or changes in space or location, which may also be purposive, but whose purpose is not indwelling. He distinguishes too between other types of change or movement (from positive to positive, negative to positive, or positive to negative, as well as between generation, or coming to be, ceasing to be, change of accidental or incidental attributes, and movement with respect to quality, quantity, or place. Not all these types of change are relevant to our point, but what is very clear is that Aristotle would not regard all temporal change as progressive, nor all achievement of ends as developmental.

Contemporary theoreticians seem to have lost sight of some of these fine distinctions in their zeal to track exactly how the changes occur. Moreover, because we are no longer in the habit of speaking in terms of final causes, the very notion of development has become somewhat of an embarrassment. Although I am by no means an exponent of Allen Bloom's (1987) *The Closing of the American Mind*, I think there is substance in his claim that we tend to be uncomfortable with any declaration of ends or preferences. It is currently fashionable to understand all goals as temporary and instrumental, all objectives as provisional, and all ideals as culturally relative or ethnocentric. Thus development—ensoulment fulfilled, as Aristotle would have understood it—is now regarded simply as the completion of a systemic loop.

Although we still do use the language of ideal states and goals, the meaning of these words has changed. In current parlance *ideal* means the same as *imagined* or *projected*, and goals have been referentially demoted to the status of boundary markers (goalposts) that define property lines or playing areas. Maturation, clearly a developmental concept, is confusedly taken to refer to the regular passage of an organism or entity through stages or levels upon a stairway that ascends to nowhere. The more detailed the description of the stages is, the less necessary it appears to be to explain why the succession from one to the next represents a move from lower to higher, from good to better, from less to more. But although the value claims are not spelled out, they are nevertheless taken for granted. We carry the baggage of our ancestors with us, embedded in our language and internalized in our psyches. No matter how charmed we are by childhood innocence, we all believe that adulthood is superior to it. I am reminded of a story by Ray Bradbury that poignantly portrays the plight of a Peter Pan-like waif, condemned to wander from home to home, as each new foster family discovers the horror of his eternal youth and his failure to undergo normal development. With similar bias, we have grown accustomed to the subterfuge of terms-of-art such as *developing* or *underdeveloped* to impart what appears to be economic information about certain nations. But the words are more likely to convey the evaluative judgment that industrialization and *modernization* mark progress, and that these nations will be improved by undergoing development. There are only a few die-hard traditionalists and feminists who dare to challenge that assumption.

Heinz Werner's (1957) orthogenetic principle asserts that: "Wherever development occurs, it proceeds in an orderly and specifiable fashion from a state of relative globality and lack of differentiation, to a state of increasing differentiation, articulation, and hierarchic integration" (p. 126). Developmental analyses in other disciplines are much the same, even where the objects they purport to explain are more abstract than cells and organisms. We have ontogenetic and ideogenetic accounts of children's understanding of causality and moral obligation, of the emergence of national identity, of ecological communities and public health hazards, and of the transformation of family businesses into corporate institutions. Behind the objective depiction of stratification is the hidden presumption that the movement from stage to stage is progressive, and that its endpoint is the fulfillment of either an inherent systemic telos or an external and absolute good.

It should be obvious, but bears repetition, that not all successful sequences of development lead to conclusions that are desirable according to all possible value scales. A full-blown cataract or cancer or economic inflation or political takeover might be a textbook example of the kind of thing it is, but it does not follow that everyone wants it. Achievement, however perfect, is often successful only from a particular perspective and might be thoroughly hateful from another point of view. Even so, there is no doubt that it is valuable to understand the sequential course of development of things for the sake of intervention. Such knowledge is as useful for purposes of elimination or avoidance as it is for bringing something about. We cannot deny the nature of the process, but we can intercede with it and bring about our own agenda to some degree. It is of the essence of Baconian science that the control of Nature depends on intimate knowledge of her ways. Human ingenuity can then be put to the service of abetting or obstructing them. Because the telos of a developmental situation can be either positive or negative, varying with the eye of the beholder, it is easy to lose sight of the fact that there always is a telos.

I am arguing that wherever a process is described as developmental, even where no telos is explicitly designated, there is an implied value judgment. It is understood that the end is in some sense better than the beginning, the means subordinate to the end, the whole of greater value than its parts. The complex is taken to be more advanced than the simple, the mature superior to the unripe, and a free-standing, autonomous system an improvement over a dependent or complexly integrated one. Because the comparative superiority of the end-state is uncritically taken for granted, no argument is offered in proof of that thesis—and yet it could be mistaken. According to Nagel (1957), it just seems to go without saying that development is going in the "right" direction if it "eventuate[s] in modes of organization not previously manifested in the history of the developing system, such that the system acquires an increased capacity for self-regulation, a larger measure of relative independence from environmental fluctuations" (p. 16). But is it really self-evident? Werner certainly believed that hierarchical integration is better than "a state of relative globality and lack of differentiation." Most of us have been taught to think so as well. We have also been taught to think that space perceptual constancy—the ability to retain a sense of absolute verticality even when our retinal stimulation is at an angle—is a good thing. Somehow it has seemed obvious that fixity and order are desirable, and that diffuseness and adaptation to context are somehow soft and submissive. The very language of normality conveys the notion that autonomy, a fixed sense of selfhood, independence of context, and sharp definition are sterling qualities, whereas their opposites are weak, effeminate, and of dubious integrity. Feminists are beginning to challenge this language and to ask whether we have been correctly educated, and we are coming up with negative answers.

Probably the most famous and well-defined challenge to these established certainties comes from Carol Gilligan. Gilligan (1982) takes on the entire gamut of developmental theories, charging that they ignore and devalue feminine orientation and therefore do not correctly describe the stages of moral development that are alleged to be universally applicable. Her criticism is explicitly directed against Lawrence Kohlberg's theory of moral development, but implicitly she indicts the entire "culpable network" that includes Freud, Piaget, Bettelheim, Levinson, McClelland, Kohlberg, and Erikson, and as one reviewer (Colby &

Damon, 1983) said: "If Gilligan's charges are justified, developmental psychology must return to the drawing board, since it has misrepresented a majority of the human race."

Gilligan (1982) outlines an ethic of care that flows in the direction of heightened responsibility, displacing patriarchal hierarchy and mechanical egalitarianism with "a weblike imagery of relationships." The inclusion of women's moral experience, she says:

> brings to developmental understanding a new perspective on relationships that changes the basic constructs of interpretation. The concept of identity expands to include the experience of interconnection. The moral domain is similarly enlarged by the inclusion of responsibility and care in relationships. And the underlying epistemology correspondingly shifts from the Greek ideal of knowledge as a correspondence between mind and form to the Biblical conception of knowing as a process of human relationship. (p. 173)

Gilligan observes that women "perceive and construe social reality differently than men" (p. 171), and she explains the difference as arising out of our distinctively different social experience. Her indictment of her mentors is based upon their refusal to attend to and take that difference seriously:

> The failure to see the different reality of women's lives and to hear the differences in their voices stems in part from the assumption that there is a single mode of social experience and interpretation. By positing instead two different modes, we arrive at a more complex rendition of human experience which sees the truth of separation and attachment in the lives of women and men and recognizes how these truths are carried by different modes of language and thought. (p. 174)

Gilligan's work exemplifies feminist scholarship without being a dissertation about it. She asserts that a pressing item on the agenda for research on adult development is "the need to delineate *in women's own terms* the experience of their adult life" (p. 173). She cites the work of Carol Stack and Lillian Rubin and others as instances of women observers who "entering worlds previously known through men's eyes, return to give a different report." The multiplication of such "different reports" is bound to lead to some radical reassessments in all fields of scholarship. It is, however, important to bear in mind that Gilligan herself does not challenge the philosophical foundations of developmental theory as such. She proposes a sequence of ethical stages that follow an alternative route to the canonic single line of moral development described by Kohlberg and others. She does not challenge the accuracy of the Kohlbergian analysis as applied to a limited (i.e., male) segment of the population. Her objection is to its universalization, and she advances the view that Kohlberg's data, drawn from male subjects exclusively, can neither describe the moral experience of women nor codify rules that would appropriately govern that experience. She argues that a more authentic and generative theory of human development could be achieved if the complexities of the dialogue between the distinct realities of men and women were properly appreciated and integrated. Moreover, a morality based upon such a theory would, in her judgment, bring to fruition the most estimable of all human potentialities and help bring about a truly universal community.

Nowhere does Gilligan deny the teleological basis of developmentalism. Indeed her work provides a reasonable explanation of the fact that women tested on the Piaget–Kohlberg scale tend to perform at a lower level of moral development than their male counterparts. The problem as she understands it is that the scale is inappropriate to women's formation. (I think there is little doubt that a sampling of men would score equally poorly if tested against a standard "ethics of care" scale, but to the best of my knowledge, no such hypothetical case study has been devised.) Gilligan's own research does not pretend to universal claims. It was derived from actual case studies of women with real moral dilemmas, and it yields a standard sequence of moral development that corresponds to their experience.

Gilligan also does not say that the alternative moral development scheme that she articulates is superior to the canonic one or produces better people. There are, of course, people who do say that or who attribute that claim to her, but they are mistaken; Gilligan, well-trained social scientist that she is, simply describes and analyzes her observations within a known empirical framework and leaves the philosophizing to others. I am less sanguine than she is about the possibility of extracting a positive, universal human ethic from the convergence of the lines of development that she has distinguished, because I believe that gender-specific evolution has always and inevitably reflected the sexist and phallocratic nature of society. We have become what we are, limited men and women, by defining ourselves and each other in that unequal struggle. I do not believe that a universal ethic can be achieved simply by merging and compounding our differences. We cannot return to a natural state of innocence by dissolving the artificial products. We cannot fabricate a seamless whole by simply declaring that polar opposites are complements. I believe that the virtues and vices of women are generated by the reality of their experience. Men are responsible for much, although not all of that experience, but they do not wholly define it. Feminists do need to articulate what that experience is to validate and transcend it.

They cannot rely upon the conceptual categories or theoretical vocabulary of patriarchy to do it justice.

DEVELOPMENTALISM IN ART

Let me turn now to the specific question: What does feminism have to say to the notion of development in art? Is feminist art itself explicable in developmental terms, or is that suggestion a contradiction? A variety of theories exists that differ as to what their authors think the telos of art ought to be. Hegel believed that art advances from the abstractness of the classical period, through a history of increasingly sensuous embodiment to the threshold of spiritual self-realization, where art will be altogether displaced. Art, he says, is a signpost that, by pointing to itself and the concrete universal it expresses, guides us to the Self-Absorbing-Other that transcends it. Schopenhauer also believed that art has its stages, passing from the turbulent presence of the Will embodied in Nature, through the plastic arts and poetry, where representation is imperfect, to the purest physical expression of the eternal Ideas grasped through pure contemplation. Schopenhauer regards music as the highest manifestation of Will, disembodied and purified, and rewarding the listener with the closest approximation to escape from Self that human beings can aspire to. These philosophers do not agree on what art is supposed to achieve, but they do share the belief that it has an end, and that progress toward achieving it can be marked. The same may be said of Marx, who, however, radically disagrees with the Idealism and determination to escape from embodiment that is common to Hegel and Schopenhauer.

For Marx, the creation of art, like all human production, is the consequence of the material conditions in which we live, and any development or change reflects the change in those conditions. The process of development can, he thinks, be scientifically studied and shown to be oriented toward human liberation. Art then becomes an instrument by means of which that liberation can be nourished. Whereas inferior bourgeois art may be rejected as a mere exudate of a period, great art reflects a critical sensitivity to the human condition and thus contributes to the betterment of human society even as it manifests aesthetic advancement. Thus development in art is equivalent to the development of human freedom and is an anticipatory expression of it.

The widespread abandonment of a general faith in progress or belief that history reveals purposes beyond those of individual human endeavor undermines the case for development in art. In industry advance can be identified with greater productivity and the more efficient use of materials, but in art greater virtuosity in the elaboration of exotic or complicated or outrageous or more beautiful materials must be seen as its own reward. Development in art is then meaningful only as a purely internal phenomenon, art feeding upon its own history (with recurrent regurgitations), but it has no point outside the domain of art.

Modernism, an offspring of Cartesian self-discovery, also undermines the meaningfulness of development in art. The art of modernism is pluralistic and bears the mark of fragmented selves cut off from a community of purpose. Its aesthetic function is the sometimes narcissistic, always subjective, self-definition of the artist. Development may occur in an artist's mastery of a style or technique, or in successive explorations of an artistic idea by several artists, hence designated a *school*. But such development is always relative to a particular artistic style or tradition and is ultimately expressed as the rebellion of one stylist against another, each struggling to affirm individual autonomy. There is no inherent logic or improvement relative to a focal aim, but only a reaction stimulated by each artist's need to establish an independent identity. Change occurs centrifugally as personal patterns proliferate in divergent directions. There is no movement toward a collective representation of a truth and decreasing confidence that such an ideal is even meaningful. This is a long way from the fulfillment of an Aristotelian telos, immanent or external, and also a long way from the communitarian objective that persists as an ideal of science.

Whatever development might be identifiable in the proliferation of modernist art forms, it seems irreconcilable with the "ethic of care and equity" that Gilligan says women's voices promote. But Modernism is entirely compatible with the phallocratic "ethnic of responsibility and equality" that marks the pinnacle of development according to the canonic theory. Where the self-aggrandizement of each man is limited only by the principled right of every other to do the same, the glorification of subjectivity that modernism expresses is right in line. Perhaps what is meant by development in art is only consistent with a more general philosophy that exalts autonomy and defines all achievement competitively.

Modernism has exploited the rhetoric of development and capitalized upon the progressive connotation that it carries. A credulous art-appreciating public (under the tutelage of art historians and commercial promoters) has succumbed to the entrepreneurial hype that welcomes as progress each successive move from classical academicism to Romanticism, Symbolism, Impressionism, Expressionism, Surrealism, Dada, Cubism, Fauvism, Futurism, Abstract Expressionism, Action painting, Minimalism, Pop, Op, Conceptualism, Environmentalism, Nouveau Realism, and onward. Evidently, these movements borrow ideas from and are outgrowths of one another, but what are they developments of or toward? Is the sheer presence of a point of departure, and that often no more than a prior moment in time, sufficient ground for claiming that a journey is to a better place? The claim that any of these stylistic innovations is a development stems from logical confusion, an error that might have dangerous consequences. It invites us to accept that any new idea, though neither good nor necessary, is both desirable and inevitable. Lacking confidence in their power to discriminate, critics are more and more willing to equate novelty with development and to applaud it for that reason alone.

The danger that I have in mind is well illustrated by an incident cited by Oliver Sacks (1985) in his remarkable book, *The Man Who Mistook His Wife for a Hat*. Sacks relates that he was called upon to interview a patient with bizarre dissociative behavior patterns who was nevertheless able to perform certain tasks extremely well and so could function almost normally in his profession as a musician. The man was also a visual artist, and Sacks asked to look at his pictures. He found these to be significantly fragmented. The man's wife, however, defended him: "Ach you doctors," she said. "You're such philistines! Can you not see *artistic development*— how he renounced the realism of his earlier years, and advanced into abstract, non-representational art" (p. 16).

Sacks affirms that our cognitive sciences are suffering from an agnosia essentially similar to that of his patient. The patient, he says, may be viewed as a warning and parable of what happens to a science that eschews the judgmental, the particular, the personal, and becomes entirely abstract and computational. I think feminists are making a similar diagnosis of our culture. We are questioning classic patterns of assessment, doubting that all linear order describes an ascent. We declare that the patient is *sick* even though the formula describes him as making progress. Surely a schema that leads to annihilation can be a development from only a perverse point of view. Why should we embrace it? Either we are mistaken in our belief that there is a telos or we have found the wrong one. (Another alternative is that Descartes was right in his conjecture—there is an Evil Genius, truly a master of perversity—but in that case all speculation is worthless, for we are systematically confused.) Some feminists believe that we have been pursuing the wrong aesthetic ideals, and that an alternative set of aesthetic criteria, parallel to Gilligan's standard for an ethics of care, can be imagined. We might think of feminist art as representing a phase in the development of a new mode of artistic expression. On the other hand, perhaps no developmental account correctly describes change in art.

DEVELOPMENTALISM IN FEMINIST ART
AND CRITICISM

There is no doubt that women's art, and in particular that made by feminists, has undergone a history of changes. It is convenient to characterize these as phases because they are, for the most part, successive and reactive. But it does not follow that they represent a development. Mary Ellman (1968) confesses in her book, *Thinking About Women*, that "the failures often seem to me successes." I too am afflicted by such miscomprehension of the apparently obvious. Ellman (1968) offers the striking image of menstruation as a reminder: 'The retraction of the uterine wall, which leaves the inflated veins to atrophy, break open and lose their absurd provisions for a non-event, constitutes an image of repeated bankruptcy. A monthly reminder that failure is as likely as success, and that failure may sometimes be as welcome as success" (p. 177). Indeed, we often pray for failure. But if that is true, what nonsense have we made of the developmental model?

Failure according to the canons of men is women's normal expectation. They can hardly do otherwise, for if they are to succeed as women, they must fail as men and thus as human, and so any success is necessarily qualified. Qualified in what sense? Not in the sense that Plato suggests that, given equal opportunity, a few outstanding women will rise to the top, so that the best women will overlap the worst men; nor in Dr. Johnson's sense, that "Like a dancing dog, the wonder is not in how well they do it, but that they can do it at all." These men missed the paradox that any woman of a certain age appreciates that to develop as a human is to fail as a woman and vice versa (see Broverman, Vogel, Broverman, Clarkson, & Rosencrantz, 1972). A woman can succeed or fail at this or that undertaking, but, unlike a man, she cannot *be* a success. The applicability of developmental standards is likewise limited.

Linda Nochlin (1971), in a famous essay entitled "Why Are There No Great Women Artists?," stressed the social and political realities that determine what art is and who produces it. Her point was that, whereas it is false that women have created no art, they have been prevented from producing great art or becoming serious artists because of the social constraints and expectations under which they have lived. She wrote: 'The fact is that there have been no great women artists, so far as we know, although there have been many interesting and good ones who have not been sufficiently appreciated. . . . The fault lies not in our stars, our hormones, our menstrual cycles . . . but in our institutions and our education" (p. 5). Middle-class women's lives, in particular, Nochlin says, were filled with activities that even women were educated to regard as trivial—providing the intimacies of domestic comfort, child care, personal ornamentation. They were not expected to excel at anything, and the so-called meaningful activities of life, not to mention exposure to formal education and the freedom to experiment, were denied them. The destiny of women was to serve others, to be forever accessible, approachable, and interruptible. No one can be expected to produce serious work under those circumstances, as Virginia Woolf had also pointed out years before in *A Room of One's Own*.

In the wake of Nochlin's article there was a flurry of efforts to retrieve women's art from the dustbins of history and the ranks of the anonymous, and to defend its merit. These first-phase art historians did turn up a number of "interesting and good" women artists who had been neglected. A small number of women have, of course, been producing works of art all along, running what Germaine Greer (1979) calls the "obstacle race" to meet the standards prescribed by men. Their work varies with the prevailing fashions in style and can be judged by the same standards that are applied to the traditional art forms. There is nothing notably feminine about it apart from its frequent failure to be recognized. One achievement of the feminist movement in its first phase has been to rectify this omission and to bring the work to critical attention. The first step of feminism was simply to win access to the art world, not to change it.

At the same time, however, a second phase of feminism was emerging. Feminists were insisting that women have been making things for centuries outside the established art circles. Moreover, although these objects are often cherished and acknowledged to be beautiful, they are denied status as art by conventional standards. Needlework, quilt making, porcelain painting, flower arrangement, and food decoration are perceived as domestic craft or left entirely unclassified. Could this identification be the consequence of their production by women and have nothing to do with the aesthetic value of the objects themselves? Why should the things that women do be denied status as art with the sole exception of a few grudgingly admitted "crossovers"? Who determines what is to "count" as art? (The ascent of women's art to the status of "art" was curiously, but unmistakably, indicated by the title of an exhibition featured at the New York Museum of Crafts—"Homage to the Quilt.")

Second-phase feminists objected to the exclusive standards by which their art was being judged: Inferiority to what and by what measure? They were waking up to the fact that critical standards are not absolute but, like the iridium bar that once defined the standard meter, swell and contract and swirl with the rotation of the celestial spheres. Physicists might be content to resort to the speed of light as an ultimate standard; but women, denied too long, insisted on women-defined units of measure and demanded that women's experience be constitutive of the reality that we know very well is socially defined. The problem is that we cannot now begin defining reality de novo. Whoever defines it faces a reality that is gendered and, as far back as we know it, one sex has dominated the other. Both men and women must read their own identity relative to that inequality. We cannot conclude that only one reading is correct, but there is diminishing support for the possibility of two "separate but equal" readings. We know all too well that they cannot have the same authority.

In the last 15 years, women have begun speaking deliberately and critically in their own voice, describing a reality that differs from the familiar, male-defined one. At first, we spoke tentatively and mostly among ourselves, but now a generation of confident feminists is arising and demanding to be heard—insisting, that is, that men listen to us and pay attention. These women, whose critical stance reflects a third phase of feminism, are looking at gender unsentimentally as a social construct that produces inequality. They mean to depose and dismantle phallocracy, but many of them recognize that its displacement with "gynocracy" would inevitably be tainted by the evil that it aims to overcome. Although the rule of the Mothers is a tantalizing fiction to some, it is an unlikely representation of our historic past and an implausible projection into the future. It is primarily a male fantasy and has, chiefly for that reason, received a great deal of attention.

Ellman (1968) spoke in her own voice very critically. Although she did not declare a distinctly feminist aesthetic, or propose new directions in feminist art, she made plain how badly we need a transvaluation of existing aesthetic concepts. She spoke out of the female experience that includes male supremacy and the sardonic knowledge of its aftermath. Unlike Gilligan, Ellman leaves the distinct impression that women could do better than men have done, relying on women's sensitive attention to detail, their sharp judgment, and their remarkable tolerance for the undramatic stresses of living.

Second-phase feminists, confronting gender inequality, demanded a vindication of women's experience. Rejecting the received opinion that the private and personal are trivial or less than human preoccupations, these feminists sought to valorize women's experience by defying phallocratic proscriptions against its representation in art. Miriam Schapiro (1972) and Judy Chicago (1975), as well as the critic, Lucy Lippard (1976), were among the first to promote such controversial and aggressively female art forms as the total environment of "Womanhouse," the use of explicitly vaginal iconography, and such traditionally domestic media techniques as needlework and collage that had a deliberately female reference. Embarrassing to some and liberating to others, these new art forms challenged even the conventions governing the materials of art, let alone its appropriate subject matter.

Refusing to accept what many of them perceived as tokenistic toleration in a male establishment, these women began exploring the world of care and responsibility. Some expressed their anger at male dominance and intrusiveness and found a haven in the common world that their art uncovered and in the sisterhood it engendered among themselves.

It should not be surprising that once women affirmed the legitimacy of their own experience they would wish to portray it in art. This is, after all, what men have always done. Art is the preservation and celebration of the most ephemeral and the most profound. We might expect that a history of radically different lifestyles would inspire women to produce art forms unlike those that men produce, and that these ought properly to be esteemed according to a different scale of merit. This is a cause for rejoicing, not for dismay. Modernism, after all, rules out an absolute measure of value in art and should prescribe that any woman's creation, like that of any man, be placed before the tradition of public judgment. If such assessments were not skewed by a long tradition that invalidates us, why should we doubt that women's art would fare as well as men's by that test? What requires explanation is why this has not been the case.

Why should art that is sexualized in a manner described as vaginal be more offensive than art that is phallic? Why should art not aim to explore women's sexuality instead of to depict women as objects of male sexual interest? Why are some so-called female functions generally thought "unfit" for public attention (e.g., menstruation and the "dull and dirty" household chores that women do), whereas slaughter and battle, commerce, and farming are eminently suitable? Why, on the other hand, are some so-called female activities, such as child care and nursing, invariably shown in an idealized light? Incredulity alone should move us to ask why the shedding of male blood on the battlefield is an apt topic for artistic representation, whereas women's monthly discharge is generally perceived as repulsive? Why *isn't* the bleeding heart of Jesus disgusting to audiences? Art that poses questions such as these to its viewers is necessarily confrontational, though not invariably feminist. It invites comparison with the art of other recent movements in art—Surrealism, Dada, and Pop-art—that have also been regarded as aesthetically and politically outrageous. But feminist art appears to be even more disquieting than these turned out to be.

Phase-two feminists created a countermovement and a style that was openly separatist and was therefore denounced by some other feminists as capitulating to phallocratically inspired essentialism. The fight between those who favor the promotion of women's art within the existing mainstream tradition and those who oppose it has not yet been resolved. Both positions are forms of critical feminism, differing along political and philosophical lines in the extent to which they regard human and aesthetic experience as intrinsically gendered.

The articulation of the disagreements between these forms of feminism led to the explicit political consciousness of third-phase feminists in the 1980s. These artists and critics directly address the issue of gender construction and the role that art plays in shaping social reality. Their commitment is neither to the creation of an alternative women's space and the glorification of women's experience nor to achieving recognition in the garrison of phallocracy. Their art and their criticism are aimed at naming the institutions that define and oppress women, and at their destruction (see Loeb, 1974; Parker & Pollock, 1981).

Although differing ideologically from the art of second-phase feminism, third-phase feminist art is continuous with it in certain respects. It shares the aspect of cultural criticism and often exhibits a collective or collaborative character both in its authorship and its relation to the public. Frequently the work of many hands, it is also seen in unusual public and private places that are not conventional display spaces. This is often necessitated by the fact of its rejection by establishment galleries. As a result, the art created by feminists is eliciting new audiences, sensitive to both its medium and its controversial political message. When challenged with bias, producers of this art defend it as a counterpart to the tacit, but no less political, content of the art of the establishment. They draw attention to the explicitly political manifestos with which such recent movements as Dadaism and Futurism began. By now, those propagandistic origins are nearly forgotten while the art is known by its aesthetic style. Feminist outrageousness, likewise, is not an end in itself, but has a uniquely critical function akin to that of those earlier 20th-century movements. Critics who dismissively subsume feminism under the umbrella of contemporary postmodernism fail to grasp its serious philosophical content (see Owens, 1983). They see only the negativism and repudiation that feminism shares with other contemporary trends, its rejection of totalistic explanations, its refusal to identify an essential reality, and its focus upon the reality that culture defines. But they refuse to attend to the affirmation that feminism expresses and the positive community that it creates.

The third stage of feminist art and concurrent criticism replaces the second-stage celebration of female nature and experience with a critique of the social and ideological construction of that nature and experience. It is more self-conscious and self-critical, but it does not repudiate the ultimate goal of stage-two feminism, the revalorization of women. Like stage-two feminism, it also challenges the traditional view of art as an objectification parallel to the theoretical specularity of science. Third-stage feminists denounce both art and science as phallocratic components of the discourse of authoritarianism and mastery. According to Tickner (1984), their objective is: "unfixing the feminine, unmasking the relations of specularity that determine its appearance in representation, and undoing its position as a 'marked term' which ensures the category of the masculine as something central and secure." These feminists exceed the political ambitions of their second-stage predecessors, whom they sometimes denounce as self-indulgent creators of myths. They do not wish to reclaim the historically feminized female; they (Broude & Garrard, 1982) deconstruct her, using the tools of contemporary postmodernist cultural criticism to "question the universal validity of those very myths and values and cultural assumptions that, in the past, have automatically excluded from the domain of Art the experiences of half of our population." No longer preoccupied with either the demand for equality with men or the celebration of women's difference, stage-three feminism has shifted attention altogether away from women to the phallocratic theory that constructs them. The Australian philosopher, Elizabeth Grosz (1987), describes this phase of feminism:

> This transition consisted in moving from a feminism which took women as its *objects* of analysis, using patriarchal theories and frameworks to discuss this hitherto excluded object, to a feminism which took theory as its object of investigation, using the framework of women's experiences. This is a significant reversal from the position of object to subject of knowledge. (p. 477)

The intention, in other words, is a radically displaced point of departure.

The aim of gender deconstruction surpasses the merely methodological or political. It aspires to demonstrate how the myth of gender has infected *all* traditional philosophizing and rendered all theory suspect—for all of it incorporates the same principles of subject/object dualism and hierarchy, the transcendent universal, the disembodied mind, and the presumedly objective and value neutral disjunction that lie at the root of the gender dichotomy. The conventional disparities of gender and the inequalities that follow from them thus turn out to be at the core of phallocracy and not accidental emanations of it that might, conceivably, be corrected.

Developmental theory is not exempt from this description, for the same principles are embodied in its structure. The telos (whether or not expressed) always represents a potential success. Development is to a state of greater perfection or objectivity, universality, neutrality, integration, or completeness. I suggested that the self-evident advancement entailed by hierarchical inclusiveness, harmonized complexity, or spatial autonomy is not as obvious to feminists as it is to developmentalists. I argue that this is not due to developmental retardation on the part of the feminists but to phallocratic bias on the part of the developmentalists. At least the phase-three feminists appear to conclude that any developmental account is bound to be phallocratic, inevitably championing values that are antifeminist and antiwoman. Not all feminists, however, are as sweeping in their condemnation of developmentalism. Some, as we have seen, favor the identification of alternative developmental criteria.

Returning at last to the original question, "Is feminist art aesthetically regressive?," I am forced to reject the developmental model that it presupposes. I described a sequential movement within feminist art and art criticism, declaring its stages to be reactive, but not developmental. Stage 1 expresses the endeavor to reclaim women's art and to assess its value on the same scale as the art of men. This phase is marked by women's vigorous effort to enter and achieve recognition in the conventional art world. Stage 2 takes the form of exalting femininity as women's unique and special nature. This stage may be regarded as the aesthetic equivalent of Gilligan's phenomenological defense of a different ethical voice. It purports to be descriptive, but its affirmative style is undoubtedly celebratory, and it does not question the origin of the difference it describes. Sometimes its advocates defend cultural separatism and political confrontation, setting it at odds with the philosophical convictions and practical aims of Stage 1, but this oppositional stance is neither dialectically dictated nor a naturally coherent successor to Stage 1.

Stage 3 is largely conceptual. Its intellectual roots are certainly to be found in Stages 1 and 2 and are obviously responsive to the same problems of gender inequality. However, its objective is a fundamental cultural and theoretical revision, and the art that is its manifestation is sometimes indistinguishable from some forms of postmodernist critical expression. But stage-three feminism is not just one of many fin-de-siècle voices crying out against totalistic woe. It is a vital political movement, at once intellectually challenging and practically optimistic. It is undergoing changes that reflect the social world from which it is emerging. And like that world, it is witness to the appearance of new organizational forms.

The fact that these new forms are intrinsically unpredictable would not alone invalidate the application of a developmental model to feminism; for it is characteristic of development that it be innovative. However, as we have seen, the concept of development does predict greater organizational complexity and hierarchical integration. Feminism, by contrast, *encourages*—it does not simply tolerate—pluralism and a multiplicity of ends (Hein & Korsmeyer, 1993). It does not subscribe to a unity of purpose, and it sometimes sacrifices the practical ends of efficiency to protect a diffuse complexity whose intrinsic value is contradicted by its developmental disadvantage. Feminism 3, thus ironically, is not dedicated to the advancement of uniquely feminine values. It holds no brief for the special quality of classical female experience. On the contrary; if stage-three feminists succeed in dismantling gender (as a socially constructed category), there will be no such thing as the feminine and no sense that can be given to Feminism 4. Like so many of the things that women do, feminism will be successful only if it achieves failure. Can this be Development?

REFERENCES

Bloom, A. (1987). *The closing of the American mind.* New York: Simon & Schuster.

Broude, N., & Garrard, M. D. (1982). *Feminism and art history: Questioning the litany.* New York: Harper & Row.

Broverman, I., Vogel, S., Broverman, D., Clarkson, F., & Rosencrantz, P. (1972). Sex-role stereotypes: A current appraisal. *Journal of Social Issues, 28,* 59–78.

Chicago, J. (1975). *Through the flower: My struggles as a woman artist.* New York: Doubleday.

Colby, A., & Damon, W. (1983). Review of Carol Gilligan's *In a different voice. Merrill-Palmer Quarterly, 29,* 473–481.

Ellman, M. (1968). *Thinking about women.* New York: Harcourt Brace Jovanovich.

Gilligan, C. (1982). *In a different voice: Psychological theory and women's development.* Cambridge, MA: Harvard University Press.

Greer, G. (1979). *The obstacle race: The fortunes of women painters and their work.* New York: Farrar, Strauss & Giroux.

Grosz, E. (1987). Feminist theory and the challenge to knowledges. *Women's Studies International Forum, 10*(5), 475–480.

Hein, H., & Korsmeyer, C. (Eds.). (1993). *Aesthetics in feminist perspective.* Indianapolis: University of Indiana Press.

Heinz Werner Institute Conference Program (1987). Development and the arts. Worcester, MA: Clark University.

Lippard, L. (Ed.). (1976). *From the center: Feminist essays in women's art.* New York: Dutton.

Loeb, J. (Ed.). (1974). *Feminist collage.* New York: Teachers College Press.

Nagel, E. (1957). Determinism and development. In D. B. Harris (Ed.), *The concept of development.* Minneapolis: University of Minnesota Press.

Nochlin, L. (1971). Why are there no great women artists? In T. B. Hess & E. C. Baker (Eds.), *Art and sexual politics* (pp. 1–44). New York: Macmillan. (Originally published in *Artnews* [Vol. 69], 1971)

Owens, C. (1983). The discourse of others: Feminists and postmodernism. In H. Foster (Ed.), *The anti-aesthetic: Essays on postmodern culture.* Port Townsend, WA: Bay Press.

Parker, R., & Pollock, G. (1981). *Old mistresses: Women, art and ideology.* London: Routledge & Kegan Paul.

Sacks, O. (1985). *The man who mistook his wife for a hat.* New York: Summit.

Schapiro, M. (1972). The education of women as artists: Project Womanhouse. *Art Journal*, *xxxi*.

Tickner, L. (1984). *Difference: On representation and sexuality* (exhibit catalog). New York: New Museum of Contemporary Art.

Werner, H. (1957). The concept of development from a comparative and organismic point of view. In D. B. Harris (Ed.), *The concept of development*. Minneapolis: University of Minnesota Press.

3

Psychoanalysis, Romanticism, and the Nature of Aesthetic Consciousness—With Reflections on Modernism and Post Modernism

Louis A. Sass
Rutgers University

> *To learn from Freud, you have to be critical.*
> —Ludwig Wittgenstein (1967, p. 41)

Psychoanalytic writers about artistic experience and expression have nearly always emphasized the central role of developmentally primitive modes of experience. In their view, the creative core of aesthetic creation and perception involves regression to forms of consciousness having one or more of several key qualities: ready access to emotional, instinctual, and sensorially concrete modes of experience; a heightened sense of fusion between both self and world and signifier and signified; and freedom from the rationality, conventional rules, and intellectual categories of everyday or scientific modes of awareness. Supposedly, the artist's creativity and, by analogy, the spectator's appreciation require a renewal of vision that hearkens back to the vitality, spontaneity, and sense of union with the world that is characteristic of early childhood. In his book on creativity, Arthur Koestler (1967) offers a succinct statement of this standard view; he describes:

> the temporary relinquishing of conscious controls [that] liberates the mind from certain constraints which are necessary to maintain the disciplined routines of thoughts but may become an impediment to the creative leap; at the same time other types of ideation on more primitive levels of mental organization are brought into activity. The first part of this sentence indicates an act of abdication, the second an act of promotion. (p. 169)

My purpose in this chapter is to locate these psychoanalytic notions in the larger realm of the history of aesthetics, and then to consider some limitations on the psychoanalytic theories that are suggested by this historical analysis. As we see later, such psychoanalytic ideas about aesthetic consciousness are remarkably similar to those of the English and German Romantics of the late 18th and early 19th centuries—to such an extent that one might almost consider psychoanalytic aesthetics to be a branch of Romanticism. Romantic aesthetic theory is not, however, the only possible conception of the psychological processes involved in art. Therefore, one might well ask if this standard picture is really applicable to all aesthetic periods or approaches—that is, whether it is adequate as a general theory of *the* nature of aesthetic consciousness. In the second half of the chapter, I consider certain aspects of 20th-century art that do not seem to fit the model offered by psychoanalysis and Romanticism. We see that, in the art and literature of the period known as *modernism*, and still more so in that of *postmodernism*, the very source of aesthetic perception and creativity often seems to lie not in irrational or regressive processes but in a hypertrophy of intellective, self-conscious awareness. A distantiated, self-monitoring form of experience may not, in these later periods, serve only a secondary or editorial function but may be the very wellspring of creativity itself.

PSYCHOANALYSIS

The psychoanalytic tendency to associate aesthetic with primitive modes of perception begins with Freud, who, in his writings on art, placed primary emphasis on the way artistic experience allows primitive wish-fulfillment fantasies to escape, at least partially, from repression, and thereby to achieve symbolic fulfillment (see Ricoeur, 1970, pp. 163–177). In Freud's (1908) view, the artist or writer tends to be someone who is characterized by a particular flexibility or looseness of repression, and who, in creating a fantasy world, essentially "does the same as the child at play" or the adult who dreams (p. 144). Freud viewed artistic creation and appreciation as essentially analogous because he believed the audience's pleasure derived from an unconscious reliving of the original experience of creation. He (Freud, 1914) wrote in "The Moses of Michelangelo": "What the artist aims at is to awaken in us the same mental constellation as that which in him produced the impetus to create" (p. 212). Most subsequent psychoanalytic writers have not, of course, equated creation and appreciation in all respects, but, like Freud, they have been less interested in distinguishing these processes than in illuminating their shared features (e.g., Kris, 1964, pp. 56, 59; Kutash,

1982; Segal, 1952, p. 204; Spitz, 1985, p. 136). They have also followed Freud's lead in emphasizing the indispensable role in aesthetic experience of irrationality and of regression to primitive states—although they have differed in just how these primitive states are to be conceptualized (see Spitz, 1985; Wright, 1984).

Aesthetic theories influenced primarily by classical psychoanalytic theory have placed major emphasis on the role of the pleasure principle and the symbolic satisfaction of primitive instinctual desires. In an essay, the art historian Ernest Gombrich (1963, p. 40) discussed the psychoanalytic view that would trace aesthetic pleasure to the instinctual gratification of the oral stage; he suggested that art that is readily accessible might tend to mobilize unconscious erotic fantasies from the passive, early-oral phase, whereas more difficult art might resonate with the more active and ambivalently aggressive experiences of the late-oral phase. Theorists influenced more strongly by later periods of psychoanalytic theory have stressed the autonomous functioning of the ego and the forms of satisfaction or pleasure this can intrinsically involve. Freud (1905) himself had mentioned the pleasure to be derived from the very activity of the psychic apparatus, but it was left to ego psychologists like Heinz Hartmann, Ernst Kris, and Rudolph Loewenstein to accord it serious attention.

The specific modes of ego functioning that, according to ego psychology, characterize aesthetic experience, setting it apart from the more pragmatic or technical modes of everyday life, are of a developmentally primitive nature; they are structurally isomorphic with the modes of consciousness characteristic of the infant or young child. According to Ernst Kris (1964), "ego regression (primitivization of ego functions)," which requires "relaxation . . . of ego functions" and involves "a greater proximity to the id" (pp. 253, 312), is a *sine qua non* of any sort of creative or aesthetic experience. Kris argues that "the intimate relation of painting and sculpture to infantile experiences and needs" (p. 53) must be understood not only in the context of psychosexuality but also in terms of early phases of ego development and of the archaic need to make or transform the environment. In similar fashion, the aesthetician Anton Ehrenzweig (1967), who combines psychoanalytic ego psychology with Kleinian object-relations theory, believes creativity is "closely related to the chaos of the primary process" (p. 35). Friedman (1960) argues that the greatness of a work of art is directly related to the degree to which primary process forms of experience are present in it. Finally, let me mention the views of Ernest Schachtel (1959), the phenomenologically oriented ego psychologist who considers the artist's curiosity and liberation from conventional modes of perception to be closely analogous to the attitude of the young child, and who argues that it is in memories of such early modes of experience that "every new insight and every true work of art has its origin" (pp. 241–244, 322).

Perhaps the most popular approaches in contemporary psychoanalysis derive from the object-relations theories of analysts such as Margaret Mahler, D. W. Winnicott, and Melanie Klein. Writers in this tradition stress the reevocation in aesthetic experience—whether of creation or of appreciation—of states of quasi-mystic union rooted in the symbiotic phase of infancy, or else of the symbolic connectedness characteristic of "transitional objects" (e.g., Bollas, 1978; Fuller, 1980; Kutash, 1982; Milner, 1957, 1978; Spitz, 1985). The Kleinian Hanna Segal (1952) has, for example, written of an acute awareness she believes to be present in the unconscious of all artists—"namely, that all creation is really a re-creation of a once loved and once whole, but now lost and ruined object, a ruined internal world and self" (p. 199). A writer inspired by a Mahlerian version of object-relations theory, Gilbert Rose (1980a, 1980b) criticizes both classical psychoanalytic and ego-psychological theories of instinctual or ego regression, yet in his own theory places equal emphasis on the developmentally primitive. Rose focuses on the vicissitudes of early relations with the interpersonal object, arguing that the aesthetic viewer's experiences of separation from and fusion with the artwork evoke the early phases of mother–child interaction. The movement of the painter's hand to and from the canvas, for instance, is said to be a revival of unconscious memories of the mother's nurturing gestures in caring for the infant (1980a, pp. 101–102). Supposedly, the " 'source' of aesthetic form arises in the fluid boundaries of the child's primary narcissism, now autonomously flexible in the adult"; the artist is one who "keeps resampling the early undifferentiated stage of psychological develop-ment" (pp. 15, 92).

In emphasizing the primitive, the instinctual, or the spontaneous, psychoanalytic aesthetic theory does not, however, deny that more advanced, mature, or rational forms of consciousness also play a role in the production and appreciation of art. Even the instinctualist model of classical psychoanalysis recognizes that the creation of a work of art, like that of a dream, must include "secondary elaboration"—the unconscious but ego-dominated process whereby raw instinctual fantasies are, par-tially in the interest of disguise, given a semblance of rationality. Further, this notion that ego processes serve primarily to disguise or sugar-coat an instinctual core has been itself repeatedly attacked by postclassical analysts who wish to give the ego a more central and essential place.

I already mentioned Kris's point that pleasure can be derived from the functioning of the psyche itself rather than from only the satisfaction of instincts. In saying this, Kris separates aesthetic experience from the id but not necessarily from that which is primitive (because the ego in aesthetic experience may be operating largely in a primary process mode). The main point of Kris's famous phrase about aesthetic regression being "in the service of the ego" is, however, to stress the role played by more rational and deliberate modes of thought generally associated with the secondary process. Thus, Kris (1964) emphasizes that, in contrast with dreams or states of intoxication, artistic regression is "purposive and controlled": "The inspired creativity of the artist . . . involves a continual interplay between creation and criticism, manifested in the painter's alteration of working on the canvas and stepping back to observe the effect. We may speak here of a *shift in psychic level*, consisting in the fluctuation of functional regression and control" (pp. 253–254). It is nevertheless clear from this and other passages (e.g., p. 59) that Kris associates the truly inspirational, productive, or generational element of the aesthetic process with regression to more primitive layers of consciousness, whereas he sees more mature, secondary process modes as serving functions that *are* secondary—namely, the editorial functions of selecting among the options offered by the primary process, of elaborating these choices, or of smoothing over inconsistencies of plot or form. Thus, Kris writes that, whenever symbols have aesthetic force, they are evoking the resources of the primary process; he concedes in one essay that artistic creation may not always derive from "inspiration," but insists that all art of high quality will have this kind of regressive source (pp. 255, 259).

It is debatable to what extent Kris's viewpoint differs from Freud's. Kris clearly puts more emphasis on the ego, but his distinction—which is both temporal and logical—between (regressive) "inspiration" and (mature) "elaboration" is very reminiscent of Freud's differentiation between a dynamic core of wish-fulfillment fantasy and a more peripheral process of "secondary elaboration." Certain later ego psychologists, such as Pinchas Noy (1978, pp. 743–744), have portrayed creative consciousness as a more intimate synthesis, a "new entity" in which primary and secondary, or instinctual-affective and rational-realistic, processes would operate simultaneously. Still, for Noy (1984/1985), as for Kris before him, "the most interesting ability of the creative individual," that which most clearly distinguishes such a person from those with conventional or noncreative minds, is "the ability to enrich his secondary-process cognition with techniques and strategies derived from the primary process" (p. 430). Noy (1972) also believes that a necessary feature of any communication that can be regarded as art is that it must use "the primary levels of experience and perception" (p. 245)—those involving concrete-sensory qualities such as timbre, pitch, and tempo of speech, as opposed to meaningful content (the latter being associated more closely with the secondary process).

A more explicit attack on Kris's traditionalism can be found in the writings of Schachtel (1959), who denies that "regression to primary-process thought" can be said to be "typical of the creative process" at all (p. 244). Schachtel, however, is primarily objecting to the notion of a creative role for the primary process if the latter is understood as serving a "drive discharge function" (p. 245). Instead, Schachtel believes that creativity is distinguished by "world-openness" in encountering the object, by the perceiver's ability to let thought and perception "wander freely without being bound by the rules and properties of the accepted, conventionalized, familiar everyday world" (p. 245). Schachtel refers to this optimal and fairly rare mode of experience as "allocentric," because he sees it as truly object directed; he contrasts this mode with the *secondary autocentricity* typical of adult experience, in which linguistic and pragmatic categories of the culture are imposed on the object world, thereby robbing the latter of its uniqueness, immediacy, and perceptual vividness.

It is true that Schachtel also distinguishes the (creative) allocentric mode from what he calls the *primary autocentricity* of the young child (i.e., from the child's quasi-fusion with a world experienced not as neutral, separate, or "in-itself" but as impinging on the child's self and as intimately bound up with affectivity). For this reason, Schachtel might at first seem to be portraying aesthetic-creative experience as being not at all primitive or regressive. In fact, however, Schachtel's comparisons of the allocentricity of adult creative or aesthetic experience with the primary autocentricity of the child are frequent and emphatic (see pp. 240, 262; whereas he seems to see allocentricity as having nothing whatsoever in common with the secondary autocentricity of normal adult perception). Schachtel (1959) asserts, for example, that

> the truth of artistic or scientific creation . . . is more likely to be encountered by the person who has continued and expanded the child's openness toward the world on the adult level and whose sensory and intellectual capacities have not entirely succumbed to the pressure of the accepted way in which everyone perceives the "realistic" world of the conventions of the day. (p. 243)

By causing the stagnation both of allocentricity *and* primary autocentricity, secondary autocentricity alienates man from objects and from his own sensory capacities; this alienation Schachtel (1959) views as the antithesis of "perception as creative experience" (pp. 238, 208). He also states that memory for early modes of experience is the mother of art and poetry (pp. 310, 317), and compares the "unseeingness" that blocks creative vision with amnesia for early childhood (pp. 243, 295), with the forgetting of the time when there was an immediate and profound feeling of affective and personal resonance in the perception of color, line, or sound.

We see, then, that primitive or regressive modes of experience are of central importance in virtually all the major psychoanalytic theories of the psychology of artistic creation and appreciation. Without denying the contribution of more mature or nonregressive modes of consciousness, such theories clearly stress, as the productive or specifically aesthetic aspect, those psychological processes that derive from and resonate with the young child's emotional and instinctual vitality and immediacy, freedom from rational and realistic constraints and categories, or lack of differentiation from objects and persons.[1]

Regressive processes have been especially emphasized in the analysis of modern, avant-garde art, sometimes as a reason for praise and sometimes for denigration. A particularly blatant example of the latter is Carl Jung's (1971) assessment of the experimental writing of James Joyce:

> If worms were gifted with literary powers they would write with the sympathetic nervous system for lack of a brain. I suspect that something of this kind has happened to Joyce, that we have here a case of visceral thinking with severe restriction of cerebral activity and its confinement to the perceptual processes. One is driven to unqualified admiration for Joyce's feats in the sensory sphere . . . [but] despite the clearness of the individual images, one wonders whether one is dealing with a physical or with a transcendental tape worm. (p. 112)

Similarly, the classical analyst Franz Alexander (1957) sees the nonobjective art of the early 20th century as an "acting-out" of the "naked unconscious," "an elemental breakthrough . . . of the primitive-disorganized impulses of the id" (pp. 357, 364). Kris (1964, p. 30) believes that, since the 18th century, all the arts had come to rely increasingly on the regressive "inspirational" processes rather than the more mature and rational processes of "elaboration." More recently, the sociologist Daniel Bell (1976) has taken a similar view of various expressions of what has sometimes been called *postmodernism*; he considers such art to be purely hedonistic and arational, a mode of experience and expression dominated by "impulse and pleasure alone" (p. 51) and that seeks to efface all separation between subject and object. A more positive portrayal of the supposed primitivity of modern art is offered by Peter Fuller (1980), a critic influenced by object-relations theory who sees modernist abstract

---

[1]In general, object-relations theorists seem less concerned than ego psychologists with pointing out the role (albeit secondary) that is played by nonprimitive processes in aesthetic consciousness.

art as affording a salutary regression that "may be compared with the individual's *necessary* regression towards a position from which a 'new beginning' (in this instance, perhaps, a new realism) was possible" (p. 176). Other examples can be found in the interesting interpretations offered by object-relations theorists and self-psychologists who view nonrepresentational art as especially suited to the evocation of archaic self-states involving highly abstract relations such as those between container and contained (e.g., Kutash, 1982).

ROMANTICISM

One consequence of the insularity pervasive in psychoanalysis is a tendency to neglect intellectual roots in other fields. For this reason, perhaps, little attention seems to have been paid, at least within the psychoanalytic community, to the important affinities between these psychological theories of art and those of Romanticism.[2] (I use the term *Romanticism* to refer to the comprehensive intellectual and artistic movement whose heyday, both in England and Germany, can be dated between the years 1790 and 1820, but whose influence extends throughout the 19th and into the 20th centuries; see Abrams, 1971, p. 11; Bloom, 1970, p. 4.)

For most of the Romantics, as for the psychoanalysts of the following century, aesthetic experience required achieving a sense of unity between self and world, a temporary escape from the self-conscious ego, and a consequent liberation of the vital organic forces of instinct and emotion, as well as a sloughing off of conventional schemata of perception and understanding. These optimal conditions for aesthetic experience were generally seen as characteristic of early childhood; to experience them was therefore to return, in some sense, to an earlier and more primitive condition of grace. The "immortal longings of the child, rather variously interpreted," writes Bloom (1970), are at the source of the revival of "romance consciousness" from which 19th-century Romanticism largely derives (p. 4). It would obviously be impossible to deal here with all the important figures in this international movement. However, to comprehend Romantic aesthetic theory—to understand its unifying themes without neglecting certain important sources of diversity as well as to see its parallels with the various psychoanalytic theories of art—it will be sufficient to focus on William Wordsworth and Samuel Taylor Coleridge, generally considered the exemplary poet and exemplary critic-aesthetician of English Romanticism.

---

[2]These affinities are, however, mentioned in Spector (1972) and in Spitz (1985, pp. 26–32). Also see Trilling (1981).

The glorification of the primitive and the instinctual is most obvious in Wordsworth, who tended to presuppose a polarity between "nature"—understood as signifying all that is instinctual, emotional, spontaneous—and "art"—understood in the special sense of signifying what is studied and deliberate, the product of self-conscious intellectual control. Wordsworth did not reject altogether any role for what psychoanalysis associates with the ego, secondary process, or more mature psyche; but, at least in his early critical writings, he relegated these to a distinctly subordinate and inferior plane (Abrams, 1984, p. 126). In his poem 'The Prelude," Wordsworth (1977) describes conscious revision as "the very littleness of life . . . relapses from one interior life that lives in all things" (p. 165); in his preface to *Lyrical Ballads*, he twice defines poetry as "the spontaneous overflow of powerful feelings" (Wordsworth & Coleridge, 1963). Wordsworth's views are, in fact, remarkably close to the position that Kris was to take more than a century later. Like Kris, Wordsworth accepts that conscious and deliberate mental processes do play a role both before and after the poem actually comes to be. For Wordsworth, the artist's outburst of spontaneous feeling must be "in the service of the ego" in two senses: it can be truly creative only in the person who has "thought long and deeply" (quoted in Abrams, 1958, p. 113), becoming practiced and skilled in his art; also, the outburst must be refined afterward by arduous processes of revision. The creative moment itself, however, was still assumed to originate in more primitive and natural impulses that spontaneously arise, without contamination by deliberation or doubt. This, in Wordsworth's view, was how the earliest poets wrote, and their work is the standard to which all valid poetry must still aspire (Abrams, 1984, p. 7).

In his *Biographia Literaria*, Coleridge (1907) subjects Wordsworth's polarizing of "nature" and "art" to a sustained critique—one reminiscent of the criticisms directed at Freud and Kris by certain ego psychologists. Like the analyst Noy, Coleridge (1907), who was profoundly influenced by German writers such as Schiller (1966), describes not an alternation but an intimate integration of more and less primitive, more and less controlled psychological processes—a process that blends both "the natural and the artificial" into a "higher third" in which there is "an interpenetration of passion and of will, of *spontaneous* impulse and of *voluntary* purpose" (II, p. 50). Emotion itself cannot, for example, be conceived of as a mere passive outburst, because, to be aesthetically useful, it will have to be "voluntarily encouraged and kept up for the sake of that pleasure" that derives from the creation of "forms and figures of speech" (p. 50). Against Wordsworth's contention that the proper diction for poetry derives directly from "the natural conversation of man under the influence of natural feelings" (quoted in Abrams, 1958, p. 120),

Coleridge (1907) stresses that a poem's elements are "formed into meter *artificially*, by a *voluntary* act," and with a particular "design" and "purpose," that of "blending *delight* with emotion" (II, p. 50). Coleridge's criticism of Wordsworth's psychology of creative expression rests, in fact, on a disagreement with Wordsworth's most fundamental conceptual distinction. Coleridge argues that one can no longer oppose "nature" to "art" or to "mind" once one understands nature itself in the appropriate organicist or biological fashion—as a domain not merely of blind or mechanical forces but of spirit and purpose. For then deliberation and control need not be thought of as antinatural; such teleological psychological processes can be understood as heightened expressions of nature's own purposiveness.

I have begun with differences between Wordsworth and Coleridge, but this should not obscure their commonalities, which are still more significant. Thus, despite his critique of Wordsworth's art–nature opposition, his emphasis on a harmonizing and blending of the natural and the artificial, Coleridge nevertheless argued that the greatest poetry "still subordinates art to nature" (II, p. 12). Coleridge may have rejected Wordsworth's tendency to treat mind and purpose as antinatural; yet, like Wordsworth and virtually all the Romantics, he was acutely aware of the dangers of a deadening form of self-consciousness and self-constraint. Coleridge believed the creative genius could not function in the presence of a certain kind of self-monitoring awareness: Like a tree that grows purposively but unconsciously, creative thoughts and perceptions must germinate spontaneously, without the deadening intrusion of rational or critical self-awareness (Abrams, 1958, p. 205). This recalls the psychoanalysts' stress on the need, in creative and aesthetic experience, for relative freedom from both the "observing ego" and the repressive superego. Also, like Kris and other analysts, Coleridge (1907) believed a certain Dionysian element was required in any act of creative expression: He agreed with Wordsworth that poetry "does always imply PASSION" and that all successful figures of speech had to be based in emotional states (II, p. 56).

Coleridge's attitude toward childhood was also similar to that of Wordsworth and many other Romantics, as well as to that of certain psychoanalysts (especially those of the schools of ego psychology and object-relations theory) who view early childhood as the condition of grace to which all aesthetic experience aspires. In a passage reminiscent of Schiller's (1966) famous essay, "Naive and Sentimental Poetry" (pp. 85, 87, 100), Coleridge writes of "a feeling similar to that with which we gaze at a beautiful infant. . . . It seems as if the soul said to herself: from this state has *thou* fallen! Such shouldst thou still become" (quoted in Abrams, 1984, p. 126). In a passage on Wordsworth that recalls Schachtel's criticism of the conventionalized perception of normal adulthood (secondary autocentricity), Coleridge (1907) describes the proper goal of art as "to give the charm of novelty to things of every day, and to excite a feeling analogous to the supernatural, by awakening the mind's attention from the lethargy of custom, and directing it to the loveliness and the wonders of the world before us" (II, p. 6). Both Coleridge and Wordsworth saw childhood as the time when such conditions were fulfilled, and maturation as a process of alienation from this state of grace. To revivify vision, the artist therefore needed to regain the spirit of childhood, as Coleridge (1907) argued in his *Biographia Literaria*:

> To carry on the feelings of childhood into the powers of manhood; to combine the child's sense of wonder and novelty with the appearances, which every day for perhaps forty years had rendered familiar . . . this is the character of genius. . . . And therefore it is the prime merit of genius . . . so to represent familiar objects as to awaken in the minds of others . . . that freshness of sensation. (I, pp. 59–60)

Coleridge and Wordsworth glorified childhood not only for its freshness of sensation but also for its greater sense of union, both within the self (where, for example, intellect and emotion were not yet sundered) and between the self and the world (where a quasi-mystical sense of participation prevailed). Indeed Coleridge was, in the words of the scholar M. H. Abrams (1971), a "compulsive monist" who always stressed the importance of "familial participation in the one" (pp. 266–267). This Romantic view of aesthetic experience, a view that sees art as recreating the original oneness from which maturation is a falling away, is echoed in the psychoanalytic aesthetics of object-relations theorists such as Segal (1952), for whom creation is a "re-creation of a once loved and once whole . . . object" (p. 199).

Abrams (1971) has pointed out that the Romantics offered an aestheticized version of a religious conception first formulated by the neoplatonist Plotinus and pervasive through the whole history of Christian thought. This was the notion of human existence as an inevitable progression away from a valued state of primordial oneness and toward a state of evil understood as "the farthest state of division, separateness, and multiplicity" (p. 147). For Plotinus, the goal of life was the attempt to return to this primordial state, to attain to a state of ecstatic union devoid of all division. With its notion of a primordial stage of symbiotic union, and its conception of "creative" experience as involving a partial return to such a condition, psychoanalysis, at least in its object-relational forms, might be said to have given us not an aestheticized but a psychologized version of the Myth of the Great Return.

It is true that Coleridge, like most of the Romantics, conceived of this return as a return occurring at a higher level of consciousness—as the curving of a spiral rather than a circle, to use an imagery they favored. Coleridge did not advocate a simple regression to an earlier state of primal oneness in which all distinctions—between, say, self and world—would be effaced, but, rather, a progression to a condition of undivided unity in which all forms of alienation (both within the self and between self and world), but not all forms of differentiation, would be overcome. Coleridge's philosophy thus combines two traditions that may seem incompatible: a naturalist or primitivist tradition that had existed since the Renaissance, glorifying wildness and simplicity, and the German philosophical tradition of the 1790s that emphasizes ceaseless striving and perpetual self-transcendence.[3] The desideratum proposed by this exemplary theoretician of English Romanticism involves a return that occurs at a higher level of complexity or sophistication. In this respect Coleridge's view is close to Schachtel's conception of creative "allocentricity," which also hearkens back to the child's freshness and sense of resonance with the world while maintaining a more mature awareness of the object's otherness. Similarly, the psychoanalyst Rose (1980a) believes that the creative impulse arises from "the early undifferentiated phase of psychological development when there is a sense of coalescence between the child and all that is," but describes the life course of the creative person as a "continuous return to sameness which is yet different [and] might be represented by a simple spiral" (pp. 91, 94).

Clearly, then, the psychoanalytic and Romantic writers on the psychology of art have remarkable affinities, both in the fundamental assump-

---

[3]The difference of opinion between two great scholars in the history of ideas turns upon this last point. In "On the Discrimination of Romanticisms," A. O. Lovejoy (1948) attacks the idea that the term *Romanticism* refers to any single, coherent tradition. The two most important of the three distinct *Romanticisms* he describes are the traditions of naturalism and primitivism and that of perpetual self-transcendence, both of which I have just mentioned. Lovejoy thinks of these as virtually antithetical and criticizes scholars who conflate them: "An ideal of ceaseless striving towards goals too vast or too exacting ever to be wholly attained has been confused with nostalgia for the untroubled, because unaspiring, indolent and unselfconscious life of the man of nature" (p. 236). In several more recent studies, Abrams (1958, 1971, 1984), perhaps the greatest contemporary scholar of Romanticism, argues that the Romanticism of the late 18th and early 19th centuries is, in fact, a reasonably unified tradition. A central purpose of his *Natural Supernaturalism* (1971) is to demonstrate the importance in Romanticism of the narrative of the "circuitous journey" from primal unity through alienation to a condition of reintegration that is both higher and more natural than what precedes it. For Abrams, then, the central concern of the Romantics is precisely to synthesize the very traditions Lovejoy sees as mutually exclusive.

For a dissenting view of Romanticism, one that aligns it more with both modernism and deconstructive criticism, and questions its commitment to organicist notions, see Rajan (1980).

tions they make and in the issues that arouse disagreement among them. There is, in both traditions, considerable argument about how the role of primitive, unconscious, or instinctual modes of experience should be conceived: Do these modes totally overshadow others that are more mature, controlled, and self-conscious? If not, how is the relationship between the modes to be conceptualized—as that of essence and disguise, as processes alternating in ascendancy, as a simultaneous interplay of opposite forces, or perhaps as a more intimate synthesis of processes whose radical differentness is really an illusion? What is not questioned, in either tradition, is the idea that an essential or necessary role in aesthetic creation and appreciation is played by processes that are closely akin to the primitive and irrational forms of consciousness of childhood or infancy. It seems reasonable to call this the *regression view* of art, as long as one remembers that this label does not imply that rational or nonprimitive factors may not also be significant.

It is important to recognize that, far from being universal, such conceptions of aesthetics are largely the product of a particular historical epoch— an epoch whose influence on the less avant-garde areas of contemporary culture is, however, still profound enough to make its assumptions seem virtually self-evident, thus invisible. The regression view does, after all, apply rather well to a great deal of art from the last 2 centuries, much of which actually inspired, or was inspired by, the Romantic ethos. To conclude from this that the regression view is adequate as a general theory of art would, however, betray a lack of historical perspective. The regression view is closely allied with, perhaps even inseparable from, what have been called *expressive* theories of art, and these are by no means the only ones to have dominated aesthetic thought in the West. *Mimetic theories* emphasized the imitation of external reality or of eternal forms, whereas *pragmatic* theories conceived of art as a form of teaching. Pre-Romantic neoclassical aesthetics were rationalistic in important respects, stressing the importance of rules and advocating a "pleasingness" based not on spontaneity but on the achievement or perception of verisimilitude in accordance with certain standards of order, harmony, and proportion. Indeed, irrationality, spontaneity, and a sense of union with the ambient world would seem to play at most a minor role in these conceptions of aesthetic experience that dominated the centuries before Romanticism. In the rest of this chapter, however, we turn to a period that comes not before but after the Romantic era. I want to consider how well the regression theories apply to the modernist and postmodernist art of the 20th century—to the very era that, as suggested previously, is often assumed to be most extreme in its regressive tendencies.

Before proceeding, a few words should be said to clarify the concepts of *modernism* and *postmodernism*. Although the boundaries of modernism can certainly be disputed, it is frequently assumed to encompass the years between the turn of the century and the beginning of World War II, with its heyday coming before and after World War I in the work of writers and artists such as Eliot, Pound, Valéry, Rilke, Picasso, and Matisse. Those who use postmodernism as a period concept usually place its advent some time after World War II, but often as late as the 1960s. Increasingly, however, the term *postmodernism* is also used to refer to a kind of art or aesthetic attitude that has been with us throughout the 20th century, especially in movements such as Dada and Futurism (see, e.g., Lyotard, 1984; Perloff, 1986). Major postmodernist figures would include the novelists Alain Robbe-Grillet and Donald Barthelme, the poet John Ashbery, the artists Andy Warhol and Jasper Johns, and the composer-conceptual artist John Cage; Marcel Duchamp is often cited as the major proto-postmodernist from earlier in the 20th century (see Sass, 1992, especially pp. 28–36, 343–350, 417–418). Clearly, postmodernist art does owe much to the modernist art that is generally seen as having preceded it; indeed, some scholars and critics would deny that postmodernism involves a significant departure. Those who do see a significant break between the two periods or styles have characterized the stylistic difference in a variety of ways, one of which involves the distinction to be developed later between *symbolic* and *allegorical* art (supposedly associated with modernism and postmodernism, respectively).

MODERNISM

Like any period of aesthetic or intellectual life, that of modernism does not just reject but also perpetuates previous attitudes and sensibilities. Accordingly, it would be foolish to deny that art of this type contains many echoes of Romanticism and of such post-Romantic or late Romantic movements as *Symbolism*.[4] (One such echo—the preference for symbolic over allegorical art—is discussed in the next section.) At least as significant in modernism's development, however, are certain radical departures from Romantic aesthetics, departures foreshadowed by the aesthetic views and practices of Charles Baudelaire, the mid-19th-century poet whose anti-Romantic tendencies have been viewed as both proto-modernist and proto-postmodernist (Abrams, 1984, pp. 109–144; Jameson, 1986).

Baudelaire viewed "nature" not as a state of grace or source of redemption but as the locus of ugliness and source of original sin; therefore he derided spontaneity and emotionalism, advocating instead a poetry produced by craft and detached calculation. The poet and painter

---

[4]The continuity of modernism with Romanticism is maintained by Kermode (1971) and Bloom (1970) among others. See also Sass (1992, pp. 343–345).

Wyndham Lewis advocated (controlled) mechanical structure over (spontaneous) organic form; the critic T. E. Hulme characterized the Romantic tradition—with its emotionalism and its quasi-mystical yearnings—as a "period of slush" and "spilt religion" (quoted in Bate, 1952, p. 560). Ezra Pound denigrated the soft-edged, merger-seeking impressionism of the Romantics in favor of the "hard light and clear edges" (quoted in Levenson, 1984, pp. 147–148) of what he considered a valid modern literature. Each of these influential modernists follows Baudelaire in refusing the Romantic and post-Romantic glorification of organic unity, spontaneous impulse, emotionality, and the seeking of a kind of fusion with the world. This implies rejecting most of the forms of primitive consciousness that psychoanalytic regression theories identify as crucial to the aesthetic mode of consciousness—the instinctual release emphasized by classical psychoanalysis, the self-delighting spontaneity of the primary process that ego psychologists describe, as well as the re-creation of wholeness of object-relations theory.

Much anti-Romantic modernist art does, however, accept the goal, first formulated by the Romantics, of renewing perception by shedding familiar and clichéd meanings; in this respect it may seem compatible with the views of Schachtel as well as those of Wordsworth and Coleridge. Such a goal is central, for instance, to such important modernist notions as the Russian formalists' notion of *ostrananie*, Brecht's *defamiliarization*, and the surrealist attempt "to live in the world as if in a vast museum of strangeness" (as the proto-Surrealist Giorgio de Chirico had recommended; Jean, 1980, p. 6). I argue, however, that crucial differences belie the surface affinities between these modernist modes of renewal and those advocated by the Romantics and the psychoanalysts who extol the fresh vision of childhood.[5]

Both the lived-world of infancy or early childhood and that of what might be called modernist alienation are, of course, very different from normal, pragmatic adult consciousness; in this purely negative sense they surely have something in common—a shared difference-from. However, if one carefully considers the overall phenomenology of the classically modernist experiences, they seem in many respects to be antithetical to infantile states. According to virtually all psychological theories of development, the world of the infant and young child is infused with an intense and dynamic sense of emotional involvement. Even inanimate

---

[5]This is not to say that certain modernists (e.g., the surrealist André Breton, 1972, p. 39) did not sometimes compare creative to childlike states. However, it is interesting to note that, at least in the case of Surrealism, the conception of the primitive and the irrational differs significantly from that of Romanticism. Thus, Breton's conception of *psychic automatism* seems more mechanistic than vitalistic (p. 26), and he conceives of childhood experience as being imbued with "a sentiment of being *un*integrated" (p. 40, italics added).

objects and space itself are perceived largely in terms of their affective resonance for the perceiving child. Further, the world of the infant is not yet felt to be a thing wholly separate from the self, for there prevails a quasi-mystical sense of union between subject and object. By contrast, the modernist experiences of defamiliarization involve a profound disengagement from reality and detachment from the processes of life. The renewal of perception they engender is associated not with mystic union and heightened emotional involvement but with detachment; it is a making-strange that is also an estrangement.

The literary scholar Erich Kahler (1957) has described the uncanny magic of many central examples of 20th-century art as manifesting a certain *schizaesthesia* (p. 182). Instead of the joyful merging sought by the Romantics, he speaks of an "insistent, overstressed correctness" or "lucid indifference" so devoid of normal emotional resonance as to result in a "disjunction of the organic, disjunction of the sensorially coherent being, of the person and of the object" (pp. 90, 159). Good examples are Roquentin's experiences in Sartre's *Nausea* and the vision of a fragmenting world and language described in Hugo von Hoffmansthal's "Letter of Lord Chandos." Although Kahler calls this *a new mysticism* in modernist art, it is better described as an antimysticism—for it involves not an embracing of all things and of self and world into a single unity but the opposite, dissociation and estrangement. Abrams (1971, p. 458) has suggested one needs the buoyancy and resilience of youth to sustain the Romantics' joyful vision of "familial participation" in a unified, organic universe; the modernist gaze—scrutinizing, penetrating, sometimes even deadening—seems that of an era less innocent and less hopeful. It is significant that Kahler describes these developments as signs not of regression but of progression—cruel consequences of the "steady growth of man's self-reflection and psychological introspection," and of a "mental microscopy" that turns on both self and world (pp. 138, 159). In one sense this attitude represents the triumph of consciousness and volitional control, but it is, in another sense, the opposite: it happens like a compulsion, and, as Kahler puts it, "the man who looks seems himself to be just an instrument, or victim, of this irresistible seeing" (p. 170). Clearly, this is not the kind of spontaneous inspiration or the progression spoken of by Coleridge and other Romantics (including the psychoanalysts Schachtel and Rose): here there is no spiraling, no escape from alienation, no recuperation of the lost unity of an earlier time.

POSTMODERNISM

Let us now turn to a somewhat different phase or aspect of 20th-century art, a mode of aesthetic perception where not only a sense of unity and resonant emotionality but also one of newness, freshness, or sensory presentness is lacking. Such forms of experience and expression tend to be especially common in what is often called *postmodernism*—that is, in much art of the last couple of decades as well as in certain avatar works from earlier in the century.

As I mentioned before, many forms of modernist art do not strive for a feeling of organic unity, either within the perceived object (which tends to be fragmented) or between the perceiver and his or her world (where the prevailing mood involves a certain alienation). We saw, however, that they do retain at least one goal reminiscent of Romanticism, that of renewing perception—what the poet Shelley (1954) described as "mak[ing] familiar objects be as if they were not familiar" (p. 282) to achieve a vision truer and more authentic than that of conventional, pragmatic perception. Whereas the modernists did not seek a child's freshness of vision, like the Romantics they did advocate a desisting from categorical perception, from the concern with identifying a perceptual object in terms of its class membership. The modernists also continued to adhere, in less ambiguous fashion, to another closely related Romantic tenet: the valorizing of sensory "presentness." For the modernists, meaning and value were to be contained in the experience of the sensory medium of the unique artwork directly present to perception, rather than in more cognitive or classificatory modes of awareness that treat the sensory object as a mere pretext, tool, or sign. As the poet Karl Shapiro put it: "The intelligence of art is a sensory intelligence, the meaning of art is a sensory meaning. . . . There is no such thing as a good work of art which is not immediately apprehensible in the senses" (quoted in de Man, 1983, p. 244).[6]

This attitude, which is shared by Romantic and modernist but not by postmodernist aesthetics, is best understood by considering the distinction, derived from Goethe but made famous by Coleridge, between "symbol" and "allegory." Coleridge glorified the true aesthetic object— what he called the *symbolic*, as opposed to the *allegorical*, image—for not depending in any essential way on a referred-to realm of meaning that exists prior to, beyond, or behind the sensory immanence of the artwork. Supposedly, in such images or "symbols," both meaning and form emanate organically from the material itself. ("Such as the life is, such is the form," wrote Coleridge of such symbols; quoted in Fletcher, 1964, p. 16.) Coleridge contrasted this condition with that of traditional religious allegories such as Bunyan's *Pilgrim's Progress*, which he considered to be overly rationalized, divided, and lacking in a crucial quality of ontological presence. The Romantics saw allegory as a self-conscious process in which

---

[6]As the critic Michael Fried (1968) put it in a famous line from his promodernist (and antipostmodernist) essay, "Art and Objecthood": "Presentness is grace" (p. 147).

preordained meanings or forms were mechanically imposed on the medium of representation—imposed in a self-conscious, deliberate, and premeditated rather than a spontaneous or natural fashion. They also criticized allegorical works for the unreal or ghostlike quality of the sensory reality they do present; hence, Coleridge's (1953) denigration of the ontological status of both the signifier and the signified in allegorical representation:

> Now an allegory is but a translation of abstract notions into a picture language, which is itself nothing but an abstraction from objects of the senses; the principal [i.e., the referred-to realm of abstract notions] being more worthless even than its phantom proxy, both alike insubstantial, and the former shapeless to boot. (p. 25)[7]

For the Romantics, then, allegory was characterized by a fateful semiotic split, a division into two separate and inevitably unsatisfying domains: a signified realm of preexistent and conventional meanings (e.g., the biblical tale that is the ultimate if indirect reference) and a signifying medium (the overt plot) that lacks primary or substantial ontological status because it is but a code pointing elsewhere (see Fletcher, 1964, pp. 13–19.) If there is a kind of "unmediated vision" (Hartman, 1954) in the presence of the true symbol, this is because, in contrast to allegory, the symbolic image never simply represents but, as Coleridge (1953) puts it, "always partakes of the reality which it renders intelligible . . . abid[ing] itself as a living part in that unity of which it is the representative" (p. 25).

This exaltation of sensory presence and immediacy in art is equally central in most forms of psychoanalytic aesthetics. Freudians have emphasized how the artist or poet—like the dreamer, child, and schizophrenic—stays in close touch with concrete, sensory aspects of experience, such as the pure sound-qualities of words. As we saw, Schachtel (1959) considers abstract, conventional meanings—"the encroachment of an already labelled world upon our spontaneous sensory and intellectual capacities"—to be the enemy of creative or aesthetic vision because these meanings come increasingly to overwhelm immediate sensory and perceptual experiences, transforming the latter into "mere recognition of the familiar" (p. 170). I have also mentioned the analyst Noy's stressing of what he calls the *primary level* of perception (i.e., the concrete-sensory as opposed to the conventionally meaningful aspects of the aesthetic object). This primary level, which

---

[7]According to Goethe, in allegory "the particular serves only as an example of the general," a mere illustration in the phenomenal plane of preexistent meanings of an abstract kind; by contrast, true poetry always "expresses something particular, without thinking of the general or pointing to it" (quoted in Fletcher, 1964, p. 13).

Noy considers to be more dominant in the experience of child and artist than in that of the average adult, is, for him, the sine qua non of aesthetic experience and communication (Noy, 1972, pp. 244, 246; 1978). Various other analysts have focused attention on the role played in painting by the sensory immediacy of paint and canvas, seeing these experiences as reminiscent of the concrete and tactile universe of the infant or young child, in whom bodily sensitivity is extreme (Greenacre, 1957; Rose, 1980a, p. 100; Sharpe, 1935).

It is just these features of aesthetic objects that have been downgraded in much of the art of recent years, where the aspiration is no longer toward what one critic (Foster, 1983) has called the "utopian dream of a time of pure presence, [the] space beyond representation" so central to the aesthetics of Romanticism as well as modernism (p. xv). According to the conceptions of some critics, in fact, it is the valuing of the previously despised qualities of allegorical art that most clearly distinguishes postmodernist aesthetics from the modernist and Romanticist notions that preceded it. Thus Fredric Jameson (1979) describes the art of the postmodernist or poststructuralist period as characterized by an aesthetic of discontinuity and the mechanical, as well as by a certain allegoricality and a gap between signifier and signified (p. 20). The critic Craig Owens (1984) suggests postmodernist art may be characterized by a single, coherent trend, best understood as "an unmistakably allegorical impulse" (pp. 204, 209). Coinciding with these developments in art has been a certain rehabilitation by critics and scholars of aspects of pre-Romanticist aesthetics, especially the concept of allegory. In several influential essays, the literary scholar Paul de Man, who had come under the influence of Jacques Derrida, defended allegory for its explicit acceptance of certain features of human signification that the Romantics had tried to escape, repress, or deny—namely, the inevitable gap between signifier and signified and the unavoidability of preordained cultural codes. In allegorical art, these features are, supposedly, accepted and foregrounded rather than repressed, for allegory is an aesthetic mode that, in de Man's (1983) words, "de-mystifies" the notion of an organic world and "renounc[es] the nostalgia and the desire to coincide [and thereby] prevents the self from an illusory identification with the non-self, which is now fully, though painfully, recognized as a non-self" (p. 207). Such allegorical art is congruent with Jacques Derrida's famous attack on the "metaphysics of presence," whereas both Romantic and modernist aesthetics seem more akin to the thought of Heidegger, a philosopher with strong primitivist leanings whose perspective Derrida (1982) describes as "an entire metaphysics of proximity, of simple and immediate presence" (p. 130).

An evaluation more ambivalent than de Man's is offered in Susan Sontag's "Notes on Camp," an essay one can read as an early description of the postmodernist sensibility. There Sontag (1969) describes the "camp" attitude as a drama of underinvolvement that "sees everything in quotation marks. It's not a lamp but a 'lamp'; not a woman, but a 'woman.' To perceive camp in objects and person is to understand Being-as-playing-a-role" (p. 281). Sontag (1969) describes how this mode of aesthetic vision can involve a curious doubling, in which the object actually perceived seems to be essentially an instantiation of something lying behind it, which may be a general category (lamp as "lamp") or else a kind of Platonic essence of itself ("In every move the aging Martha Graham makes she's being Martha Graham, etc., etc."; p. 287). Camp involves a sense of detachment rather than union with the world. It is a predominantly cerebral rather than emotive kind of experience. Instead of focusing on the concrete sensory presence and uniqueness of the object, one adopts a form of categorical perception in which the object seems but an instantiation of some absent, abstract, or more general meaning.[8] Also, rather than adhering to Ezra Pound's famous modernist advice— "Make it new!"—such postmodernist art may offer an apotheosis of the familiar or the ordinary that trades upon the already known or even clichéd quality of its object (Wilde, 1987, p. 149; also see Calinescu, 1977, pp. 225–262, re "kitsch").

Camp is not, however, the only example of what has been called a widespread *allegoricality* in postmodern art. In a rather different type of allegoricality, *presentness* is attenuated in favor of concentration on what seems a distinct but elusive meaning, one that retains an irresolvable ambiguity and to which the immediately present, sensory subject can only allude. This is particularly evident in Marcel Duchamp's famous work, "The Bride Stripped Bare by Her Bachelors, Even,"—known as the "Large Glass"—a piece Duchamp himself described as "allegorical appearance" and that seems to exemplify this artist's stated ambition to escape from "the physicality of painting" (Cabanne, 1971; Owens, 1984, p. 204). The "Large Glass" presents, between panes of glass, a number of precise but mysterious forms that inevitably provoke—and just as inevitably frustrate—a desire in the viewer to figure out just what preexistent meaning is being signified.

A related kind of allegoricality is exploited by the performance artist Laurie Anderson, who sometimes uses conventional or clichéd images to demonstrate the curious ambiguity of signs, which never intrinsically contain their meanings but rather rely on the (often ambiguous) cultural

---

[8]It is true that, as in the case of the camp perception of Martha Graham, the meaning alluded to may constitute a pseudocategory, because it includes only one member, the actual object perceived. But this does not negate the fact that the experience of sensory presentness is minimized or eliminated. For related discussion, see Sass, 1994, pp. 97–116.

context. In one performance, for example, Anderson projects an image that was emblazoned on the Apollo 10 spacecraft: a nude woman and man, with the man's right arm raised. But how, Anderson asks during the performance, will the extraterrestials for whom this is intended know how to read this sign? How will they know whether the image indicates hello or goodbye, or whether, for instance, it simply depicts the position in which the right arms of men from the planet Earth are permanently fixed (see Owens, 1984, pp. 219–220)?

Art of this kind can hardly be described as escaping the preoccupation with conventional or abstract meanings that Schachtel associates with secondary autocentricity: either it provokes the viewer to seek conventionalized meanings lying behind the sensory appearances (as in Duchamp's "Large Glass"), or else it causes the viewer to contemplate or sense, in an alienated and intellectualized fashion, the curious phenomenon of referential meaning itself (as in Laurie Anderson's performance). It is worth contrasting such experiences with those of the Romantic "symbol." In the experience valued by the Romantics and their followers (which, at least on this issue, includes the Symbolist as well as modernist schools), the experience of the aesthetic object does not seem to imply some distant and expressly conventional meaning, or some other, more real version of the object. Hence the experience is not imbued with the kind of doubledness that in the allegorical experience makes the visible object seem a pale copy of itself or of some abstraction, or a cipher to be decoded. As a result, the Romantic image is devoid of that tantalizing doubledness, that ever-frustrating feeling that reality always lies elsewhere that is so central to much of postmodernism.

The ways in which postmodernist allegory differs from more traditional allegories like Bunyan's *Pilgrim's Progress* or Dante's *Inferno* should also be noted. Whereas the latter were products of relatively unified cultures, whose members could assume the same sacred canopy of religious and cosmological meanings, the postmodernist allegories tend to be idiosyncratic and elusive; the realm they refer to seems unstable, ambiguous, perhaps even nonexistent. In the words of one critic (Owens, 1984), these contemporary allegories "proffer and defer a promise of meaning"; unlike traditional allegory, "they both solicit and frustrate our desire that the image be directly transparent to its signification. As a result they appear strangely incomplete—fragments or runes which must be deciphered" (p. 206). Such allegories might better be termed *pseudoallegories*, because, when followed through, the deciphering they invite may not lead anywhere but only circle back to the image or cipher with which one began.

We see, then, that in many examples of postmodernist art, the last vestiges of Romanticism still present in modernism—authenticity of perception, presentness, uniqueness—are jettisoned, to be replaced by a virtual cult of inauthenticity and absence. In the postmodernist modes of perception, a certain estrangement or alienation is central, but, paradoxically enough, this seems rooted in the disconcerting impact of a certain experience of recognition (or, pseudorecognition) rather than, as in many examples of modernist art, in a more straightforward process of defamiliarizing the familiar. The feeling of strangeness characteristically evoked by postmodernist art does not stem from a sense of newness or uniqueness characteristic of primitive consciousness, but resides instead in certain uncanny feelings of inauthenticity, doubling, or disconcerting familiarity. The sensory presence of the work recedes in favor of a more cognitive quality of enigmatic meaningfulness.

Postmodernism, we might say, rejects the last vestiges of Romantic aesthetics. Therefore it is a sensibility to which traditional Romanticist psychologies of art, whether in philosophy or in psychoanalysis, are almost wholly inapplicable.

CONCLUDING REMARKS

Once one stops taking it for granted, it may seem odd that theories of the general nature of aesthetic expression or appreciation should ever have been sought. In his famous discussion of "family concepts," Wittgenstein argued that, just because there is a word, one should not assume all things designated by that word must necessarily share a common essence. The category art, or *aesthetic consciousness*, seems hardly more likely to be based on a single essence than that of *games*, Wittgenstein's main example. Rather than having a single positive attribute in common, members of such a category may only share the absence of some quality—or there may not even be that degree of negative commonality. Here I do not attempt to answer this larger question of the very possibility of a general theory of aesthetic consciousness. What I have tried to do in this chapter is only to demonstrate the limitations of one especially influential attempt at such a theory.

We have seen that the modes of aesthetic consciousness most prominent in modernism and postmodernism are quite different from the regressed, Dionysian, quasi-mystical modes emphasized by so many aesthetic theorists who, wittingly or not, have adopted a Romantic or post-Romantic view. To apply the concepts of Romantic aesthetics to such art is, I believe, more likely to distort than to illuminate its actual nature. Romanticism associated aesthetic perception with a certain openness to the world, with what Schachtel (1959) described as willingness "to remain in the flux of the fully allocentric encounter"—to desist temporarily from categorical perception (which he calls "secondary autocentricity") and thereby to give up the pragmatic but ultimately alienating need "to take hold of the object and fix it, to wrest it from the infinite process of world and life, and to fix it at a definite point where we can take hold of it again, recall it, refind it" (p. 200). F. Scott Fitzgerald, in this and other respects a post-Romantic artist, described this aspect of Romantic aesthetics very succinctly when he wrote that "To observe you must be unwary." The modernist or postmodernist novelist Nathalie Sarraute (1963), by contrast, has described the modern period as an "era of suspicion." The kind of perception characteristic of much modernist and postmodernist art does seem to be infused with a hyperscrutinizing or constantly wary watchfulness.

The orientation toward experience involved in many of the forms of 20th-century art discussed in this chapter might, in fact, be compared to that of such thinkers as Erving Goffman or Ludwig Wittgenstein, writers who defamiliarize the world, whether of everyday social interaction or of philosophical discourse, by their capacity to stand back from, and render explicit, what normally comes so naturally as to remain unnoticed. In my view, this type of creativity is closely allied with the alienated and hyperconscious scrutiny that the Romantics and their followers have deplored. It has little to do with the chthonic unconscious forces, the freewheeling spontaneity, or the capacity to merge with the All that have been emphasized in regression theories of aesthetic consciousness, whether in Romanticism or in psychoanalysis.[9]

REFERENCES

Abrams, M. H. (1958). *The mirror and the lamp: Romantic theory and the critical tradition.* New York: Norton.

Abrams, M. H. (1971). *Natural supernaturalism: Tradition and revolution in Romantic literature.* New York: Norton.

Abrams, M. H. (1984). *The correspondent breeze: Essays on English Romanticism.* New York: Norton.

Alexander, F. (1957). The psychoanalyst looks at contemporary art. In W. Phillips (Ed.), *Art and psychoanalysis* (pp. 346–365). Cleveland: World.

Bate, W. J. (Ed.). (1952). *Criticism: The major texts.* New York: Harcourt, Brace & World.

Bell, D. (1976). *The cultural contradictions of capitalism.* New York: Basic.

---

[9]For further discussion of the role of alienated consciousness in modernism, see Sass (1990, 1992). I am not aware of any psychoanalytic interpretations that explicitly address these increasingly common forms of pseudoallegorical artistic expression. One might, however, be tempted to consider the applicability of Freud's own analysis of experiences of what he called "the uncanny," for such experiences do include the "deja vu" experience, which is also common in postmodernist art, or, at least, is akin to the kind of mood involved in pseudoallegorical doubling. For critical discussion of this issue, see Sass (1990).

Bloom, H. (Ed.). (1970). *Romanticism and consciousness.* New York: Norton.

Bollas, C. (1978). The aesthetic moment and the search for transformation. *The Annual of Psychoanalysis,* 385–394.

Breton, A. (1972). *Manifestoes of surrealism.* Ann Arbor: University of Michigan Press.

Cabanne, P. (1971). *Dialogues with Marcel Duchamp.* New York: Viking.

Calinescu, M. (1977). *Faces of modernity: Avant-garde, decadence, kitsch.* Bloomington & London: Indiana University Press.

Coleridge, S. T. (1907). *Biographia literaria* (2 volumes) (Ed., J. Shawcross). Oxford: Clarendon Press.

Coleridge, S. T. (1953). *The statesman's manual.* In R. J. White (Ed.), *Political tracts of Wordsworth, Coleridge, and Shelley* (pp. 1–53). Cambridge: Cambridge University Press.

de Man, P. (1983). *Blindness and insight: Essays in the rhetoric of contemporary criticism.* Minneapolis: University of Minnesota Press.

Derrida, J. (1982). The ends of man. In J. Derrida (Ed.), *Margins of philosophy* (pp. 109–136). Chicago, IL: University of Chicago Press.

Ehrenzweig, A. (1967). *The hidden order of art.* Berkeley & Los Angeles: University of California Press.

Fletcher, A. (1964). *Allegory: The theory of a symbolic mode.* Ithaca & London: Cornell University Press.

Foster, H. (Ed.). (1983). *The anti-aesthetic: Essays on postmodern culture.* Port Townsend, WA: Bay Press.

Freud, S. (1905). Jokes and their relation to the unconscious. *Standard Edition, 8,* 3–258 (complete volume).

Freud, S. (1908). Creative writers and daydreaming. *Standard Edition, 9,* 141–156.

Freud, S. (1914). The Moses of Michelangelo. *Standard Edition, 13,* 209–240.

Fried, M. (1968). Art and objecthood. In G. Battcock (Ed.), *Minimal art: A critical anthology.* New York: Dutton.

Friedman, S. (1960). One aspect of the structure of music. *Journal of the American Psychoanalytic Association, 8,* 427–449.

Fuller, P. (1980). *Art and psychoanalysis.* London: Writers & Readers Publishing Cooperative.

Gombrich, E. (1963). Psychoanalysis and the history of art. In *Meditations on a hobbyhorse and other essays on the theory of art* (pp. 30–44). New York: Phaidon.

Greenacre, P. (1957). The childhood of the artist: Libidinal phase development and giftedness. *The Psychoanalytic Study of the Child, 12,* 47–72.

Hartman, G. (1954). *The unmediated vision: An interpretation of Wordsworth, Hopkins, Rilke, and Valery.* New Haven, CT: Yale University Press.

Jameson, R. (1979). *Fables of aggression: Wyndham Lewis, the modernist as fascist.* Berkeley: University of California Press.

Jameson, R. (1986). Baudelaire as modernist and postmodernist. In C. Hosek & P. Parker (Eds.), *Lyric poetry: Beyond new criticism* (pp. 247–263). Ithaca, NY: Cornell University Press.

Jean, M. (Ed.). (1980). *The autobiography of surrealism.* New York: Viking.

Jung, C. (1971). "Ulysses": A monologue. In C. Jung, *The spirit in man, art, and literature.* (pp. 109–134). Princeton, NJ: Princeton University Press.

Kahler, E. (1957). *The tower and the abyss: An inquiry into the transformation of man.* New York: Viking.

Kermode, F. (1971). *Romantic image.* London: Fontana.

Koestler, A. (1967). *The act of creation.* New York: Dell.

Kris, E. (1964). *Psychoanalytic explorations in art.* New York: Schocken.

Kutash, E. (1982). A psychoanalytic approach to understanding form in abstract expressionist and minimalist painting. *International Review of Psycho-analysis, 9,* 167–177.

Levenson, M. H. (1984). *A genealogy of modernism: A study of English literary doctrine 1908–1922.* Cambridge: Cambridge University Press.

Lovejoy, A. O. (1948). On the discrimination of Romanticisms. In A. O. Lovejoy, *Essays in the history of ideas* (pp. 228–253). Baltimore: Johns Hopkins University Press.

Lyotard, J.-F. (1984). *The postmodern condition.* Minneapolis: University of Minnesota Press.

Milner, M. (1957). *On not being able to paint.* New York: International Universities Press.

Milner, M. (1978). D. W. Winnicott and the two-way journey. In S. A. Grolnick & L. Barkin (Eds.), *Between reality and fantasy* (pp. 37–42). New York and London: Jason Aronson.

Noy, P. (1972). About art and artistic talent. *International Journal of Psycho-analysis, 53,* 243–249.

Noy, P. (1978). Insight and creativity. *Journal of the American Psychoanalytic Association, 26,* 717–748.

Noy, P. (1984–1985). Originality and creativity. *Annual of Psychoanalysis, 12/13,* 421–448.

Owens, C. (1984). The allegorical impulse: Toward a theory of postmodernism. In B. Wallis (Ed.), *Art after modernism: Rethinking representation* (pp. 203–235). Boston: The New Museum of Contemporary Art/David R. Godine.

Perloff, M. (1986). *The futurist moment: Avant-garde, avant guerre, and the language of rupture.* Chicago & London: University of Chicago Press.

Rajan, T. (1980). *Dark interpreter: The discourse of Romanticism.* Ithaca, NY: Cornell University Press.

Ricoeur, P. (1970). *Freud and philosophy: An essay on interpretation.* New Haven, CT: Yale University Press.

Rose, G. (1980a). *The power of form: A psychoanalytic approach to aesthetic form.* New York: International Universities Press.

Rose, G. (1980b). Some aspects of aesthetics in the light of the rapprochement subphase. In R. F. Lax, S. Bach, & J. A. Barland (Eds.), *Rapprochement: The critical subphase of separation/individuation* (pp. 353–373). New York: Jason Aronson.

Sarraute, N. (1963). *The age of suspicion.* New York: Braziller.

Sass, L. (1990). Surrealism and schizophrenia: Reflections on modernism, regression, and the schizophrenic break. *New Ideas in Psychology, 8,* 275–297.

Sass, L. (1992). *Madness and modernism: Insanity in the light of modern art, literature, and thought.* New York: Basic.

Sass, L. (1994). *The paradoxes of delusion: Wittgenstein, Schreber, and the schizophrenic mind.* Ithaca, NY: Cornell University Press.

Schachtel, E. (1959). *Metamorphosis.* New York: Basic.

Schiller, F. von. (1966). *Naive and sentimental poetry and On the sublime.* New York: Ungar.

Segal, H. (1952). A psycho-analytical approach to aesthetics. *The International Journal of Psychoanalysis, 33,* 196–207.

Sharpe, E. F. (1935). Similar and divergent unconscious determinants underlying the sublimations of pure art and pure science. *International Journal of Psychoanalysis, 16,* 186–202.

Shelley, P. S. (1954). *Shelley's prose* (D. L. Clark, Ed.). Albuquerque: University of New Mexico Press.

Sontag, S. (1969). Notes on "camp." In S. Sontag, *Against interpretation* (pp. 277–293). New York: Dell.

Spector, J. (1972). *The aesthetics of Freud: A study in psychoanalysis and art.* New York: Praeger.

Spitz, E. (1985). *Art and psyche: A study in psychoanalysis and aesthetics.* New Haven, CT: Yale University Press.

Trilling, L. (1981). Freud and literature. In P. Meisel (Ed.), *Freud: A collection of critical essays* (pp. 95–111). Englewood Cliffs, NJ: Prentice-Hall.

Wilde, A. (1987). *Horizons of assent: Modernism, postmodernism, and the ironic imagination.* Philadelphia: University of Pennsylvania Press.

Wittgenstein, L. (1967). Conversations on Freud. In L. Wittgenstein (Ed.), *Lectures and conversations* (pp. 41–52). Berkeley & Los Angeles: University of California Press.

Wordsworth, W. (1977). *The prelude, 1798–1799* (S. Parrish, Ed.). Ithaca, NY: Cornell University Press.

Wordsworth, W., & Coleridge, S. T. (1963). *Lyrical ballads* (1798 ed., with additional 1800 poems and prefaces). London: Methuen.

Wright, E. (1984). *Psychoanalytic criticism: Theory in practice.* London & New York: Methuen.

II

Artistic Processes in Ontogenesis

Development as the Growth of Repertoires

Dennis Palmer Wolf
Harvard University

On the occasion of the opening of "Le Salon des Refusés," Paul Saint-Victor wrote (Denvir, 1987): "Imagine Goya gone **native** in the pampas of Mexico, daubing his canvases with crushed cochineal, and you have Manet, the most recent of the 'realists.' His pictures in the Boulevard des Italiens are like pages from **a coloured comic**" (p. 23). Reviewing the second Impressionist exhibition in 1876, Albert Wolff, writing in *Le figaro*, had these words about that display of new work (Denvir, 1987):

> It is a spectacle which is as afflicting as the sight of that poor **lunatic** whom I saw at Bicêtre; he held in his left hand a coal shovel tucked under his chin like a violin, and with a stick, which he took for a bow, he kept playing, or so he said, *The carnival of Venice*, which he claimed to have played before all the crowned heads of Europe. If you placed this virtuoso at the entrance to the charade in the rue le Peletier, the scenario would be complete. (p. 101)

These reviews were written and read as damaging because both writers and readers shared one of the most fundamental images of modern Western thought. It is a picture of change over time as progress that ascends in ladder-like certainty from the primitive to the advanced. Beyond the core notion of ascent, this image carries with it two other pictures. The first is the shape of progress: It is linear—all beings or states can be rank-ordered with respect to its teleology. There are no sidebars or varietal routes. The second image is that on the lower rungs of any development are not just ancient beings and states but all kinds of "primitives": the natives daubing cochineal, the low art of popular colored comics, the lunatic, and the child. At the height are not just modern individuals but artists who understand and uphold what the centuries' long practices of realism have accrued, the high art of museums, the rational, "normal" observer of the poor man with the coal shovel violin, and the adult observing the child's scribbles. In this vision of progress, we have established a yardstick against which we measure all forms of human living and work: It is what we call *development*.

But much as Manet and other Impressionists used their canvases to upset the 19th century's notions of artistic progress as headed for pictorial realism in the visual arts, perhaps it is time to rattle the cage bars about the broader notion of development that produces such characterizations as "primitive," "underdeveloped," and "childish" versus "advanced," "developed," and "mature." In that vein, this chapter explores several linked issues. In the first section, I unpack the image of development as an ascendant line of progress, tracing out at least three of its core assumptions: linear progress, the coherence of the organism, and the vision of growth as an orderly series of stages or ranked behaviors. In the second section, I turn briefly to three major attempts to teach us to see human development in more complex ways. These are to be found, not surprisingly, in the writings of Darwin, Freud, and Heinz Werner. What each of these theorists offered—albeit uneasily and partially—is an image of development, not as a series of orderly replacements but as the generation of a *repertoire* of possible behaviors. This is development envisioned, not as a ladder, but as Darwin (in Beer, 1985) would have it, as a "branching coral." Finally, I turn to specific illustrations of how a too-linear and progressive notion of development precludes us from understanding the more complex texture of development over time or patterns of human choice within a moment. First, I look at the specific instance of young children learning to draw. Subsequently, I turn to examples taken from the work of an adult image maker, a contemporary filmmaker. In all cases the effort is to break out of the received categories of primitive and mature, low and high, and to reveal these categories as "provisional, mutable positions within a larger circle of creation" (Varnedoe & Gopnik, 1990, p. 12).

INHERITED CONCEPTIONS OF DEVELOPMENT

One very particular notion of change over time—that of ascendant and unilinear progress—so permeates our thought about the history of organisms and civilizations that it is frankly difficult to conceive of narratives of growth that diverge from the images and verbs of "later is higher and better." It is a notion of change that is so deeply embedded in Christianity, Western politics, and everyday language that to root it out is to be left virtually silent or incoherent. We speak, habitually, of base instincts turning into higher principles, basic skills becoming educated toward higher order thought, deep depression giving way to an elevated mood, and the rising action of a story as it reaches its climax. Conversely, we speak of the decline of civilizations and regressive behaviors. This view of history and change as progress has perhaps no greater legacy than in the construction of the narratives of individual development within the field of psychology.

This is hardly accidental: Medieval and Renaissance accounts of society are based on a great chain of being leading from serf to monarch (Gould, 1981; Kamin, 1974). Shakespeare's history plays portray an orderly and productive world as one in which just such order prevails. Authors like Dante and Milton—fundamental architects of our imagery and language—envision the good life as progressing from the lower depths of Hell, struggling through Purgatory, and ascending finally to Paradise. Anyone who would challenge such a description—whether Darwin, Freud, or their successors—has had to struggle with the weight of an inherited language that urged a view of change that was orderly rather than random, and ascendant rather than simply variant (Gould, 1981).

Inherent in this view of development are at least three critical and linked assumptions: the notion of a singular teleology, the fiction of coherence, and the conception of replacement as the frequent, if not necessary, consequence of development. Only once we understand these assumptions is it possible to see how powerfully the conception of development as ascendant progress has shaped—and even distorted—our understanding of what it is to learn and then to exercise that accomplishment.

The Notion of a Singular Teleology

Most familiar concepts of psychological development are organized around a unified teleology; that is, each proposes one end or *telos* toward which all productive growth is described as moving. Consequently, major developmental theories each can be characterized by a cardinal decision rule that arrays individuals, their behaviors, or their works in an ordered series on a single defining measure. In Darwin, it is the degree of adaptation to an ecological niche. In Freud, there is the ascendance of civilization over instinct, that is, of secondary over primary process thought. In Piaget, development is defined in terms of the increasing use of logical thought structures in investigation, the use of evidence, and argument.

These same kinds of decision rules prevail outside of theories of psychological development as well. Until quite recently, art historians, for instance, have built a narrative for the development of Western art as turning on the gradual discovery of techniques that would permit the recreation of a three-dimensional world captured through forms inscribed on a two-dimensional surface (Baxandall, 1972; Gombrich, 1969). Similarly, observers of the process through which children learn to draw have argued for that same course of change: scribbles, then shapes, then look-alike outlines, followed by volumetric forms (Freeman, 1980; Gardner, 1980).

The Fiction of Coherence

A concomitant of such a linear view of development is a fiction of coherence, or the presumption that any individual, species, or civilization is, at any given moment, located at *a* position along a unilinear arc of progress. It is only once such an assumption is made that it becomes possible to say that a child's drawings are at "the scribbling stage," or to argue that Bronze Age imagery was a step backward from that of Graeco–Roman times. A similar belief informs statements such as the one that Byzantine painters never reached the stage of realism or that Rousseau was a primitive painter. Each of these propositions presumes that a sample of behavior will reveal all there is to know about the individual, the period, or the people. It presumes, fundamentally, that the organism or the work is one system, rather than a network of competing or counterpoised systems. Curiously, it leaves us no very interesting way to describe the fact that a 4-year-old child who "has learned to make pictures" draws a house as a dot if she is making a map, as the cartoon box topped by a triangle when making a picture of an imaginary place, and as intersecting planes implying volume when depicting her own house containing her room. Nor does it account for a painting by Donald Judd where enormous lemons loll on a tarry, black surface. In certain regions the painting is about lemons—their oval outlines, their nubbed ends, their porous skins. But elsewhere the painting is not a representation but a frank exploration of the tactile surfaces of black oil paint scrubbed onto canvas. It is picture, calligraphy, or gesture—depending on where you look.

The Tenet of Replacement

A third presumption in many developmental theories is that less sufficient responses emerge early and are replaced by later emerging and, therefore, more sufficient approaches. Thus, within the individual, we assume that a child's early scratchings lose their meaning and use once that child discovers how to produce the recognizable, representational forms we know as pictures. Similarly, on a cultural plane, all but the most recent art histories presume that the appearance of perspectival rendering or the technology of the camera obscura "naturally" drove out any interest in the more planar forms of landscape characteristic of medieval times. Conversely, any sign of an earlier emerging form in an older organism or a later time has been viewed as regression, a return to the primitive forced by deprivation, stress, illness, or ignorance. Hence, Freud viewed the urgent presence of dream imagery in adulthood as revealing, but primal, and Piaget (1962) described play and fantasy as rightly fading in later childhood. However, such a view makes it difficult, if not impossible, to describe the 20th-century planar renditions of painters like Milton Avery, Arthur Dove, or more recently, Alex Katz, as choices and inventions, rather than echoes or returns. We are, in effect, without a way of understanding that an early-appearing form of behavior or symbolization continues to evolve in its uses and meanings. Dove's blunt and simple contours are substantially different from the 7-year-old's.

The result of this trio of assumptions is a constrained set of images for describing development, whether it is physical, cultural, or psychological. In fact, we have had, until very recently, only three such images. There is the rising and unilinear growth curve where height and weight, or number of words in the vocabulary, are plotted against time. There are the ladder-like diagrams often used to portray the stages of development between infancy and adulthood. Or there are the right progressing time lines that portray the chronology of periods in art history. Each of these images carries in it the presumptions of unilinear or teleological progress, the fiction of coherence, and the presumption of replacement. None of them provides a satisfactory way to describe the most basic facts of our image-making lives: that even as children we possess a range of visual strategies; that we often gerrymander these strategies into new combinations to create novel meanings; or that early approaches can evolve toward quite sophisticated uses.

As indicated, this view of development is problematic. It cannot, in fact, account well for many of the most fundamental characteristics of developing systems. First, it cannot account for the fact that individuals, species, or cultures may move toward multiple endpoints. For instance, that Aboriginal and contemporary American art styles are each articulate without being the same. Second, images of linear progress preclude us from entertaining the possibility that what an organism reaches is not some singular final stage as much as a repertoire of responses that may have arisen at different times in development, and which can be called upon again, taking on new uses and meanings. Thus, we cannot, within this framework, capture the essential heterogeneity of any developing system or organism—a heterogeneity that may be essential to continued growth. Consider, for instance, the way that young children's ability to read pictures far outdistances their ability to make images. This is, in all probability, a major source of change. So too is the tension between the systems of popular and "high," familiar and exotic art, technology and art, in any given culture (Varnedoe & Gopnik, 1990). Finally, such a vision argues that early-emerging strategies are necessarily primitive. When they are used late in life they are regressive. But this offers a thin account of visual image making. For instance, it precludes us from understanding the fact that a powerful visual image draws on many strategies for making meaning.

Until we question the usefulness of these assumptions, it remains impossible to capture the nature of what it is to engage in behaviors as complex as inventing or reading a visual representation.

THE SEARCH FOR ALTERNATIVE IMAGES OF DEVELOPMENT

Given these confines, we have to search for alternative images of development. Of particular interest are formulations that might break with the single teleology and its overly simple notions of progress or growth. There are hints of this conceptualization in the work of Darwin, Freud, and finally, Werner—each of whom managed, at least in part, to pull away from or at least to raise questions about, the language and imagery of orderly progression that they inherited. Of particular importance is the recurring urge to describe development as branching, rather than linear.

This view appears first in Darwin's work, where he proposes two quite different images of change over time. On many occasions and in many places, Darwin talks about "nature's tangled bank." This image stands in stark contrast to the orderly language of fixed species and phyla invented by Linnaeus working on classification. Once he had blurred and unglued fixed biological categories, Darwin went on to suggest that the development of any particular species could not be conceived in terms of unilinear or assured progress. Rather, depending on what happened in the surrounding environment, any particular branch of variants might flourish or die out. Hence, survival (whether or not that was to be thought of as progress) depended on myriad variation. This is the image of evolution as a branching coral. Thus, as early as the mid-19th century, there is a competing notion of development that is both equipotential (any branch could become the survivor) and highly mutable, rather than foreordained (success does not inhere in the organism but in the extremely protean relations between the organism and the environment). In fact, much of the tension in Darwin's own writing derives from his struggle to replace the assured, progressive narrative of growth with the much dicier notion of evolution. If we take Darwin seriously, the notion of unilinear progress becomes an orderly fiction, not up to capturing the divergent, and finally, random quality of evolution.

Roughly half a century later, Freud took on the notion of simple progressive development. If Darwin's challenge came from the chance nature and systemic complexity of evolution, Freud's challenge emerged from looking at behavior as more than what meets the eye. Beginning with his enormous curiosity over his colleague Breuer's hysteric patients, Freud followed out the possibility that what had previously been conceived of as **the** mind was in fact profoundly composite. The conflicts that Anna O. could return to in an unconscious state of mind (under hypnosis) were unknown to her conscious mind. The consequences of this formulation were significant: Despite a single brain and nervous system, the individual was fractured, or "of several minds." In spite of his persistent use of language that describes a fixed hierarchy for these different modes of experience, Freud's writings also insist that these other minds or modes of thought could not be described simply as ancient or primitive. Without the "primitive" imagery of dreams or mistakes, the censorious conscious mind would never admit to irresolve or pain. The fissures in everyday behavior are what permit insight and realization. The human system cannot be characterized solely in terms of its rational and conscious self. The system is a tense negotiation between several ways of being that are all constantly alive and kicking. In many respects, Freud's legacy to developmental theory is less his orderly progression from primary to secondary thought, or from oral to anal to phallic pleasures. Instead, subsequent generations of psychodynamic theorists have from Freud the insistence that human behavior is inevitably and appropriately diverse, and that development depends on the conflicts or conversations between these several minds or states of being. Hence, if we attend to Freud, the notion of a coherent individual who could be characterized comfortably as being at this or that stage of development becomes untenable.

Finally, it is Heinz Werner who provides a powerful alternative to the image of the ladder or ascendant series of stages of behavior. This is particularly evident in his work with Bernard Kaplan, *Symbol Formation* (Werner, 1957; Werner & Kaplan, 1963/1983). Like Darwin and Freud before him, Werner presents a radical view of development as the emergence and continual evolution of *a range of differentiated choices*. Like Darwin's, Werner's theory stresses the proliferation of possibilities in the organism. Even more than Freud's notions of a dynamic interplay between primary and secondary process, Werner's proposal—if pushed—argues that the sophistication of an organism should be characterized, not by the last step achieved in a series but by several quite different qualities. These can be illustrated if we look at Werner's and his associates' experiments with drawings.

Symbol Formation (Werner & Kaplan, 1963/1983) contained a provocative section on children's drawings:

> Another child (in Muchow's studies of children's drawings), before copying a narrow triangle presented to him, stretched out his tongue and then made rapid forward movements with his stretched-out forefinger; following this, he drew angular strokes so sharply that he tore the paper with the pencil. It was as if the presented triangle were grasped in terms of bodily movement—penetration, etc.—and then drawn in terms of bodily depiction. . . . It seems that for the young child, in the transition from scribblings to graphic representations of visual content, there is a stage where the line drawings are basically a translation of gestural imitations descriptive of presented contents. (p. 90)

It would have been enough that this observation captures the vigor and complexity of so early a drawing. But Werner and Kaplan go for a larger point. They argue that these early-emerging ways of making meaning **remain** present: under special conditions in healthy individuals and more permanently in the instances of mental illness or brain damage. For instance, the chapter on "Nonverbal (Linear) Naming in Normal Adults" in *Symbol Formation* contains illustration after illustration where competent **adults** use the fused, gestural drawing style of Muchow's children. Thus, a word like "longing" can be illustrated by a low arc swinging off and open to the left. Although we don't see illustrations in the book, presumably these same adults could also depict "longing" by showing two stick figures with their arms outstretched toward one another. Thus, Werner and Kaplan argue that it is possible for fully functioning, normal individuals to *"take* a physiognomic attitude," *choosing* to illustrate "longing" with long, thin lines that stretch out in "yearning" arcs across and up the page. Or, they can elect to sketch this experience in a more "distanced" and conventional manner—for instance, by depicting two figures leaning in toward one another. In other words, central to this conception of development are the notions of diversity, choice, and evolving meaning, in place of linear progression, coherence, and replacement.

If followed out to its logical conclusions, what may appear to be only an intriguing laboratory illustration is, or can serve as, a continuation and an extension of Darwin's view of development as imaged in the branching coral or Freud's several minds breaking in on one another. Repeatedly, Werner and Kaplan describe development not in terms of a simple progression but as "differentiation and hierarchical integration." Implicit in this formulation are three distinctive ideas about the nature of development. First of all, there is, as in Darwin or Freud, the idea that what matters is that the organism generates a range of behaviors. As mentioned, an adult can make a picture of longing that plays off physiognomic properties **or** he or she can draw two figures with their arms outstretched toward one another, using the conventions of Western figural representation. Second, there is the ability to select among that range in ways that are tuned to the moment, to a particular cultural task, or to a given audience. An individual making a dictionary illustration of ''longing'' would probably sketch two figures rather than an abstract open arc. Finally, there is the difficult, but critical, notion that behaviors, once generated, continue to develop as they are used in increasingly complex circumstances. Muchow's boy knows no other way to copy the very pointy triangle in front of him. But if he were to keep that visceral, gestural approach in his repertoire, as many artists do, it might become one of several choices he can make when he wants to symbolize the fierce, ruthless quality of the form. Think, for instance, of the jagged, teethed forms that show up in Francis Bacon's paintings, complete with their aggressive brushwork. Bacon, in **choosing** a physiognomic or gestural rendition, transforms it. He delivers these savage, broken, or yearning forms with a killing craft, using them as dark and complex personal emblems, and doubling as recognizable cultural forms (the mitre of a bishop, a dog's open jaws). So delivered, these gestural forms are anything but primitive. They are a deliberate "detour into the archaic," which permits us to understand in more than one way what Bacon referred to as "the brutality of fact."

These points about the gestural quality of children's and artists' drawings may seem a small corner of the matter—nice, but minor. However, they have very wide implications. In effect, they propose a model of development based on a widening repertoire rather than an ascending scale. If we were to incorporate the notion of repertoire with its concepts of diversity, choice, and evolving meaning into our understanding of development, our conception of growth would be considerably enriched. The implications of this view are wider than the few drawing studies presented in *Symbol Formation* make apparent. In particular, once we take up this view, our understanding of the onset, the elaboration, and the final exercise of visual image making shifts.

In essence, we have inherited two quite different images of development: the ladder and the branching coral. The ladder has large powers—it is ancient and long running, it provides order and prediction. The coral, like the tangled bank, is natural and noisy. But it may, via its notions of diversity, choice, and evolving meaning, teach us to think quite differently about both growth and the sophisticated conduct of image making. In other words, what would we realize if we were to take the impulse in Darwin, Freud, and Werner seriously, rethinking prevailing descriptions of the development and conduct of visual image making?

RETHINKING UNILINEAR PROGRESS:
THE CASE OF EARLY DRAWING SKILLS

Across any number of years and theories, it has been assumed that graphic representation occurs in children's drawings with the onset of their ability to produce simple look-alike forms or what might be called *pictures*: A rough circle enclosing a few dots can stand for a face; an oblong atop two small circles can be used to represent a car or truck. In other words, we do not accord representational status to children's marks until children produce forms that encode the relative sizes, spatial locations, and shapes of objects in ways that echo the conventions of Western pictorial drawing. Given the amount of eye–hand coordination and planning required for even simple look-alike drawings of this kind, it has long been observed that children under the age of 3 draw only what many have labeled *scribbles* or *sensory explorations* (cf. Kellogg, 1969).

This description of early drawing provides an excellent illustration of the difficult presuppositions of progressive and unidimensional models of development. In this formulation, all drawing development has been viewed as progression toward mastery of Renaissance-derived illusionist rendition; that is, the ability to simulate both volume and depth with nothing more than a pattern of marks on a two-dimensional surface. Consequently, any graphic activity prior to or different from the appearance of forms that resemble conventional picturing has been treated as primitive and necessarily unrepresentational. But the result is, quite simply, an impoverished account of the development of graphic symbolization.

Between the ages of 1 and 3, children exhibit a rampant exploration of symbolization. During these 2 years normal children construct the basic rules for linguistic and gestural forms of reference. Moreover, they combine these forms into rather sophisticated representations of events in symbolic play. There is also strong evidence that children this young read graphic representations with a fair degree of sophistication. Although they may not be able to interpret information about perspective and diminishing size, young children are able to make sense of highly stylized line drawings (Hochberg, 1978). Finally, data on early metaphoric productions suggest that children can "discover" meaning in quite a wide range of visual patterns that were in no way specifically tailored to picture information. Thus, a 2-year-old can bite into a cookie, produce a crescent, and call it "moon" (Winner, 1979).

Given these early-emerging forms of visual-spatial representation, and what appears to be a kind of pervasive interest in cross-modal analogies, it is not at all surprising that there are extremely early forms of graphic representation that long precede iconic and illusionistic drawings. Perhaps the earliest hints of what will be graphic symbols occur in what have been termed *object-based representations* (Wolf & Perry, 1988). They emerge as early as 15 months, contemporaneous with the onset of simple language and symbolic play abilities. In fact, in this type of representation, children handle the marker and paper precisely as they handle other objects in the course of short episodes of symbolic play. A child might, for instance, roll up a marker inside a sheet of paper and comment, "Night-night," or "Bye."

Slightly later, there emerge the first kinds of graphic strategies in which the process of making lines or shapes (not just the objects used) carries meaning (Wolf & Perry, 1988). These include both tally-marking systems and forms of gestural representation not unlike that described by Muchow earlier. In tally-marking systems 2-year-olds can "draw a person" by making marks for each of the figures in a dictated series. A request to make "eyes" will produce two slashes in the upper regions of the paper. A request for "tummy" provokes a slash in the middle region; a request for "feet" provokes two more marks at the bottom of the paper. (The ability to be correct about number and placement is often fragile, breaking down if too many features or too many features out of spatial order are requested.) Gestural representations emerge when children perform depictive motions while holding a marking tool, for instance, hopping a marker across the paper, and leaving a trail of squashy dots, which might be labeled "rabbit going." Although neither of these routines results in conventional drawings, the products do have several novel qualities when compared to the earlier emerging object-based representations: Meaning is transferred to the process of marking, if not entirely to the marks themselves. Those marks occur on the plane of the drawing paper. Some primitive spatial relations such as "next to," "past," or "connected to" are being transformed, if not represented, on the smaller, horizontal drawing surface. At the very least, they are being rendered with visual qualities that are not literal replications of actual distances and sizes. Obviously, there are limits on these traces as effective graphic symbols: Children are often encoding motions, not the static visual aspect of objects such as size, shape, and color—the key conventions in the Western notion of pictures as views (Baxandall, 1972). Consequently, gestural properties such as speed, emphasis, and pause are the vehicles for meaning. Although these properties carry meaning for the maker, they can be imperceptible to perceivers who encounter only the final swath of the marks. Significantly, it is often in the context of pursuing these kinds of gestural patterns that children produce detailed-enough contours that they stumble on the notion of distinctive contour, or shape, which essentially allows them to break the simplest kind of code for making the look-alike drawings that they see and read in their daily lives.

This is a remarkable illustration of how the proposed end goals of development are not matters of neutral observation but of cultural decision making. Much past and contemporary research on drawing assumes that the child's intention is to capture views or scenes, but if we split apart notions of graphic representation from notions of picturing volumetric objects or drawing perspectival views, then we see quite a different pattern of events. In fact, as a result of broadening the definition of early graphic representation, researchers have observed the staggered appearance of several systems for encoding visual-spatial information, long prior to the onset of picturing (Wolf & Perry, 1988). In rapid succession, the younger child elaborates the early-emerging forms of many different drawing systems: those based on objects, on gestures, on expressive forms arranged on a plane, or on the illusion of volumes and distance. But rather than replacing one another, these systems continue to exist, growing up and differentiating in one another's presence.

RETHINKING THE FICTIONS
OF COHERENT SYSTEMS

Once drawing systems appear, they provide a repertoire of possibilities. A 7-year-old can elect to make a cartoon, a map, or a portrait, depending on what is required or desired. For those individuals who continue to make visual images, the point is often much more than accurate representation. Often it becomes a question of *rendition*—in which of several possible ways shall the image be crafted? For instance, consider what a young adolescent has to say about the changes in the way the "same" line functions even within a single drawing of a shell:

> Last term I started drawing shells. I wanted to learn to draw things from life so I decided to draw the same object over and over and over. While I was working on them, I started to see a lot about different kinds of lines. Shells force that. As you move around drawing one of them, you have to

draw sharp edges, folds, flaps, round shoulders. I went from pencil to charcoal because I couldn't get the pencil line to do all that, but with the charcoal you can get a hard edge and a blurry soft form. The more I worked, the more I saw each one of the lines as a story. It would start at the front edge all clear and hard and then travel up toward one of the shoulders and I would change it, make it thicker and softer as it went. (Wolf, 1988, Interview with Lea Wolf)

Thus, at the front edge the line represents the details of observed contours. Unable to portray the recession of form into space, the young artist *chose* another route where soft-broad gesture (i.e., traveling) captured the full bulk of the shells.

Similarly, visual images can be read according to any number of rules. Even within the compass of a single work, a viewer becomes alert to diverse languages of the image. Here is the same adolescent, thinking aloud about Munch's print, "The Kiss":

When I look at the print I notice right away how unevenly the figures divide the space. In my mind I imagine how different, how still it would have been if he had placed the figures dead center. The figures have an extraordinary simplicity. Their features aren't defined. So in a way, more than the figures, you absorb the softness and roundness of the shapes. That's what says, "This is a kiss." When I look at the one shape for two people, I think about the way he cut the block, getting those long lines that aren't, but are, the real shapes, hard as that is in wood. But I know that if I imagine the figures with elbows and lips, the power drains out. (Wolf, 1988, Interview with Lea Wolf)

To read "The Kiss," the viewer has to apprehend that the image is at once the trace of a physical act of cutting into the block, a kind of gesture of fusion in which two forms melt together, *and* a picture of two figures in an embrace. In other words, to make or to make sense of a visual image is a fundamentally protean act. It requires not one way of imaging or imagining meaning but a laminated response that draws on all that past development has yielded. Adaptation, skill, or success is inherently heterogeneous.

WHAT BECOMES OF EARLY SYSTEMS?
THE CASE OF GESTURE AND PORTRAITURE

But there are also problems that arise from presuming that as later emerging, increasingly illusionistic kinds of drawing emerge, they necessarily replace earlier emerging strategies for making visual meaning.

A much more satisfying account of drawing development emerges if we take Werner and Kaplan's notion of "differentiation and hierarchical integration" seriously. The major result of this stance is that we recognize that children as young as age 3 and 4 are developing a number of distinct systems for rendering visual meaning (e.g., a differentiated repertoire), which is integrated and moderated by the ability to choose an appropriate response out of the many possibilities. Thus, if we look carefully at children's drawing processes, we can see that it would be wrong, or at least insufficient, to describe a child simply in terms of his or her last acquired drawing system. In fact, early-acquired systems do not atrophy or become courts of last resort. Rather, they continue to evolve. These different rendering systems are quite unlike unwanted tails or webbings that drop out in biological evolution or primitive pointing and groaning that give way to language. Each of these systems, once it has emerged, continues to grow, becoming not "the way to draw" but "one way to draw."

This continuous and mutual differentiation of drawing systems is not just a peculiarity of the early years when young children have to work through the demands of learning how to draw realistically. It persists well into adolescence and adulthood, long past the basic stages. Here, too, a specific illustration may be helpful. It comes from the portfolio of an adolescent in a studio art class. It is taken from a moment in her development when she turns away from life-drawing exercises and a careful study of the anatomy of faces, bodies, and postures, and moves toward the development of a radically simplified, personal imagery. In a series of closely spaced drawings made over the course of some 9 months, this student reclaims the kind of gestural and physiognomic drawing system that Muchow described in her 4-year-olds and that Werner and Kaplan describe occurring in adults' drawings of emotional states. This reclamation is not a regression, rather it is the rediscovery of the distinctive kinds of visual strengths of an earlier invented system. In that process of rediscovery, it is also a moment when an earlier invented system comes newly of age.

In her senior year, Ella Macklin begins work on a series of portraits. Like many students she struggles with drawing a nose head-on, making the eyes look recessed, and making cheekbones that look modeled, rather than just pasted on. At some point she begins what she calls *family portraits*, based on recollections and old photo albums (Wolf & Pistone, 1991). One of these images is of her father holding her on his hip. Throughout the drawing, she fights with drawing his right arm so that it looks—in good illusionistic style—as if it curves around back of her body, reappearing at her side, and hooking in front of her waist. Looking back at her portfolio, Ella comments:

I drew it pretty much as his likeness—his high cheekbones, his Indian part of him—and I like that. But here, where his arm is coming around my waist, I felt that I didn't draw the arm right. But I changed my opinion of it when we talked about Matisse and I saw pictures in art magazines where the arms are somewhat distorted. My dad is just like that arm. I mean, he's really protective. And when I was growing up, he was with me a lot. I mean, he wasn't the kind of father that says "Go play, go play by yourself." You know, if I wanted to play, even though he was tired he'd say, "Come here." I think that arm wrapping around me shows his personality, his character a lot. (Wolf, 1989, Interview with Ella Macklin)

In saying this, Ella recognizes that she can work this drawing from at least two angles: She can go for the muscles and the foreshortening and she can recognize and claim the gestural and expressive properties of drawing—much as Werner and Kaplan's (1963/1983) adults do when they make their line drawings of "longing." Moreover, she is recognizing that these gestural forms are not just defaults, they have a power, a history, and a set of exigent demands all their own. For example, if she works within that gestural and expressive system, it is not enough simply to line up likenesses of her cousins and uncles. She has to create a design—albeit simple—that carries information about more than size, shape, and position. She says:

I tried to express in my work that sense of family, that sense of togetherness, that emotional quality. And when I was looking in the book, *The Harlem Renaissance*, one of the artists, William H. Johnson, he was saying that his aim was to express in a cultural way what he felt both emotionally and spiritually about all that's been saved up in his family of primitiveness and tradition. And that's what I think basically says the same thing about my work. We're a family, we're proud of our black heritage, of black traditions, and our culture. Basically, I think what he was saying primitiveness and tradition is, when you walk into someone's home, it is the way it is, and that expresses who they are. (Wolf, 1989, Interview with Ella Macklin)

In light of working within a drawing system where the expressive and gestural qualities of simple shapes carry meaning, Ella begins to rethink the usual obligations of illusionistic representation. She comes to recognize that in this other system, an artist chooses what to represent. Just because there is a nose, doesn't mean you have to draw one:

When I went to the museum, I'd been used to seeing pictures that have the eyes, the nose, the face—everything's there for you. What I've learned to like about pictures that are just simple and don't have everything there is that, when you look at them, you are able to bring something to them. For example, here I just have the eyes, the expressions on my relatives' faces, but I don't fill in the nose, the mouth, because you know there's a nose, there's a mouth. I think the eyes (stay)—they say that the eyes are the windows of our souls—because eyes give a different feeling. (Interview, Wolf, 1992)

In the weeks immediately following this reflection, Ella carved out a different approach to portraiture—one that was deliberately simplified, pared down to the essential shapes. Thus, when she lined up her cousins on the family couch, she drew them as if they were Giorgio Morandi's bottles or Romare Beardon's figures—in a cascade of overlapping shapes. The eyes were only accents, capturing the individuality of attention, silliness, or a serious stare. Moreover, she began to question what it is she wants these simple gestural shapes to represent. Gradually, the answer shifted from "family" to "a family":

> I was tired of doing my family. And because I want work to be something that everybody can enjoy. I'm sure that if people looked at my art work, they'd say, "Oh that's beautiful, that's nice, but it's your family. What can I see in it for myself?"
> This (a pastel drawing from her portfolio) began the universal series, that I later developed, in which you have an adult holding a child, a mother holding a daughter, whoever. It happens to be my mother holding me on a swing. And I wanted it to be where anybody could look into the picture and see their own mother holding them, having fond memories of their own childhood. I didn't want to put in any features because then it would be, "Oh, it's my family and not yours." I wanted anybody to look at it and have the same feeling. (Wolf, 1989, Interview with Ella Macklin)

On a visit to a museum, Ella took her understanding of the potentially gestural quality of visual images a step further:

> I like the way the quality of Giacometti's *Walking Man* was rough (she had recently seen it in the museum); it was a very rough bronze statue. And I attempted to create that same roughness. Even though you have good relationships with your parents, you still have arguments. You have rough edges in a relationship. So I left that rough quality. Because to smooth everything would be very unrealistic.
> That rough quality started off as a mistake, because I originally wanted it to be silver smooth. But then I thought, "Wait a minute, life isn't like that. Not everything in life is totally smooth. Your best relationships, as I said before, with your parents can be rough at times." So, that's what I like about it. I tried to show the very fact that he's holding up the child. Lots of times you see parents walking with their children, down by their side; they're taking the children by their side, and it's sort of pulling along the children in life. You're taking the child everywhere you want to take the

child. Here I think the figure is lifting the child, saying, "Hey, I'm trying to get you up in life. I'm trying to make you be better than I was." So I think it has a lifting-up quality. (Wolf, 1989, Interview with Ella Macklin)

What Ella has here is a system for making visual images that, at one level, resembles the physiognomic, simplified, and expressive forms of much younger children. But this is hardly a regression; her work is reflective and full of deliberate choice; it is the result of prolonged experiment, not accident; it is connected to a growing knowledge of art history. In many ways, it forces a deep-running reconceptualization of drawing development. Rather than a series of stages leading up to illusionistic drawing, we need the notion of diversity so evident in Darwin, Freud, and Werner. As mentioned earlier, in rapid succession, the younger child elaborates the early-emerging forms of many different drawing systems: those based on objects, on gestures, on expressive forms arranged on a plane, or on the illusions of volumes and distance. But rather than replacing one another, these systems continue to exist, growing up and differentiating in one another's presence. At any given moment, children exhibit their understanding and control of the drawing process by making appropriate choices about which system to use and how to make it expand. Drawing, in this light, is the parallel growth of any number of mutually influential options for making visual meaning.

The same might be said even of the most sophisticated visual art. The system of object-based representations evident when 2-year-olds roll up crayons in paper saying, "Bye," reappears transformed, sly, and lovely in Man Ray's "Pêchage," where three voluptuous peaches rub cheeks inside a wooden box painted to look like a country scene: fluffy clouds above and green swath below. The gestural drawings of 3-year-olds elaborate a set of options for translating motion into marks that is fully realized in Arabic and Chinese calligraphy and again in the handwriting and notations of Abstract Expressionist painting by contemporary painters like Tobey or Twombley.

Thus, certain strategies may appear at particular ages—earlier than some, later than others—but that is a peculiar way in which to think about their developmental sophistication. What counts with respect to the developmental sophistication of a behavior is its application (can the behavior be an adaptive choice, can the organism use it well?) and its evolving meaning (can it continue to take on meaning as the organism matures and uses it to more complex and demanding ends?).

Thus, drawing development cannot be thought of as a linear progression through a hierarchically tiered series of stages with primitive and inferior stages being gradually replaced by more advanced, and superior, ones. Rather, at every phase in development, the symbolic systems used are legitimate and powerful systems capable of capturing different kinds of essential information (Smith, 1983; Smith, Fucigna, & Goldsmith, 1986; Wolf & Perry, 1988).

CONCLUSION: BEYOND DRAWINGS

The heterogeneity and lamination discussed here are not peculiar to the act of drawing. Rather they characterize much of visual—and perhaps other—symbolic activity in and outside the world we recognize as "art." Here, for instance, is an adult filmmaker thinking aloud about an assignment to photograph an image of a young girl, for a "spot" for the American Bible Society. Essential to doing his work is a constant choice between a simple, close-to-the-bone retail approach and a more "art" look:

> There is this other piece which has this bit of a girl which has her reading the Bible and being happy about it, but . . . which has a lot of time where nothing really happens. Here the point was to make a high class item, beautiful, even. So we made the shawl umber to pick up on the walls, we put an amber/umber kind of filter on the camera too . . . um . . . the softness is a product . . . somewhat . . . of the smoke in the air, that is why it looks so painterly. The potatoes are arranged on the table, so that they cast long shadows.
>
> That's different from when I do Stop & Shop potatoes. If you take the retail approach all you have to do is show what you have for sale, and just turn on the camera to say so. You only have to show it in a normal way that demonstrates all the bells and whistles and doesn't have shadows, pretty flat.
>
> When you shoot, you know these two points of view go all the way up and down the line in everything that you do, all the decisions you have to make, in terms of lighting, in terms of camera, in terms of what happens on the screen . . . in terms of the way you pick out the potatoes and arrange them on the table. And whether the spots on them are pattern and contrast, or a reason for going in the back and getting perfect ones. (Wolf, Interview with Austin de Besche, 1991)

The retail, plain look is easier to achieve, faster to learn, and quicker to deliver than the "arty," painterly one. But as a filmmaker, both are part of his repertoire. If we want to understand his development—his level of sophistication—as an image maker, it isn't indexed only by his being able to turn potatoes painterly. Rather it is indexed by his ability to know "when is retail" and "where is art."

This is what Darwin, Freud, and perhaps, most centrally, Werner have to say to us about the nature of development. It is about repertoire and choice, rather than unilinear progress. Development is also systemic. It inheres not in the organism but in the relation of that organism to an environment. A filmmaker who makes art where retail belongs is out of sorts. And finally, development is human and so, mutable. Goya's choices that once made him the "native" daubing with cochineal now make him "a master."

ACKNOWLEDGMENT

This chapter is dedicated to Nancy Ray Smith, who was a long-time student of the works of Heinz Werner. Because of Werner, Nancy devoted much of her very forceful life to "getting straight" the difference between the mythical forward motion of development and its actual course—full as that is of milling about and refusals to give up fierce intuition and immediate sensation, no matter how ancient and uncivilized they are.

REFERENCES

Baxandall, M. (1972). *Painting and experience in fifteenth century Italy.* Oxford: Oxford University Press.

Beer, G. (1985). Darwin's reading and the fictions of development. In D. Kohn (Ed.), *The Darwinian heritage* (pp. 543–588). Princeton, NJ: Princeton University Press.

Denvir, B. (1987). *The impressionists at first hand.* London: Thames & Hudson.

Freeman, N. (1980). *Strategies of representation in young children.* London: Academic Press.

Gardner, H. (1980). *Artful scribbles: The significance of children's drawings.* New York: Basic.

Gombrich, E. (1969). *Art and illusion.* Princeton, NJ: Princeton University Press.

Gould, S. (1981). *The mismeasure of man.* New York: Norton.

Hochberg, J. (1978). *Perception* (2nd ed.). Englewood Cliffs, NJ: Prentice-Hall.

Kamin, L. J. (1974). *The science and politics of IQ.* Potomac, MD: Lawrence Erlbaum Associates.

Kellogg, R. (1969). *Analyzing children's art.* Palo Alto, CA: Mayfield.

Piaget, J. (1962). *Play, dreams, and imitations.* London: Routledge & Kegan Paul.

Smith, N. (1983). *Experience and art.* New York: Teachers College Press.

Smith, N., Fucigna, C. E., & Goldsmith, L. (1986, April). *The development of children's ability to render edge shape, surface contour, and form.* Paper presented at the annual meeting of the American Educational Research Association, New York.

Varnedoe, K., & Gopnik, A. (Eds.). (1990). *Modern art and popular culture: Readings in high and low.* New York: Abrahms.

Werner, H. (1957). *Comparative psychology of mental development* (rev. ed.). New York: International Universities Press.

Werner, H., & Kaplan, B. (1983). *Symbol formation.* New York: Lawrence Erlbaum Associates. (Original work published 1963).

Winner, E. (1979). New names for old things: The emergence of metaphoric language. *Journal of Child Language, 6*(3), 469–491.

Wolf, D. (1988). Interviews with Lea Wolf, Boston, MA.

Wolf, D. (1989). Interviews with Ella Macklin. Schenley High School, Pittsburgh, PA.

Wolf, D. (1991). Interviews with Austin de Besche. Moonlight Motion Pictures, Arlington, MA.

Wolf, D., & Perry, M. D. (1988). From endpoints to repertoires: Some new conclusions about drawing development. *Journal of Aesthetic Education, 22*(1), 17–34.

Wolf, D., & Pistone, N. (1991). *Taking full measure.* New York: The College Board.

5

Development in Architectural Designing

Gabriela Goldschmidt
Technion-Israel Institute of Technology

A few years ago, I had the good fortune to spend a day with 4-year-old Naomi, from the new town of Yuvalim in Israel. We passed the morning at a swimming pool compound. Naomi, who did not as yet know how to swim, had a fabulous time in a small, round toddlers' pool, adjacent to two large swimming pools. In the afternoon, Naomi used wooden blocks and other playthings to build what she described as "a model of Yuvalim" (Fig. 5.1). She had seen models before, including one of her family's house that was under construction at that time.

Naomi made houses from her materials and put little people in front of them; she built bomb shelters, electricity poles, and a long path (all features of Yuvalim; long paths provide pedestrian access to an inner row of houses and are favorite play areas for young children). She then completed her model by building a round structure at the end of the path. When I asked what the round structure was, she said: "a pool." "A swimming pool?" I asked, knowing there is none in Yuvalim. Astonished at my naïveté, she looked at me and replied: "No, of course not! It's a pool for children my age!"

Naomi departed that evening. I kept the model she had constructed on the floor, intact, for days. I was thunderstruck. That 4-year-old child had redesigned her hometown! She improved it, as it were, by adding a new, attractive feature to it, which she situated within easy reach of the places

FIG. 5.1. Naomi's model.

that for her were the central loci of the environment. She showed herself able to incorporate her newly gained experience in the toddlers' pool into an imaginal projection of a novel physical environment, thereby transforming that environment in a most plausible way. Until that day, it had never occurred to me that a child could design, indeed, that anything constructed by an "unqualified" designer could be worth taking seriously. "Design" by "nondesigners" of whatever age could, I thought, be charming and picturesque but belonged in some other category of activities, having little to do with what I have always taken to be "serious" design.

My understanding of the process of designing was never the same after the lesson I learned from little Naomi. I began to entertain the possibility that the *capacity* for designing might be inherent. Rudimentary questions regarding design skills and education kept me preoccupied. As a design educator, I now began to ask myself how it was possible for new students in schools of architecture to produce anything sensible at all in response to design tasks given to them as of their first day at school. The continuum I had formerly seen, beginning at the outset of vocational training and culminating in professional maturity, now expanded into a longer sequence, starting with a young child's first construction game and possibly even earlier.

The seeds of the experimental work that I have since undertaken to obtain a better grip on the design process were sown at the time of the startling discovery that I owe to Naomi. This chapter, whose aim it is to trace development in design competence from childhood through limited expertise in adulthood, summarizes the results of that experimental work. I use the analysis of findings of three design workshops, carried out with children, with novice architectural students, and with advanced students of architecture, who worked on the same subject.[1] The analysis is used to illustrate and support my emerging theory of development in architectural designing, a theory formulated primarily in the course of work on the materials of the workshops in question.[2] I should stress that because the entire endeavor has been carried out within the domain of architectural designing, any extrapolations outside that context must be taken as tentative. However, because architecture, the "mother of arts," likely shares much with other manifestations of creative venture, it may be worthwhile to indulge in speculations that transgress the diffuse borders of that particular realm. As a final caveat, it is important to emphasize that it is not Architecture that this chapter addresses, nor Design. *Architectural Designing*, or rather its *front edge*, is the subject. I concentrate on the *process* alone, with not attempt to evaluate the products.

THE BILBY WORKSHOPS

Bilby is the beloved heroine of a well-known children's story (Lingren, 1974), which was also made into a full-length movie as well as a television series. ("Pippi" was renamed "Bilby" when the work was translated into Hebrew.) The daughter of a ship captain who pays rare visits home, Bilby lives on her own with her horse and her monkey and plays with her next-door neighbors, Tommy and Anika. She is very strong and independent and knows how to do everything and cope with any situation. When Anika quarrels with her mother one day, she and her two friends decide to run away from home and be vagabonds. In the story, the three runaways go through a long series of adventures before they finally decide to return home. In our workshops, we ignored the end of the story; for us, Bilby and her friends were homeless. The task for all the designers was to design a house for them.

All the participants in the workshops were familiar with the story, which served as a scenario for the given task. No further information, instructions, requirements, or recommendations were offered. It was a

[1]Group I consisted of some 20 third and fourth graders (ages 8 and 9) in the Haifa Experimental Open School. My warmest thanks to Judy Hill, the school's principal at the time, to the teacher, Adina Shpiler, and to Benny Avigdory, a former student, for their help and support in conducting this workshop. Group II had in it one dozen first-year students at the end of their second month in the Faculty of Architecture and Town Planning at Technion, Israel Institute of Technology (ages 20–25). Group III was comprised of six advanced students, toward the end of their fourth year in the Faculty of Architecture at Technion (ages 24–28). Documenting the workshops was made possible by grant #20-331-9 from the Technion VPR Fund.
[2]The students' workshops were undertaken after an analysis of the findings of the children's workshop was summarized in my monograph, *House for Bilby: Children as designers* (Goldschmidt, 1985).

design-as-you-go activity that involved, primarily, the construction of models out of cardboard, wood, and other materials, an abundance of which was made available to the designers. Protocols including photographs of the models and drawings made by participants, as well as transcriptions of taped discussions with them and amongst them, were prepared and served as data that inform this study.

A DESIGN SPACE

To design is to plan for the making of something new; in the case of architecture—an artifact of the physical environment. Designing entails generating, transforming, and refining images of different aspects of that still nonexisting artifact and making representations of it that enable the examination and sharing of the images. The front edge of designing, manifested in preliminary representations indicating how the designed entity would look, feel, and function, is what we are looking at in this study. Based on an analysis of the processes involved, I assert that development in design competence can be discerned with maturity, training, and experience. Competence in design is the ability to identify relevant design problems and to generate satisfying solutions to them on the basis of knowledge accessible to the designer. Development of design competence is a function not only of training and experience but also of maturity, by which I mean a sensitivity to and comprehension of the kinds of issues with which design concerns itself. Age contributes to maturity, but not exclusively so. I propose the notion of a *Design Space*, within which designing and its development can be described and explained.

Three interconnected underlying premises, on which the concept of a Design Space rests, may be summarized as follows: First, that there is what I call a *capacity for designing* that is inherent in human cognitive structures. This design capacity enables us to perform as *laydesigners*, something all of us do, often beginning at a very young age. Second, I claim that laydesigning is of a kind with sophisticated designing performed by experts. The basic processes of designing in all cases can be described by the same parameters, and the path from laydesigning to expert designing is a continuum. The third premise is that the development of *design competence* (from basic capacities to expertise) is multidimensional rather than unidimensional, or linear. No amount of progress along one of several dimensions of designing is by itself a sufficient indicator of advancement in design skills. Rather, development involves the ability to interconnect and interrelate the different parameters at a higher level in a network, systemlike manner.

The multidimensional Design Space I am talking about is metaphoric. I propose it as a model through which it is possible to conceptualize processes of designing, both in a single-design episode and as a developmental trajectory over time. I describe three dimensions of this space, which are not of a kind: Contextual Worlds, Structuring, and Making. Whereas Worlds pertains to entities, Structuring refers to mental operations. Making, on the other hand, is pertinent to operations that are both mental and physical, cognitive as well as affective. Despite the disparity, maybe because of it, I think these three dimensions are necessary and sufficient to define the Design Space and to use it effectively in analyses of design processes. Designing engages all three dimensions and establishes complex networks and systems of interconnectivity among them. Design Spaces are both personal and dynamic; they change with the designer's perspective on that part of reality that is experienced as the domain of designing. Keeping in mind the three premises I just outlined, I describe, illustrate, and discuss development in terms of the dimensions of the Design Space.

CONTEXTUAL WORLDS—WHAT AND HOW DOES A DESIGNER KNOW?

A designer at work taps knowledge-based sources that gain relevance through the contexts in which they have been stored, as well as those in which a design task is seen as being embedded at a given point in time. Contextual worlds[3] are acquired and developed through design-related experiences, both active and passive. They differ from the "worlds" all people share (if any) in that they are series of blowups and reflections of selective framed portions of larger, "generic" worlds (Bruner, 1986); they are reinforced with networks of espoused commitments based on awareness and affiliation. Contextual worlds are largely shared by microcultures, such as styles, even minicultures, like schools, to which a designer fully or partially subscribes. They can be appropriated by nondesigners, notably thinkers about design such as historians or critics, but also sponsors or clients. Contextual worlds do not involve action, although they may contain considerable knowledge about action. Online action is incorporated in the two other dimensions of the Design Space, Structuring, and Making.

Contextual worlds deal with function and with form and with ways the two are—or can be—fitted to one another. Laydesigners who have never dealt with design before do not possess preexisting contextual

---

[3]The term *contextual world* is, in a way, a hybrid between Schön's (1983) *design world* and Ciborra and Lanzara's (1987) *formative context*. Schön formulated his term after Nelson Goodman's *worldmaking* and uses it in a sense too wide for what I have in mind. Ciborra and Lanzara, who coined their term to analyze organizational behavior in institutions, use it in a somewhat too narrow sense for my purpose here.

worlds, but they are able to use knowledge derived from their other worlds or realities to create ad hoc contextual worlds for design purposes. My view of design and designing is necessarily somewhat wide if it allows the inclusion of laydesigning in it. I accept broad orientations toward design such as expressed by Victor Papanek (1985): "Design is the conscious and intuitive effort to impose meaningful order" (p. 4). "All men are designers. All that we do, almost all the time, is design, for design is basic to all human activity" (p. 3). However, I must take issue with another extended vision of design that strips it of its uniqueness vis-à-vis other cognitive operations. Such a view is tacitly implemented by David Perkins (1986), who studies knowledge through metaphorically likening it to design. His definition of design reads as follows: "In general, one might say that a design is a structure adapted to a purpose" (p. 2). The two approaches are diametrically opposed, although this may seem difficult to detect at first. Whereas in Perkins' view design and knowledge are synonymous, Papanek's argumentation suggests that designing is *acting on* knowledge. Both are concerned with knowledge-in-action; but for the former design is in knowledge, and for the latter knowledge is in design. This distinction is crucial to my understanding of designing and to the concept of contextual worlds.

I look at developmental trajectories in these worlds in terms of construals of the task, the way form and function were thought of, and finally, the type of worlds the designers operated in and their understanding of it.

Construal of the Task: Who Is the Design for?

We discern three types of houses in terms of whom the designers actually had in mind as the ultimate inhabitant: a generic house, a house for self, and a house tailored for Bilby. Roughly, we see a progression from a universal house to one that is crafted specifically for Bilby as we move from children to novices to experienced students. This fits with Werner's (1940/1957) view of ontogenetic development from cognitive globality to specificity. Piaget's notion of movement from egocentrism to a greater differentiation between self and "other" (Piaget & Inhelder, 1969) is seemingly contrasted here, but we may well say that "generic" or "universal" might be closer to self, in some cases, than what is particular to Bilby. I describe the construals and the contextual worlds that generated them.

Most children (almost half) paid little attention to Bilby and her companions and made House, or Home, the focus of the undertaking. The designers in this category chose to concentrate on either exterior aspects of a house (Fig. 5.2a) or interior layouts and furnishing (Fig. 5.2b)

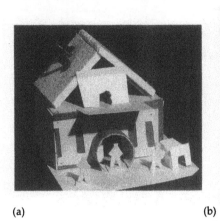 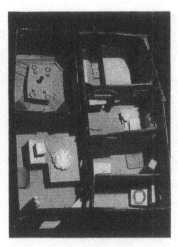

(a)   (b)

FIG. 5.2. Children's models for Bilby's house: (a) exterior, (b) interior.

of what looks rather like apartments, subdivided into rooms. The children knew what they were doing, as we learn from the exemplary comments two of them made postfactum:

"[The house is on columns] because a normal house is."

"[The house] is not for Bilby nor for me . . . for whoever will want to live here . . ."

In some cases the house was generic but included concessions, remembering the "givens." For example, one house included a space labeled "living room for the horse." Those designers who were interested in interiors produced, for the most part (girls more so than boys), very detailed models, including typical fixtures, all the way down to a towel rack or a clothesline. Accuracy and truth to reality as experienced by these designers seemed to be the major concern.

A second, smaller group of children (27%) used the task as an opportunity to design houses for themselves, or by extension, for children in general (Fig. 5.3a, 5.3b, 5.3c). They drew on their own worlds, their own priorities, with a very strong sense of children having requirements all their own. Here are two of their comments:

"But we thought more [of ourselves], we forgot Bilby altogether and we just made a fun house."

". . . and will mess up here. Grownups who come will be shocked . . . In the playroom all can be played, whatever pleases."

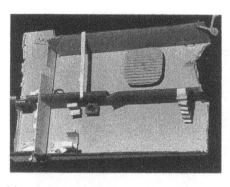

(a)

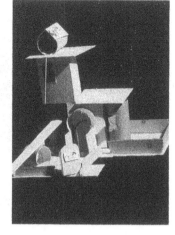

(d)

(b)

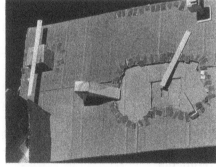

(e)

(c)

FIG. 5.3. Children's models for Bilby's house—continued: (a,b,c) first, second, and third floors of a house, (d,e) houses.

In many of these schemes conventional parts of houses that were of little significance to the children, such as kitchens, were left out. Dominant features were playrooms, playgrounds, swimming pools (in one house there were two of them), as well as items such as an ice-cream stand, a dovecote, and even a space rocket. Two girls affixed a nameplate with their names to the entrance door. These children constructed for themselves contextual worlds in which a wide range of that which interested and concerned them most directly was present, and that which seemed irrelevant was simply left out.

In the third type of houses (27%) the designers had Bilby very much on their minds (Fig. 5.3d). Her salient characteristics provided the scenarios and the reasoning for design decisions: her playfulness, her strength, her independence. The houses designed for her are full of swings and slides, are entered by climbing ropes or by jumping from one play item onto another. Play opportunities were so important that in one case the need for a house to contain them was ignored altogether (Fig. 5.3e). These designers tried to accommodate Bilby's needs, as they saw them, as best they could:

"I thought of Bilby for all that, because we made a playroom very suitable for her and we thought of making a rope first."

"We thought we would give her some toys and would give her some amusement. Where will she play with them [Tommy and Anika]? Here she will jump, slide down the rope . . ."

The designers in this category did not try to reproduce familiar "House" realities, nor was it enough for them to improve their houses by adjusting them to their own needs. Thus we have, for example, one house that is a collection of play facilities, about which the designer said she did not like it, but she thought Bilby would. These designs were the least constrained by what all children associated with generalities of house in reality, and the contextual world they created for the purpose of housing Bilby was narrowly defined and most specific to play, which epitomized and symbolized her world.

When we look at how novice students construed their tasks, we notice many similarities between them and the children. On the whole the same three categories pertain, but those who designed a relatively "normative" dwelling unit are small in number (25%).

Because these designers are adults, designing for children was not an extension of designing for themselves but of designing for Bilby, the "super child." There were those, however, who said they used themselves as yardsticks for the users' needs and wishes and tried to re-create in their designs spatial features derived from their own experiences, such as, for example, "an attic like in the house I live in." But most tried hard to cater to Bilby's special needs, which, like in the children's workshop, were identified primarily as play and were typically translated in a "one to one" manner into design attributes (Fig. 5.4a):

> "She likes to jump and she has all kinds of ways. There is a slide here with a steep slope . . . Why did I want columns? Because I wanted her to have an unconventional bed, a hammock [tied between columns], and she likes to climb."

When Bilby was seen as a representative of "childkind," designers reasoned about what is appropriate for children and tried to convey that in their models (Fig. 5.4b):

> "This is a house that all the kids in the neighborhood would have come to."

These novice designers understood that they were to operate in contextual worlds that differ from their everyday nondesign-related experiences, although there was a lot of confusion about such a distinction. The question of whether and how their own preferences should or could be incorporated was a major concern to most. Many students felt they had not received enough information and protested the lack of guidelines. There was a sense of the existence of some right answers, unavailable to them, which they must try to find out. They shied away from taking the liberties that many of the children took, having a more constrained idea of what should guide their designing:

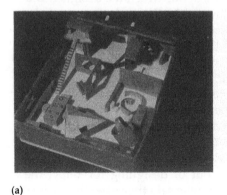 

(a)   (b)

FIG. 5.4. Novice students' models for Bilby's house: (a,b) houses.

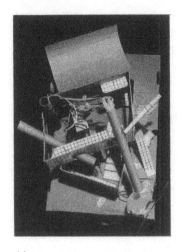

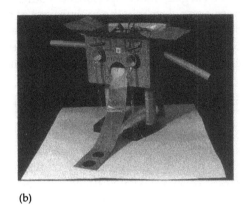

(b)

(a)

FIG. 5.5. Advanced students' models for Bilby's house: (a,b) houses.

"A really absolute definition is necessary of all conditions and needs and all that is consequently called for."

But also:

"First of all I wanted to break conventions."

The means by which they tried to achieve their design goals were partial and "extraneous." They are discussed when we talk of form and function.

Our advanced students did not even consider proposing generic houses. All of them were highly aware of having to accommodate Bilby's specialized needs. Some confined themselves to her playfulness (Fig. 5.5a, 5.5b), much like many children and novices, but were conscious of the limited potential of such a restricted choice:

"Actually you may say it is superficial . . . we designed according to one criterion [only] and this is not what designs are like, usually . . . we were carried away by her character and that's it. Nothing else interested us."

These more experienced designers were able to tap a repertoire of concepts and images taken from sources specific to their preshaped contextual worlds, like the history of architecture. One of them, for example, used the classic concept of "the primitive hut" as a reference.

Privileged, more specialized contextual worlds, though still limited ones, were clearly in the background of operations by the more advanced students. Their worlds included a wider range of resources for architectural "solutions," and as a result the designs were more integrative and extraneous ideas were readily transformed into architectural ones.

Form and Function: Knowledge and Its Implementation

Knowledge of prevailing conventions of form and function in architecture and normative fits among them, as well as a possibility to project unconventional fits, is essential to designing. Developmentally, we would expect form to precede function as a design concern (e.g., drawings by autistic children). We discovered that this was not the case.

When talking about their designs, all children gave primarily functional reasons for doing what they did. They had *activities* in mind most of the time, be they play or ordinary scenarios for life in a house. Consider this remark by one of the girls:

"For instance the kitchen. I think the kitchen is very nice, because from here, if she doesn't want to see the food, [she] jumps and it is very nice, such an open house, not walls that enclose."

But beyond the explicit reasoning used, we find surprising evidence of knowledge of functional interconnections in the children's designs. Kitchens were placed next to dining and living rooms, bathrooms next to bedrooms. Adjacencies of furniture items were sensible. Whether this reflects a conscious understanding of behavior or is just an unconscious reproduction of familiar patterns is hard to say.

Knowledge about form–function relationships are even more striking. The children displayed a good working command of typical sizes, proportions, and internal relationships of spaces. Pitches of roofs; sizes of rooms relative to whole houses; heights of walls; the size of doors and windows and their sill heights—all these are faithfully rendered in all the designs. It is possible to attach scale definitions to almost all models (most fall in the range between 1:100 and 1:50). The children asked no questions about sizes or scale; the novices did ask and were upset when these questions were not answered at the outset of the workshop. Some of them commented at the end that, whereas they did not think they learned much from this exercise, they found it possible to implement in it some of the knowledge about dimensions and ergonomics they had acquired in their 2 months at school. This is a particularly interesting point, because the children's' models were at least as detailed and at least as accurate as those of the novice students.

Issues of pure form took the shape of distinction between rectangular and nonrectangular forms. With very few exceptions, all our designers built spaces that had rectangular plans. It is interesting to look at the unusual cases in which other forms were used, or at least attempted, and understand the designers' motives for such choices. As a rule, nonrectangular forms were considered to break away from orthogonal shapes and create something unusual. They were abandoned due only to technical construction difficulties. A child and a novice student told us, respectively:

"First, we wanted to make a round house . . . And then we wanted to make a round living room, square rooms and triangular rooms. And it did not come out well."

"I wanted to make it triangular. That it would be round or triangular, that it wouldn't be square. But then it didn't come together . . . because of cardboard constraints."

Designers who took an additive approach and constructed one room adjacent to another ended up with irregular shapes, intentionally or by accident. This is the case of two mazelike houses, one by children (Fig. 5.6a), one by a novice student (Fig. 5.6b). The spaces suggested by the advanced designers, however, were all rectangular.

Classifying orthogonal shapes as "usual" and other, in particular, round shapes as "unusual" and therefore reserved, as building forms, for special purposes is consistent with architectural practice as we know it. In classical architecture there were clear rules about usage of round forms; in modern architecture the question is both more subtle and idiosyncratic and the introduction of nonorthogonal shapes usually

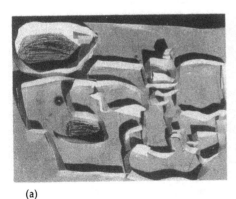
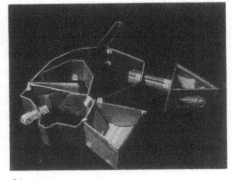

(a) (b)

FIG. 5.6. Mazelike houses: (a) by child, (b) by novice student.

requires a "case" to justify it. It is interesting that our less experienced designers were relatively unconstrained about wishing to use round forms, in comparison to their experienced colleagues who were less inclined to do so. In all cases, though, the designers clearly started with the notion that rectangular forms were the base from which to make deviations when so desired. In contrast, the history of human construction starts with round structures in almost all civilizations, to be replaced with rectangular forms and orthogonal ordering principles only later in time (Wachman, 1959).

Although "knowing that" and "knowing why" are two distinct states and may sometimes represent different developmental stages, I argue that both lead potentially to "knowing how" in designing, in a nonhierarchical manner. For example, a child may know that a house has a slanted roof because he or she sees it. An architect knows that a particular roof gradient is necessary to properly handle snow loads. Both know how to represent the roof in their respective designs. Seen in this light, the knowledge children possess as applied to the houses they designed in this workshop is far more extensive than is usually expected. This finding supports the notion that contextual design worlds are fabricated and can be made of "materials" of reality as perceived by observers of a varying degree of experience and expertise. Whereas it is true that a specific design background introduces into contextual worlds elements that cannot be there in the absence of experience, it is possible for laydesigners of all ages and levels of training to construct ad hoc contextual worlds, enlisting knowledge transferred from other "worlds."

Surrogate Worlds

Experienced architects are conscious of distinctions between contextual worlds that provide the framework for their design activities and their other worlds, pertinent to different domains of their lives. At the same time the different worlds are interdependent and the realities of one do not conflict with those of other worlds. Instead, in each situation different aspects are brought to the fore and given primacy within a coherent conceptual framework. In our workshops novices recognized that distinctions should exist but often felt that their contextual worlds are still too limited or nonexistent all together. All adult designers are aware that contextual worlds are *virtual* (Schön, 1983), that they differ from "reality" per se in that they have their own knowledge bases and their own rules. They are also virtual in that design products in these worlds are only representations of that which is being designed and which is normally to be brought into being by parties other than the design party.

We found that this is not the case of children, whose contextual worlds can be seen as *surrogate* more than virtual. For the children their models were the real houses for Bilby. They were real not in the sense that the children confused them with real-size mortar and brick structures but in the sense that they were ultimate design goals, not representations of something to be later built on a concrete site. As pointed out eloquently by Werner and Kaplan (1963/1983), it is common in young childhood for a symbol to be taken as the thing it represents. Although the children in our experiment were not so young (8 and 9 years old), I am not surprised to find surrogacy in this case. This is an important point, because it is one of the few distinctions we can make between children and novices who otherwise perform very similarly, having about the same amount of design experience and expertise.[4]

I think we should see the surrogate nature of the children's designs in light of their relating to designing much like playing. As in play, everything was taken to be real, and therefore a space rocket in one of the schemes was no more unlikely than a staircase or a seesaw (the designer said the rocket was real, not a toy). Mental imagery of anything a child associated, however loosely, with the Bilby story, had no trouble finding its way into the design. Children who filled a box with small objects that stood for playthings carefully chose or shaped each of them to resemble a particular toy. But when an advanced student filled a box with many unspecified small odd objects to suggest play opportunities, the objects were abstract symbols and did not resemble concrete toys. Virtuality is related to an ability to work abstractly.

The issue of play and its relation to designing leads to the question of stories in designing, which I discuss in the next section.

STRUCTURING—HOW DOES THE DESIGNER INTERPRET?

> We structure knowledge in pursuit of meaning. For pieces of knowledge to gain specific meaning and for the meanings of different pieces to be coherent as a larger whole, we have to interpret them by structuring. Structuring makes the pieces adhere to one another in an interactive and mutually supportive manner. We structure and interpret to "make sense" of a situation, which means turning it into a "story." A design story is the designer's personal framing of a situation with which he or she is presented,

---

[4]How similar the results seemed we can learn from the following: The 9-year-old daughter of the instructor in whose class the novices' workshop took place joined the students for this occasion. When all finished models were placed on a desk, several design instructors were asked to point out which model was made by a child. None of them was able to identify it correctly.

the basis for the reasoning that shapes the design on all its levels. Manipulating knowledge takes the form of making design moves, to both generate "leading ideas" and substantiate them when they preexist.

There are two major structuring "strategies," vertical and horizontal. We structure vertically by deriving one design question from another, by nesting problems in an hierarchical order, until we define them in a way that is manageable for us. When engaged in horizontal structuring, we use analogy and metaphor to switch among parallel or alternative ways of seeing and classifying form. Seeing things in more than one way is essential to producing coherence because it enables consolidation and convergence. An inherent aspiration in architectural design is for entities to achieve meaning beyond that of their constituent parts.

Design Stories

In designing one responds to a "design situation" that is described and defined by all one knows and assumes to be relevant to a task at hand. One does not follow a set of instructions; designing entails the production of rules for intervening in the physical world. A design situation is what a designer *reads* into a given task. It is not the task itself but its *appreciation* by the designer, revealed by his or her responses to it. The reading of a situation presumes what I call metaphorically a *design story*, and it is this story that the designer attempts to translate into physical form. The design story is virtual in that it is not the design situation but the designer's interpretation of it, as seen from his or her specific perspective at a particular time. In this way it resembles a scenario and is akin to the story a reader constructs in response to a text he or she reads, which is, as pointed out by Iser (1978), a reformulation of a reality that seeks to uncover through interpretation its hidden meanings.

Design stories are dynamic and evolve throughout the process of designing; they can be best understood and articulated in retrospect, when the design has been completed (on any level). I distinguish between lower level illustrative stories and higher level transformational stories. Whether these reflect developmental distinctions I am not sure, but they certainly represent hierarchical levels in design expertise.

Illustrating Stories

Our children, most novices, and some advanced students reacted to the strong messages of the Bilby story by making "one to one" responses to them in their design proposals. They identified salient features in the Bilby design situation and literally illustrated them by constructing appropriate physical environments for them. Said one introspective advanced student:

"Everything [in this design] has its story. Here inside the horse stands on a seesaw and then Bilby flies and then she slides down right into the mud . . . It was some sort of a paste-up, a collage of sorts. We glued on more and more things . . ."

Seesaws, swing-ropes, treasure boxes, and the like, as well as more holistic concepts such as a treehouse, a maze, or a space vehicle, were typical of these projects. In all cases the designers highlighted characteristics of the story and made design moves that responded to them. The design moves were typically generated one at a time and were combined in an additive manner, as suggested by the student's observation: "We glued on more and more things." A succession of single additive design moves is typical of laydesigners, who are not practiced in considering and manipulating different design aspects concurrently, and who lack experience in generating and evaluating alternative framings of situations. The act of illustrating a story in architectural design bears a remote resemblance to set design in the theater. A simple-minded set is appreciative of the plot and creates an environment in which it can be enacted, but nothing more. Other arts have their share of illustrative efforts, which are usually considered to be at the lower end of artistic interpretation. Let us look at a vignette from a musical composition class, in which a piece by one of the students is criticized for being too illustrative.[5]

Student: "The intention here was to take a text and explore it in a musical way . . . The instruments, of course, are a very important component in there . . . It wasn't always my intention to describe each word. Rather generally the atmosphere. In some passages it's as though the conversation has developed and the instruments continued it. Or in some places the narrative was concurrent with playing . . ."

Classmate: "The music is illustrative . . . very illustrative . . ."

Professor: "Perhaps you will allow me to say something. I think that when he [classmate] pronounced the word "illustrative" he was being critical and I think that whenever a musician says "illustrative" it means criticism. In my role of teacher . . . I suggest you write, with your free imagination, something more absolute, in some way. I mean, not to support the extra-musical thing you are conveying, even if it is inside you or in your program."

[5]This class was taught in 1972 at the Rubin Academy of Music in Tel Aviv by Professor Abel Erlich, an Israeli composer. It was recorded by the Israel Radio Network, who made the tape available to me. The text the student used was a children's story-poem, "A Tale of a Cat and a Cop," by Miriam Yalan-Schtekelis.

Contriving a design story is the most important basic mental operation that must take place as a prerequisite for architectural design; but just as in music, illustrating the story is a relatively unsophisticated and nonarchitectural way of interpreting the task. Sophistication grows when an interpretation *structures* the design task by subjecting the basic story to transformations.

Transformations

Our advanced students were aware of a difference between their first reactions and a complete, appropriate, and meaningful design they thought they were expected to produce (and which they awaited of themselves). We remember one student's comment on the "superficiality" of using but one design criterion. Let us look at another comment:

> ". . . The first image [was] to take a box and put a million odds and ends in it . . . [But] I tried to think one step ahead with my images."

One student explained why he likes the first phase better than the rest of the design process:

> "When I approach a project, at the phase of the conceptual model, the idea, at the very beginning . . . I feel full, I feel [it is] much more integrated . . . In later phases, I have difficulties inferring exactly from it [the conceptual model]. It isn't just hesitations, but a matter of confidence . . . [At first] you don't owe anything to anyone. I look at this [the Bilby project] as a conceptual model."

There are a number of important lessons to be learned from this candid commentary. The most significant, probably, has to do with the notion that a designer "owes" something to someone. Although the student did not articulate what is owed and to whom, it is clear that he has a notion of design criteria that must be satisfied, regardless of the designer's initial responses and wishes. There may be a specific party whose requirements are to be met, such as a teacher or a client. But I think we can generalize that a design owes to Architecture at large, seen as having domain-specific legitimate imperatives, independent of the designer. We can now paraphrase what the student said in terms of our concerns as follows: Initially one contrives a design story; that is both easy and fulfilling. Then one must make good the story by *transforming* it into architecture that can be evaluated in its own terms; that is less easy. It could well be that this student expected that transforming a story would become easier with experience, and indeed this is normally the case. Transforming an initial story into a work of architecture through designing is analogous to the process of musical designing as manifest in yet another comment the professor made in reaction to another piece in the musical composition protocol quoted earlier:

"I think that your thinking isn't quite 'cooked' yet, not entirely mature. I have the feeling you confuse a few things. The preparations don't have to be what you call 'musical,' only the results."

The ability to make structural transformations is a prerequisite if one is to progress from laydesigning to professional designing. It involves online assessment and evaluation, something the children and most novices in our sample did not do. A few of them offered posterior evaluations, mostly on the level of 'like–dislike,' with no reference to design criteria. A striking exception was a child who had the following to say about his work (Fig. 5.6a):

"Perhaps it [the house] is wise and all, but it isn't particularly beautiful . . . the house itself that we made [the walls] of thin paper, and it collapses all the time, that is actually not beautiful in this house. But what is nice is that there is that living room here and this mazelike [form] and all that."

The child appreciated the plan but not the aesthetics of the model. The ability to distinguish between the two is very unusual for such a young laydesigner. At the same time the child's appreciation of the excellence of the plan and the completion standards of the model as two complimentary things provides us with yet another potent example of the surrogacy of children's worlds, in which the model and what it is meant to represent are inseparable.

Structural transformations in early stages of the design process can be categorized as vertical or horizontal. Ultimately, they turn generic problem solving into specific architectural problem solving, but initially this distinction does not exist. Manipulation and transformation of form (as well as its perception and representation) have been shown to be at the basis of what Gardner (1985) calls *Spatial intelligence*, without which it is hard to imagine physical design of any kind. The examples that follow demonstrate that even novices possess impressive structuring capabilities.

Vertical Structuring. Vertical structuring takes the shape of *nesting problems* derived from an evolving formulation of the task, until a suitable question, or story, is mapped out. Let us look at one of the beginning students' design for Bilby. The "house" he presented in class was not a house at all but a warehouse storing prefabricated wall elements (Fig. 5.7a).

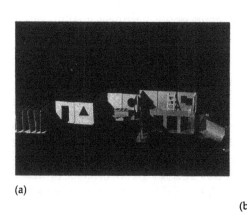

(a)

(b)

FIG. 5.7. Novice students' models: (a) vertical structuring, (b) horizontal structuring.

He explained that because Bilby was a very strong as well as a strong-willed person and did whatever pleased her, he thought it best for her to design her own house and be able to change it at will. He therefore provided her with suitable building elements, and the configurations he drew and built, made later upon request, represent a few possible floor plans illustrating how Bilby might design her house. He said at the outset:

> "Suddenly an idea presented itself . . . I couldn't get it out of my head until I knew something special I was going to do, I didn't want to make . . . a conventional house. It [the idea] was strengthened because there are clear phrases in the book [saying] that she does whatever she wants."

An initial framing of the problem reads more or less like this: Find an idea for a nonconventional house (or: Find a nonconventional idea for a house) that can be supported by evidence from the literal "givens." Once a solution was formulated that said "let Bilby design her own house," this very solution became the next problem: How is she to do that? The answer: by using prefabricated elements. Then the problem evolved into one of identifying properties of such elements:

> "It was clear to me that I would do it this way, I wasn't clear about the dimensions . . ."

We have here a series of nested problems, derived from one another. The actual experimentation and physical *gestalting* had to do with features of the prefabricated elements, such as methods of erection and joining, or shapes of openings. This state of affairs differs radically from one in which a designer engages in "illustrating a story." The student's design story was several levels removed from the text he had read in the book; yet he did not, at any stage, lose track of the original story: He found new ways of relating to it.

Horizontal Structuring. Horizontal structuring involves *multiple vision* of design situations, problems, and solutions and the ability to move back and forth among parallel alternative ways of seeing and classifying the preceding. We have one unusual example of children displaying a remarkable facility with multiple vision. A pair of kids who worked together got interested in round forms and, like many other children (and adults), they were attracted to the cardboard rolls they found among the model-making materials (toilet paper cores). They developed a complex rationale for the use of cylinders in a multipurpose fashion (Fig. 5.3d). First, there was the structural need:

"At first I thought that this would be like columns . . . It will simply hold this floor, the top."

Second, a spatial idea emerged:

"I thought it could serve as an idea to put in a window, and it can add, as if it were another room."

But we have not reached the end yet; other cylindrical segments appear in the model and windows are made to be arched. We have a third exposition, one of style:

"We also wanted a style . . . we wanted to make such an Arab style, an old style. We didn't want such a new style, really."

The ability to respond with one solution to several problems is what multiple vision is all about. These children's performance in this respect is highly surprising and unusually sophisticated.

The next case of horizontal structuring I found was one in which a novice student used metaphor to generate a design solution. She chose to make the house of macaronilike elements (Fig. 5.7b) and explained:

". . . Not the conventional things of shoes and mushrooms . . . I thought of food . . . I read that somewhere [in the Bilby story] or saw it in the movie . . . About the macaroni, it's something she can produce at will, cook and make. The house changes all the time. It's made of pipes she can climb on and slide in, and make a seesaw with . . ."

The student consciously and actively searched for an appropriate visual metaphor from children's stories and went through a few of them before she made her choice. The picture she had seen provided the macaroni image that gave her a handle on the design, and her proposal consisted of an assembly of large tubes. When criticized for the restricted nature of a house made entirely of pipes, she said:

"I can't relate to it [the Bilby story] as something realistic. We have to know whether we are talking about reality or imagination. As soon as we try to square them out we completely lose the base."

This "either–or" approach prevented her from taking the next step and detaching the actual design from its metaphoric origins so as to be able to submit it to evaluation according to architectural criteria. Her contextual world was still semisurrogate, and she could not as yet see that "face value" can be manipulated until an interpretation is reached that "works" from diverse points of view.

MAKING—ITS VISUAL LANGUAGES

Architectural designing results in propositions for built spaces and volumes. Because it deals with physical form, it is obviously highly visual. The crucial constituent of design activity clearly consists of conceiving, composing, and representing forms and their properties. The language in which architecture can be brought into being, explored, and expressed is that of visual simulations of spaces, spatial qualities, and spatial relationships: drawings and three-dimensional models. Although models are more concrete than drawings, the latter constitute the major language of architectural making. Of the different kinds of drawings designers make, sketches are the most important, because they serve as tools for generating, exploring, communicating, and assessing design ideas. Partial and incomplete representations can become rich sources of clues for possible interpretations, reframings of situations, unanticipated relevant knowledge. Abstract sketches become suggestive of meaningful "gestalts" for designers who interact with them. Visual images lend themselves to gradual or abrupt transformations as a designer makes them, reads into them and remakes them, especially when tracing techniques are used. The most abstract of diagrammatic sketches can become a personal shorthand notation of design intentions and may

play an important role in the process of making interpretations and testing
their validity and viability in terms of physical form.

Very few designers manipulate design ideas exclusively in their minds
and represent them only when the end product is fully conceived and
elaborated. Frank Lloyd Wright was a case in point, at least according to
his own testimony. Most designers, however, from children to great
masters, need to experiment. They begin with visual representations of
partial ideas to inform the generation of consequent design moves, single
or in chains. The making of representations is an important part of
designing; and as pointed out by Arnheim (1969), visualization is a mode
of thinking, not a mere documentation of it. In our Design Space,
visualization does not *follow* probing one's contextual world, nor is it the
result of structuring. It puts form into effect and makes it subject to
purposeful manipulation.

Drawings and models are the two major modes in which designers
traditionally represent space. It is important that we remind ourselves
that we are dealing with the "front edge" of designing only. Modes of
representation are of interest to us as conceptualizations of space rather
than its presentation to third parties. In our workshops novice designers,
children and adults alike, found model building a far more attractive and
useful design tool than the making of sketches. The findings in this respect
are systematic and correlate with those of other researchers, as we see
shortly. Drawings were made by children to represent their designs *after*
they were completed, but not beforehand (with one exception). The few
novice students who attempted sketches (less than 20%) readily abandoned them. It is interesting to look at this phenomenon because model
building has not been widely researched.

Generally speaking, I think we should look at this question from two
points of view: The first has to do with the activity of construction versus
the activity of drawing; the second considers the respective advantages of
concreteness versus abstractness to the conceptualization of space and
assumes that a priori models are more concrete and drawings more
abstract. Ontogenetic development progresses from appreciation of the
concrete to understanding the abstract (e.g., Werner, 1940/1957). Because,
regardless of age, our inexperienced designers preferred to work with
models, we must assume that concreteness is advantageous to design
thinking until the designer gains fluency in the utilization of a sophisticated
system of abstractions via drawings. This is the case of our advanced
students. We can support this claim with historical evidence. It was during
the Renaissance that the method of interrelated formal projections was

introduced into design practice (architecture as well as mechanical engineering, inasmuch as they were differentiated at that period). The three projections of plan, section, and elevation made it possible to accurately describe any space and volume and therefore also to explore them. When the system of formal projections was disseminated suffi- ciently among practitioners, a decline was experienced in the use of models. Wilkinson (1977) noted: "even in the 15th century, drawings were beginning to replace models in architectural practice" (p. 142). The following are comments on the use of the two modes of making and their role in the process of designing.

Model Making

The concreteness of three-dimensional models brings them close to representing space the way we perceive it in reality. How scale affects our mental representation when using model simulations is not clear enough yet; some researchers believe scale is not important (De Long, 1976), whereas others maintain that it is. Experiments in user participation in design have confirmed that, whatever the scale, models prove to be more efficient design tools than drawings for adult laydesigners involved in designing their homes (Lawrence, 1987). Our children would not make drawings at the beginning although it was suggested that they do so. Yet they could barely wait to secure building materials from the assortment offered to them and to start building.

As a rule, the children did not preplan their construction. They designed as they went along. Said one child:

"First it was this and this combined like that at this side, because I didn't know what to do . . . And then I already had an idea. So . . . I took that thing and I cut a little here . . ."

The making of models was an involving and exciting activity for the children. We observed the following: (a) All the children in the class participated in the workshop, although it was made clear that it was not obligatory; the teacher of this class said that this was unusual; (b) all the children finished their models. More time than was originally scheduled was allowed, in view of the general excitement; (c) although none of the children had ever built a model before, not one was inhibited by lack of experience or skills. Technical difficulties were overcome by learning "online" (cutting, gluing), when it became useful, or by substituting something that seemed feasible for something that did not (such as making round forms); (d) many children expressed genuine joy at their designing/model-building activities and at the finished results:

"It is also fun to take it home and play with it; at home I have plasticine I play with; I put all kinds of things of plasticine in the house."

The novice students performed quite similarly. They enjoyed model building less and, because theirs was not a surrogate world, they were more interested in the model as a representation of ideas about the design task they had to perform, regardless of their particular interpretation of it. More preplanning went into the construction of their models (yet not much more technical skill), but there were exceptions:

"Concerning what I did, I simply glued things together in space and then the solution developed."

The experienced students thought of model making in this task as a "fun thing to do," in which they did not have to justify every move; this seemed a big relief, compared with habitual "serious" designing:

"You know what, give me an exercise like this every week, to just build a model."

We can assert, then, that model building is an effective as well as an attractive design tool at the front edge of designing. Advantages manifest themselves both when it is seen as adequate replacement or supplement to sketching and when a more abstract tool like sketching is not accessible or of limited use to an unskilled laydesigner.

I think models are as serviceable as they are because, in addition to the concrete simulation they offer, making them is emotionally involving, as is the making of *artifacts* in general. The making of artifacts is known to create a commitment to their completion, as expressed by one of our children:

"What I like best is to see how it comes out."

Jerome Bruner (1979) talks about the Zeigarnik completion tendency in terms of the "freedom to be dominated by the object," which acquires an independence and sets its own terms of completion as it takes over.

This conclusion seems to be true for children and adults alike, and in architectural practice and teaching it is easy to observe great attachment to models, more so than to sketches. Emotional involvement is generally thought to be an important contributing factor in both making and learning (I recognize, of course, that overinvolvement can lead to a predicament). In the case of children, although not uniquely so, making models seems to also bear a kinship to *playing*, which explains why it is so enjoyable. I distinguish between two separate ideas here: First, the finished artifact, the model, is seen as a toy, in this case rather like a dollhouse. Second, the making of the model is a variety of a construction game, classified by Piaget (Piaget & Inhelder, 1969) as one of the modes of playing in childhood. In addition to three principal categories of play (Exercise play, Symbolic play, and Games with rules), he talks about a fourth category "which serves as a transition between symbolic play and non-playful activities or 'serious' adaptations . . . Out of symbolic play there develop games of construction, which are initially imbued with play symbolism but tend later to constitute genuine adaptations (mechanical construction, etc.) or solutions to problems and intelligent creations" (p. 59).

I have shown elsewhere that playing is a fundamental mode of search in designing, which is undertaken by adults as well, and not exclusively in model building (Goldschmidt, 1988). The construction of models, however, seems to provide particular play opportunities that may not otherwise be available to nonsketchers like laydesigners. How basic this play-design activity is we can learn from the Yuvalim model constructed by little Naomi at age 4.

The last aspect of model building as a design tool on which I comment here has to do with the maximization of resources. Maximizing resources and opportunities is an important design goal under any circumstances. We talk about design creativity demonstrated in turning constraints into opportunities. In terms of model building, we want to look at how designers utilized the materials made available to them and in what way some materials became instrumental in generating design ideas. We have seen how manipulating materials gave rise to ideas; we saw the contribution of rolls. Our advanced students were able to start working without foreplanning, with an assurance that through manipulation of materials ideas will surface (Fig. 5.5b):

"I had the boxes. She [teammate] had the two rolls in her hands. And then we put them one on top of the other . . . Then we added those . . . Then we realized that it looks like Bilby."

Another experienced student told us of how the availability of round wooden disks affected her thinking before she made any design moves:

"I was also influenced by what I saw there was, working materials. The minute I saw these wheels, I had to do something with wheels . . . There are wheels; would I not use them in a model?"

In a sense, designers work here like sculptors might with "objects trouvés." The reasoning, or the contriving of design stories, may be after-the-fact phenomena, but they are based on selective, critical perception, which must take place for design thinking to occur. Whereas some critics find after-the-fact reasoning unacceptable, I think that on the contrary, it is an indispensable form of design transformation and should be encouraged in practice. The only thing unacceptable is a design story that overlooks or contradicts relevant issues of the task; but whether these issues are recognized and brought into play before, during, or as a result of experimentation is irrelevant to the results. In fact, good designers typically make use of any opportunity to enhance, frame, and reframe their thinking on a design task, at any phase in the process. Experts do not only use but actively search for *clues* that carry the potential to generate design interpretations. Such a search is by definition mostly visual and therefore effected by materials for models just as it would be by features of a site in a "real-life" situation. Opportunities for cluing are among the most important advantages of sketching in architectural designing. Let us now look at this second, primary, mode of visual making.

Sketching

Drawing is one of the earliest representational devices used by humans. As a tool for the *conceptualization* of space, however, it requires harnessing that is acquired only through particular training and is therefore usually not available to laydesigners, who have trouble using it effectively. Here are some statements by our novice students:

> "I made one sketch but stopped it in the middle and started building. I threw it away because . . . actually it didn't say anything . . . maybe some single element can be drawn . . . but the totality, when they [elements] come together, is much easier to show in a model."
>
> "I was first going to make do with the sketch, but saw that it was very limited . . . When I started to work [on the model], I noticed that there are many possibilities I didn't think of in the sketch."

These reflections provide important evidence as to the nature of the predicament that renders sketching useless to untrained designers: For them, drawings capture only partial aspects of spatial configurations; combining these partial images into a whole is beyond reach. As pointed out earlier, the coordination of different images or views of spaces or volumes into one whole via drawing was facilitated by the invention of a formal projection system. This system must be learned and practiced beyond an acquaintance with its conventions before one can effectively synthesize partial representations into a coherent full image.[6] Designers learn to do that, and when they do they can also *infer* from one representation to complimentary ones.

Once this is achieved, the abstractness and partiality of drawings turn from a predicament into an important asset. *Abstractness and partiality are precisely the factors that account for an ease of manipulation of images when they take the form of sketches.* An experienced designer, well versed in contextual worlds and practiced in structuring and interpreting design tasks, will use sketching to generate clues, experiment with their meanings, and evaluate their consequences. The case I discuss as an example is taken from the work of two advanced students, who collaborated on this task. They brought together ideas that were initially conceived and expressed individually. This is how they described their separate beginnings:

> Student 1: "I thought that it [the house] is somewhat raised. That it is possible to enter underneath the house. There is some instability to it: A house above something . . . I suddenly thought of a flying house. A house that can move . . . The house is on wheels."

> Student 2: "I thought of three things . . . That there should be one open space, and tunnels. A "Mies Van Der Rohe space" and something that contrasts, with lots of play nooks . . . Contact with the exterior will not be through a door . . . but something like a tree which penetrates the house . . . The house is subterranean; this is a very important point."

Both students accompanied their thinking by sketching. Student 1's first sketch is figurative and describes a house on rollers that raise it from the ground and permit it to be moved (Fig. 5.9a). Student 2 sketched three abstract *diagrams*, supplemented with a written list of the three requirements he set for himself (Fig. 5.9b). Diagrammatic sketches are of particular interest because of their ultimate abstractness. They are used here, like in many other cases, as *personal, idiosyncratic, shorthand notations*

---

[6]One of the children, son of an engineer, knew the convention for indicating a door in a plan and used it in his drawing (he was the only child who made a drawing prior to building a model; Fig. 5.8a). Two boys who did not know the convention but wanted to mark doors in their postmodel drawing invented their own symbol (Fig. 5.8b), based on an observation of their model. The invention and use of the symbol occurred in a most matter-of-fact manner.

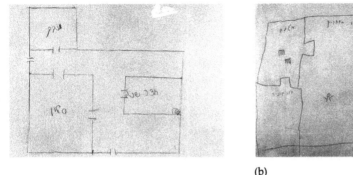
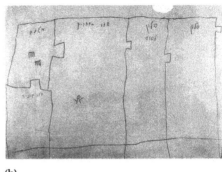

(a)

(b)

FIG. 5.8. Notation of doors in children's drawings: (a) by child who knew the formal convention, (b) by children who did not know any convention.

a designer makes up ad hoc for him or herself. Graphic shorthand notations are not unique to designing but their sequential usage in developing spatial ideas seems to me to be an exclusive design activity. To better comprehend this point, which I take to be crucially important to the understanding of designing, I attempt a brief reconstruction of the process Student 2 went through when making his diagrams and the following process in which both students made combined diagrammatic sketches to conjoin their ideas.

In his three successive diagrams Student 2 developed the notion of a large space connected to several small "play nooks." First the large space only is represented, with arrows that signify that it is meant to relate to other spaces. Next the space is shown with smaller spaces surrounding one side of it. At this point the student must have felt ready for a somewhat firmer commitment, which he depicted in the third, larger diagram. A rectangle represents an underground territory. In it a meandering line encloses the large "Miesian" space, which is tangential to four round "nooks."

When the two students decided to converge their schemes, they made five small diagrams around Student 1's earlier sketch of an elevation of the house she had in mind (Fig. 5.9c). We look at the three significant ones: 1, 2, and 4. The first thing they did was to abstractly superimpose an "upper house" (Student 1's house on wheels) on a lower house (Student 2's subterranean house). Next the result was drawn in form of a section, about which Student 1 said:

"We could have such a section. Here there are such tunnels. The outside continues as if there were no house."

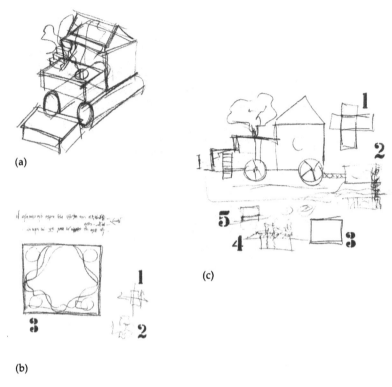

FIG. 5.9. Advanced students' drawings: (a) Students 1's sketch, (b) Student 2's sketch, (c) combined sketch.

The section was further elaborated to capture some of the forms in Student 1's elevation. We notice that it is the designers' fluent switches from plan to section and elevation that made it possible to adjoin two concepts that initially had nothing in common. This operation could not have taken place without the designers' freedom to represent abstractions of forms and relationships among them, using the formal system of plan, section, and elevation projections. The students' command of the representational system rendered sketching useful to them as a design tool for the conceptualization of space.

At this point the students abandoned their sketches and started building a model. They continued to transform their shapes while building, but they did not alter the basic concepts. The house on wheels became a tent on wheels, to enhance "impermanence." The subterranean component became a large rectangle divided into two squares, a large open one separated from a mazelike one by a wall perforated with several openings.

I dwell on the sketches with insistence because I think they illustrate cogently the nature of design expertise in the making. To make these sketches the designers had to have the images that generated them, which were abstracted from a contextual world that had in it reference-based repertoires acquired through design experience.[7] For example, the raised house was likened by the students to the classic "four-column [primitive] hut." The large open space was described as a "Miesian" space. Further, the designers had to be able to structure their interpretations of the task, which in this case evolved throughout the process:

Student 2: I feel the idea as a whole is good, as a scheme: The upper house, the connecting tree. The tunnels and the subterranean qualities remained . . . Beyond that, slowly, as we progressed, we thought of impermanence. We developed that."

Student 1: "When I look at it now . . . it really convinces me. The more I talk about it, the more pleased I become . . . Because of the [initial] image of taking a box and stuffing a million odds and ends into it . . ."

I believe that neither the structuring of the task nor its anchorage in the particular contextual world that gave rise to some of the initial images would have happened in quite the way it did, if it were not for the sketching that occurred at the early stages. It is basically through sketching, complemented by the building of a model, that these designers were able to bring their design expertise to bear on the task. The resultant project was the most sophisticated piece of architectural design produced in our Bilby workshops.

IN CONCLUSION: THE DESIGN SPACE REVISITED

The three categories in which the Bilby projects were analyzed, let us remind ourselves, are the three dimensions of what I called a Design Space, within which design operations take place. By way of summarizing, I quickly review where in a design space each of our constituencies performed.

---

[7]The notion of building repertoires as a way of developing know-how (and not only knowledge) seems important to me. Dennie Wolf (this volume) sheds light on this issue in regard to drawing. Her conclusions can be extended to other domains of developing knowing-in-making.

Children. The youngsters used their experiences in the world and the information they drew from the story they were presented with to make up a world of contexts for their design task. They did not and could not utilize specialized design knowledge as they had never faced an architectural design task before. What they had access to, though, was enough for each of them to rely on in this endeavor. The ad hoc worlds created this way were largely surrogate and what happened in them was, for the children, a substitute for reality. This may explain the perfectly uninhibited nature of their designing. Issues of function took primacy over issues of form. I understand this as being related to the illustrative nature of the children's designs. The design stories they construed were predominantly plot related and therefore directly transformable into function-oriented interpretations. The structuring of the task took the form of making single moves and combining them in an additive manner until all important issues seemed to have been taken care of. The language in which the design moves were made was one of producing concrete spatial simulations in the form of three-dimensional models. Because of the surrogate nature of the children's worlds, the models became the ultimate design goal and product.

Novice Students. The novice students had no more design experience or skills than the children. But they had different experiences in the world, and different expectations. Whereas they, too, had to rely on their generic experiences to frame contextual worlds for the task, they were aware of a need to tap specific design knowledge that they felt they did not have as yet. By and large their worlds were virtual, in that they took their actions and products to be aimed at the creation of full-scale structures for which they specified intentions, if not yet instructions. Some were able to apply successfully problem-solving strategies derived from other domains of experience. Those who did structured the task through transformation, vertically or horizontally, and as a result were able to make interrelated design moves in chains. Nonliteral more than illustrative interpretations of design stories differentiated them from the children and from their less advanced peers. The thinking was still done exclusively in the concrete language of three-dimensional models, in absence of fluency in the application of strategies of manipulating form by way of sketching.

Advanced Students. This group worked in a fashion closer to what would be considered expert designing. There were manifestations of subscription to specialized contextual worlds and some ability to tap their resources. Such worlds did not altogether replace "generic" worlds but were superimposed onto them. They were fully virtual, not surrogate.

We discern clearly for the first time the primacy of form. Function is not necessarily subordinate, but form is seen as the primary variant in a truly architectural interpretation of a task. Moves are made in chains and transformational structuring occurs almost as a matter of course. Design stories undergo transitions as online evaluation provides corrective cues. Coherence is sought in the form of holistic meanings that transcend that of the participating partial ingredients. Thus the work is no longer illustrative but truly interpretative. The "laboratory" used to explore form configurations is, for the first time, that of sketching. Advantages include fast production, easy generation and evaluation of alternatives, tentative commitments to principles with sufficient "open ends" to accommodate transformations. Most importantly, sketching is a compact yet rich medium for clues as it is combined with structuring skills and wide contextual repertoires.

I hope I have demonstrated the continuum between lay and expert designing. In a design space, development consists of growth and gradual transitions in loci of operation as defined by the three dimensions. Interdependence among the dimensions is crucial and takes the form of networking in design performance. Individual developmental trajectories vary, but my observations suggest that the patterns I have described are generic.

REFERENCES

Arnheim, R. (1969). *Visual thinking*. Berkeley: University of California Press.

Bruner, J. (1979). *On knowing: Essays for the left hand*. Cambridge, MA: Harvard University Press.

Bruner, J. (1986). *Actual minds, possible worlds*. Cambridge, MA: Harvard University Press.

Ciborra, C. U., & Lanzara, G. F. (1987, May). Change and formative contexts in information systems development. *Proceedings of the IFIP Conference on Information Systems Development for Human Progress in Organizations*, Atlanta.

DeLong, A. (1976). The use of scale models in spatial-behavioral research. *Man Environment Systems*, 6(3), 179–182.

Gardner, H. (1985). *Frames of mind*. New York: Basic.

Goldschmidt, G. (1985). *House for Bilby: Children as designers*. Technion, Haifa, Israel.

Goldschmidt, G. (1988). Interpretation—Its role in architectural designing. *Design Studies*, 9(4), 235–245.

Iser, W. (1978). *The act of reading*. Baltimore: Johns Hopkins University Press.

Lawrence, R. J. (1987). *Housings, dwellings and homes: Design theory, research and practice*. Chichester, UK: Wiley.

Lingren, A. (1974). *Pippi Longstockings* (Hebrew translation from the Swedish original). Tel Aviv: Am Oved.

Papanek, V. (1985). *Design for the real world* (rev. ed.). Chicago: Academy Chicago Publishers.

Perkins, D. N. (1986). *Knowledge as design*. Hillsdale, NJ: Lawrence Erlbaum Associates.

Piaget, J., & Inhelder, B. (1969). *The psychology of the child*. New York: Basic.

Schön, D. A. (1983). *The reflective practitioner*. New York: Basic.

Schön, D. A. (1988). Designing: Worlds, rules and types. *Design Studies, 9*(3), 181–190.

Wachman, A. (1959). *Circular and orthogonal building (A morphological study in evolution of circular and orthogonal forms in building)* (Unpublished master's thesis). Technion—Israel Institute of Technology, Haifa, Israel.

Werner, H. (1957). *Comparative psychology of mental development.* New York: International Universities Press. (Original work published 1940)

Werner, H., & Kaplan, B. (1983). *Symbol formation.* Hillsdale, NJ: Lawrence Erlbaum Associates. (Original work published 1963)

Wilkinson, C. (1977). The new professionalism in the renaissance. In S. Kostof (Ed.), *The architect* (pp. 124–160). New York: Oxford University Press.

III

Development of the Artist

Interconnective Evolvements from One Medium to Another

Leonard Baskin

I must, at the very onset of this chapter, proffer several disavowals. I stoutly believe that artists should be seen, not heard! And Sir Joshua Reynolds urged that artists have their mouths sewn-up, and *that* from the painter whose Royal Academy lectures (discourses) are still important in any consideration of philosophical aesthetics. Sir Jacob Epstein declared, somewhat sententiously, "I rest quiet in my work," and proceeded to write three books explicating his sculpture. Under no circumstances that I can think of would I undertake to explain my work, granting that I could. I am a firm believer in the role, indeed the crucial role, that *ambiguity* plays in works of art. Levels of meaning can be vested in a work beyond the artist's intention or wish. Response to profound works can *only* be *generally*, not specifically, controlled. Plastic forms lack the precision of words: I can hear the guffaws from the phenomenologists; try writing a law in sculpture. Think of the delightful but utter chaos that would ensue if bank statements and accounts were rendered in aquatint or mezzotint. Ergo, I desist from offering linguistic equivalents or explanations of my works. My second disavowal declares my somewhat distressed feeling of being an interloper in this volume, placed here through ancient friendships and the specious presumption that I might somehow contribute to this volume honoring the memory and achievement of Heinz Werner. In reality I have not the scantest notion of advances in concepts of developmentalism. But I must have perceived some relationship, however tenuous, between these festivities and the evolving nature of my work, which allows me to present my thoughts. I am now done with palliating demurrals, and proceed with foolhardy bravado to the pith of this piece. I have ever had a devout interest, perhaps devout *passion* is more apt, in pursuing an idea, or theme, or subject in successive series of works, and further and more to the point, exploring and driving the concept from one medium to another. Not all subjects and not all media, but a sufficiency to permit thought *about* the interdependent developmental enrichment that flows from, forgive the expression, intemedial deployment. We are all variously burdened by the timeless cliché "Jack of all trades, master of none." I resent the restrictive, the stifling, the repressive nature of that old saw. The Oxford English Dictionary gives *jack* 38 distinct definitions, beyond the slang usages. Interalia, the word pertains to a certain kind of young greenpike, to a hawk, to several usages in plant names, to machine parts, and to the object aimed at in the game of bowls; pertaining to people it implies boors, rude fellows, and the like. Jack of all trades is thus pejorative and nasty, a put-down from every point of view. I pronounce a new jimcrack, a fresher formulation, that is, "Jack of all trades, master of all," and I hope it develops into a cliché. Blake in "The Auguries of Innocence" intones the beautiful and heartening line, "Bless relaxes, damn braces," meaning to condemn all that retards, halts, impacts, and denies, and to celebrate all that releases, refreshes, and enriches. And Blake with the divine afflatus firmly fixed like a golden nimbus or under the benevolent influence of a doubled dose of Epsom salts further urges upon us in the "Marriage of Heaven and Hell" that "the road of excess leads to the palace of Wisdom." We must stretch ourselves on a benign procrustean bed; we must be protean in attitude and in achievement. Gauguin, who is an honest witness, tells us "that nothing can be achieved by taking the moderate route." We are exhorted to an extreme reached, impelled to a red-hot commitment, urged to partake of stellar aspiration. The notion of specialization has become so prevalent that one is looked upon with suspicion if one strays off into a medium not normally associated with one's name. For me, specialization has inherent negative and retardiaire connotations. However specialized in function parts of the brain are asserted to be, they must work in cohesion with and as part of a greater operating whole. Pavlov's stimulation of the hypothalamus to good gnarling and gnashing effect, of that severed dog's head, has perhaps improved us, but I rather imagine that the dog was wildly desperate for the rest of its body. With no basis in the deep wells of sapience, and with no layered structures of knowledge to buttress the grave misgivings and hostile suspicions with which I regard the new learning that subdivides the brain into smaller and smaller quotients, indicating ever more highly specific activity, my deep-rooted ignorance tells me, *beware!* this stinks of a newer behaviorism, a mechanistic reduction of the complex to the simple, a drive to disentangle the ganglion web, an attempt to separate and particularize the integrated workings, to reduce the interdependent syncopation of physiology to computer-like compartmentalization. If I am pressed, I own that this brain localization is subtle and sophisticated with possible elements of truth in the findings. But I would urge upon the discoverers of centers for right-sided vowel capacity an equivalent concentration on the consorted efforts of the parts striving together to frame the "fearful symmetry" of our living organism. On securer ground, let me affirm at once that I am not proposing a mindless or heartless shuffling about without mastery or wanting in intention, or not impelled by historical or personal imperatives. I wish to, indeed I am, caviling at the universal pigeonholing that characterizes our time. This caterwauling is a preamble to my averral that I am smitten with the notion of immersion in and mastery of as many media as I can manage. It has been, for instance, a lifelong struggle to restrain and contain my desire to write. I turned to the scribbling of poetry when young, perhaps to compensate for my youthful incapacities in sculpture and drawing. I mention this, not to reveal autobiographical irrelevancies, but to assert that the easy movement from one medium to another was suspect behavior, was considered irregular, certainly not the normal procedure; a painter was expected to paint, a sculptor to sculpt, and so on. But I have never been able to resist the blandishment of erupting into another medium. My work clearly reveals my tendency to traverse the plastic media with the exception of painting in oil; I have no proclivity for the medium that Fuseli called "his coy mistress." I seem to be avid to explore themes and subjects, motifs and ideas, which are clearly and closely related. I also tend to penetrate a theme by doing a long series of drawings or numbers of prints and as the idea seems to be exhausted, conceiving of the theme *anew* as a long bronze relief or a large woodcarving; the subject is reinvigorated and reinvested with newfound meanings, or aspects of meaning or new levels of meaning. I am not simplemindedly suggesting a mechanical device to extend the life or liveliness of a subject, but if one can move with natural ease from modeling to carving, from woodcut to etching, from drawing to lithograph, a manifest possibility exists for a deeper reach, an expanded range, an extended scope. The veering among the media tends to lengthen the possibility of a concept taking on a renewed life, or the newfound force of regeneration. "Bless relaxes, damn braces," indeed! In this age of general indifference to content, with the inevitable concomitance of an unintended decorativeness, expressed with diverse subjective tendencies, works do not achieve that degree of differentiation that the probing I have described within the modalities of realism *allows* or permits. The flagging spirits of the developmentalists should lift at the sound of differentiation. To differentiate is to mark the passage of developmental time, to annex charged space and to invent inevitable forms, which when in compaction with one another shape a content of complexity, of ambiguity, and replete with terraces of meaning. Differentiation is not a Rothkovian blanket of subsuming orange, nor is differentiation defined by gestures that I once categorized as expressing "visceral anxiety and fecal despair." To differentiate is to build complex interconnective structures expressive and communicative of that many-chambered reality in which living humans render meaning to cellular and all other diologies, give credence to theories of developmentalism and other psychologies, make palpable the totality of knowledge about human life. I mean, that works of art that differentiate hold a mirror, however dessicated or dissolute, or pure or preserved, the mirror can be cracked or whole, but it is held up to nature and reveals ourselves to ourselves. Each medium abounds in characteristics that are peculiar to it alone. And within a medium, great and startling differences exist: Consider sculpture; how different its three classically fundamental materials are. The resonances that exude from stone, wood, and bronze are inimitable and language is reduced to feeble incapacity in attempting verbal equivalents. That richness of variation is strikingly obvious when comparing woodcuts, etchings, and lithographs, and one can further compound the differences in confronting etching's capacity to be worked in aquatint and mezzotint, drypoint, roulettes and rockers, soft and lift grounds, and so on. It is the exploitation of these aggrandizing modalities of difference that cross-fertilize, that allow an artist an ever deeper probe, a more febrile or cooler sensibility, a greater and broader breadth of understanding. It may be said that Blake urged us to spill ourselves out of our containing vessels, to overflow our ever-tightening and encroaching boundaries, to see in specialization a spurious and meretricious enterprise. And to loose the dynamics of our artistry into programs and systems of variegated diversity. I press the blessings of excess upon you and I exhort you to passionate exuberance in the long pursuit of an idea.

Michelangelo, Early Childhood, and Maternal Imagery: The Sculptor's Relation to Stone

Robert S. Liebert
College of Physicians & Surgeons,
Columbia University

It is my purpose to explore the contribution that psychoanalysis can offer to the understanding of the meaning of artistic images as well as the medium in which the artist works, as a natural complement to the scholarship of the art historian. In this endeavor I consider several of Michelangelo's earliest and last works, all involving the motif of mother and son, and his relation to stone—that particular substance through which he expressed, more than through any other medium, his inner world.

In the psychoanalytic study of an artist the biographer is intent, foremost, on stressing an intimate connection between the inner life of the artist and the unique character of his creative works. After all, we know Michelangelo only because of the fruits of his creativity. What follows is speculation, a narrative that attempts to move beyond plausibility to probable truth in establishing the complex and often contradictory elements that were the basis of Michelangelo's psychic life, and then to explain these in relation to his art.

Our explanation with respect to Michelangelo and his works is, of course, no better than the correctness of our theory and the adequacy of our primary data. Michelangelo is unique among artists of the past in that a wealth of deeply personal statements, in the form of 480 letters to family, friends, and patrons, and 800 letters from them to him and between them and about him, as well as 327 poems, have been preserved. In addition, we have two biographies by his friends: one by Giorgio

Vasari (1598/1967), the Florentine artist and biographer of Italian Renaissance artists, and the other, published in 1553, when Michelangelo was 78 years old, by Ascanio Condivi (1553/1975), a young assistant to the artist. Scholars agree that the Condivi biography is largely an autobiography based on recollections and letters supplied by the master. Further, there are lengthy characterizations of Michelangelo by contemporaries in the literary form of dialogues. These documents are supplemented by the facts of Michelangelo's infancy and childhood, and of his family, as they are known. We actually know far more about Michelangelo than any other artist until the 19th century (see Liebert, 1983).

MICHELANGELO'S EARLY LIFE

Before addressing the main issues of this chapter, I briefly summarize some of the facts about Michelangelo's early life and what I infer to be major constellations of fantasy that bear on the problems before us.

Michelangelo was born in 1475 and lived to be 89 years old, working until 6 days before his death. We cannot account for his extraordinary endowment as a sculptor, painter, architect, and poet. No one in the Buonarroti family had ever been concerned with such pursuits, and his early inclinations toward art were vigorously opposed by his father. An initial formidable problem is the role of his mother and her surrogates in his early life. It is therefore usual to gather together what is known about his early mothering and speculatively fill in certain additional pieces. In contrast to the documented knowledge about so many aspects of his life, information about his mother and her relationship with him is extremely sparse. All that we know is his mother's name, and that she died at age 26, when her second born was 6 years old. We do not know what she died of, whether her death was unexpected or followed a long illness. I presume the former, because Michelangelo's youngest brother was born the same year. The only reference to her in all of Michelangelo's writings is not very illuminating and occurs in a letter to his nephew, written when the artist was 79 years old. There is a question not simply about the quality of the mother–son relationship, but about whether there was even continuous contact between Michelangelo and his mother during the 6 years in which they coexisted.

In the Condivi biography the one reference to mothering tells us that Michelangelo was boarded at birth with a stonemason's family on the small Buonarroti farm to wet nurse. Condivi (1553/1975) recounts:

> Michel Angelo used to say jestingly, but perhaps in earnest too, that it was no wonder that he delighted in the use of the chisel, knowing that the milk

of the foster-mother had such power in us that often it will change the disposition, one bent being thus altered to another of a very different nature. (pp. 6–7)

Thus, Michelangelo describes himself as the passive object of the mystical power and active force of the foster-mother's milk, which he felt endowed him as a sculptor. The force apparently stood in opposition to that of his natural mother and father as his procreative source and identification.

Because Michelangelo's experience of being boarded with a wet nurse is so alien in our century, yet so formative in his life, it is necessary to understand this part of his personal history in the context of the childrearing practices of the time. In a comprehensive historical study, Ross (1974) established that it was the usual practice in 15th-century Italy to board an infant from a middle-class family with a wet nurse. The norm of the early childhood experience then is so foreign to us now that Ross's description deserves to be quoted in some detail.

What were the infant's first contacts with the world outside the womb? Birth in the parental bed, bath in the same room, and baptism in the parish church were followed almost at once by delivery into the hands of a wet nurse, generally a peasant woman living at a distance, with whom the infant would presumably remain for about two years or until weaning was completed. Immediate separation from its mother, therefore, was the fate of the new-born child in the middle-class families of urban Italy . . . It became wholly dependent for food, care, and affection upon a surrogate, and its return to its own mother was to a stranger in an alien home, to a person with whom no physical or emotional ties had ever been established. (pp. 184–185)

Unfortunately, we know no more about the stonemason's wife than we do about Michelangelo's natural mother. So, again, we are left with countless questions about her specific influence on Michelangelo and the nature of the maternal care he received. We can only draw inferences from his later character structure, relationships with women, sexual orientation, and representations of women in his art. One must also bear in mind that wet nurses were generally lower class women, either grieving the loss of, or concurrently nursing, their own infants, and doing this on a business basis.

As for Michelangelo's early life, we have little more to draw upon than the average expectable circumstances for a Florentine middle-class child. To that extent, my reconstruction is based upon probabilities strengthened by some facts. I assume that he remained with the stonemason's family in Settignano for approximately 2 years but had some contact with his family, because it was their farm and it lay just outside of Florence. There is no reason not to conclude that, once weaned, he rejoined his natural parents, who were then living with the family of his father's only brother in a very small communal household in the Santa Croce quarter of Florence. Michelangelo's mother may be presumed to have been reasonably healthy as she bore three more sons during the 4 years following his birth.

To recapitulate my reconstruction of Michelangelo's first 10 years: He was boarded with a wet nurse of unknown character for perhaps as long as 2 years. His weaning was then associated with an abrupt separation from this mothering woman. At this time he was returned to his natural mother and father, both of whom were relative strangers to him, as he was to them. His reentry into his mother's life, particularly as her second son, probably elicited minimal emotional investment on her part, inasmuch as she was subsequently pregnant for about half of the 4 years that remained to her. Thereafter, he was a member of a two-family collective household until 10 years of age, with no known adequate maternal surrogate, and a ne'er-do-well father who, apart from whatever grief he may have experienced following his wife's death, must have felt his five young sons to be a substantial burden.

We are now faced with the problem of translating this particular childhood history, or to be more accurate, my version of Michelangelo's childhood, which was not unusual for the 15th century, into the constructs of 20th-century theory and analysis. It must be assumed that, regardless of the norms and prevailing practices during the Renaissance, there are certain invariable laws of human behavior that include, on the one hand, universal psychobiological impulses, and on the other, restraints and ethical concerns shared by all social orders. In each environment, however, certain predominant pathways of discharge and sublimation of drives and the derivatives are more or less accessible and acceptable. Therefore, in a given society, some patterns of resolution of conflict and behavior will be facilitated and others impeded. Even by the standards of the time, Michelangelo's childhood was traumatic—marked by inconstant care when he was totally dependent, abrupt losses of the persons responsible for his protection and nurturance, and by little experience with the continuity in attachments and the dependable and consistent environment that are necessary to provide for the development of stable self and object inner representations.

INFLUENCE OF CHILDHOOD ON MICHELANGELO'S ARTISTIC IMAGES

Having outlined what is known and inferred about Michelangelo's early years, I now turn to the question of whether his childhood influenced his artistic images and, if so, how, and whether these artistic solutions in turn yield insight into his inner experiences of his personal history. As a preliminary effort in this direction, let us consider one of his earliest sculptures, *The Madonna of the Stairs* (see Fig. 7.1). This work commands attention, for it is Michelangelo's earliest artistic statement about mother and child.

The *Madonna of the Stairs* was completed at age 16 while Michelangelo was living in the household of Lorenzo ("the Magnificent") de' Medici. Art historians are divided as to whether this work is Michelangelo's first or second sculptured work. This low relief is extraordinary for the originality with which he treated the most common subject in Renaissance art—particularly striking because, at the time, Michelangelo was very young, a student, and just learning the technique of carving. Although the work bears some resemblance to an earlier 15th-century Madonna by Donatello (the *Pazzi Madonna*), it appears that Michelangelo drew his primary inspiration from ancient Greek marble reliefs. He rejected as his model the typical contemporary Tuscan Madonna, in which the Madonna was almost always represented as a young bourgeois, with Jesus depicted as the blessing savior. In these contemporary works the Virgin was rarely shown seated in profile and, with a single exception, never in an upright position. Rather, Michelangelo looked back in time to a particular genre of works, the ancient grave reliefs in which a deceased woman is forever commemorated by her image in stone. The stelae, incidentally, often present a dead mother being bade farewell by her child. Michelangelo's *Madonna* shares not only the position of the women of the stelae but also their mournful solemnity. Instead of the idealized maternal image of the Renaissance, in which the Virgin sometimes has her gaze averted in sad foreknowledge of the tragic destiny of her son but is nonetheless in nurturing contact with Him, Michelangelo's *Madonna* is stone-like and detached. Her appearance is all the more striking because of the circumstances depicted—nursing a child.

As one studies this work more closely, several other revealing ambiguities emerge. Jesus appears to rise from His mother's womb to nurse at her breast. However, rather than nursing, He appears to be asleep. But it is the sleep of death, which is communicated by the symbolism of His pronated right arm. The arm in this attitude derives its meaning from the iconographic vocabulary of Roman sarcophagi. A similar pronated arm reappears 60 years later in the dead Christ of the Florence *Pietà*, which Michelangelo intended for his own tomb. Moreover, for the first time in Renaissance art, the child Jesus is shown with His back to the viewer, thereby both increasing the ambiguity of His meaning and emphasizing the primary role of the Madonna.

To interpret an artist's motivational currents on the basis of a single work is a hazardous undertaking. Rather, it is more fruitful to consider

FIG. 7.1. Michelangelo, *Madonna della Scala* (Madonna of the Stairs), Casa
Buonarroti. Scala/Art Resource, New York.

the work as just one part of the fabric of attempted solutions to the unconscious challenge of a particular motif. At this point in Michelangelo's adolescence, however, certain lines of thought are suggested by the innovations in the *Madonna of the Stairs* that might tentatively be brought together in the following formulation.

Michelangelo was attracted to the task of creating a figure who embodied the idealized, nurturing mother of the Christian world. In his search for this woman, he was unconsciously compelled to reject the available contemporary repertoire and, instead, sought the image from the prehistory of Christianity—from a figure of a dead mother, remembered and preserved by only her presence in stone. This is not one of the several traditional Marys—sad yet maternal. Rather, she is cold and stone-like, and strikingly unresponsive to her child. She represents the fused image of Michelangelo's wet nurse and natural mother, both of whom were forever lost to him. The yearning to recapture the lost sense of well-being in a symbiotic union with the breast remained an intense moving force within Michelangelo, as is indicated by the wet nurse anecdote in Condivi. However, to yield to this regressive yearning was also to risk death—both in the union with the dead mothering one and in the unleashing of the impounded rage connected with the sense of abandonment so early in life. Thus, it was the power of these unresolved, traumatic childhood experiences and the continuing unconscious attitudes toward his mothering figures and their object representation that found sublimation in this remarkably innovative treatment of the Madonna.

THE MEANING OF THE MEDIUM

I have offered an explanation of why Michelangelo's first sculptured Madonna assumed the image that it does. This image is consistent in its unique and personally distinctive aspects with his four other sculptured Madonnas (*Bruges Madonna*, ca. 1503–1505; *Taddei Madonna*, ca. 1503–1505; *Pitti Madonna*, 1503–1505; and *Medici Madonna*, 1521–1534). But it is dramatically different from his one painted Madonna, in *The Holy Family* (Fig. 7.2). This difference in the representation of the Madonna in sculpture and painting leads us to inquire further about the meaning of the medium itself to the artist.

Michelangelo viewed himself first of all as a sculptor and often signed his letters "Michelangelo the Sculptor." Although also a painter, architect, and poet, he clearly preferred working in stone. Therefore, let us turn our attention to his intimate relation to stone.

FIG. 7.2. Michelangelo, *Holy Family* (Doni Tondo), Uffizi, Florence. Alinari/Art Resource, New York.

In examining the chronology of Michelangelo's career, it is striking that he periodically spent extended periods of time in the mountains at the quarries of Carrara and, later, of Pietrasanta. In 1497–1498, he spent 6 months at Carrara, seeking marble for the *Pietà* at St. Peter's; in 1505, 8 months obtaining marble for the Tomb of Pope Julius; in 1516–1518, he spent periods of 3 months, 7 months, and 1 month at Carrara in search of stones for the tomb and the facade of the Church of San Lorenzo; and finally, in 1518–1519, he spent 18 months at Pietrasanta. During these sojourns he was away from family, friends, the mainstream of art, patrons, and the familiarity of Florentine and Roman urban life. How can we understand these periods of isolation in the remote mountains?

It is fair to assume that Michelangelo had a deeply vested interest in ensuring that the block of marble with which he was to enter into so intimate a relationship be free of veins and other obstacles to his carving. Yet the wish to oversee the selection and stages of the cutting does not seem a full explanation for his long immersions in the quarries.

A starting point for understanding Michelangelo's relationship to the quarries is his statement in a letter written from Pietrasanta (Ramsden, 1963): "In trying to tame these mountains . . . I've undertaken to raise the dead" (Vol. 1, letter 123). This stark phrase suggests that Michelangelo's consuming absorption with these raw sources of marble had its origin in his earliest experiences—the first year or two of his life, spent with the stonecutter's family among the blocks at the farm in Settignano. Let us recall Michelangelo's statement to Condivi that his wet nurse had been both the daughter and wife of stonecutters, and that his delight in the use of the chisel was transmitted to him through the milk of the foster-mother, which possessed the power to shape the personality of the infant. I would postulate that the later retreats to the quarries also represent the search for his lost maternal and nurturing origins. The search was undertaken again and again, while most of his statues remained in some state of incompletion and all his sculptural programs, such as the 12 Apostles for the facade of the Cathedral in Florence, the Tomb of Julius, and the facade of the Church of San Lorenzo, were far from finished.

Michelangelo wrote a madrigal in 1544 in which he equated stone and maternal rejection in words that also convey the intensity of his ambivalence (C. Gilbert, Trans.; Gilbert & Linscott, 1963):

> . . . just as I am made by her,
> And always seem to take
> Myself for model, planning to do her.
> The stone where I portray her
> Resembles her, I might
> Well say, because it is so hard and sharp;
> Destroyed and mocked by her,
> And yet if art can keep
> Beauty through time only if she endure
> It will delight me, so I'll make her fair.
> (poem 240)

Thus Michelangelo states his conflict in identifying stone with woman; he sees as futile his attempts to convert this "stone mother" into anything more nurturing, yet he cannot abandon hope. Out of his despair over ever finding "her," Michelangelo seems to state that he can only rely on himself.

At the deepest level of unconscious thought, the marble face of the mountain represented the maternal breasts. As Sterba and Sterba (1978) suggested, the quest in the quarries for the intact, perfect block of marble was part of a restitutive process. An intrinsic component of this form of restitution was the venting of Michelangelo's rage at the oral and maternal deprivation to which he had been subjected. In contrast with the farmer who works the earth's surface by agricultural means to yield nourishment, Michelangelo had to attack this obdurate and intransigent material with sharp and harsh weapons to make it his. On a drawing for the lost bronze statue of *David*, Michelangelo wrote, "David with his sling and I with my bow" (Daviete cholla frombe/e io chollarcho). In this written fragment the artist played with the word *bow*, which, in addition to being a weapon, was the term for the sculptor's hand drill. The bow, hammer, and chisel were Michelangelo's tools for attacking the block. By making an analogy with David, who with his weapon slew the hated enemy, Michelangelo reveals his unconscious view of the mountain stone as something to be conquered and forced into relinquishing the image imprisoned within. Throughout his long life, the hope of recovering the idealized state of early union with his mothering figure brought him back to its most primitive symbolic origins—the buried sources in the earth—to reengage in the struggle to regain the unfulfilled promise. It was a struggle composed of exhilaration and fury. As the phrase "to raise the dead" implies, it was Michelangelo's inner imperative to breathe life and movement into this most inert of the earth's substances. Indeed, the most animated of all of Michelangelo's images is found in one of the sketches for *The Resurrection* (Fig. 7.3), in which the tomb of stone has miraculously yielded up the soaring and triumphant Redeemer.

No image in Western art has commanded the awe and popular response of the *Creation of Adam* (Fig. 7.4), with its vision of an anthropomorphic God who, with transcendent grace and power, soars to the apogee of his celestial journey. He bestows his compassionate gaze and tender procreative gesture upon Adam, whose concave and receptive form reaches out for the mysterious infusion of physical strength and spiritual purity already latent in him. The miraculous event-to-be exists outside of time. As has been said (Freedberg, 1970), "For the moment Michelangelo and God's roles merge: God acts as the classical sculptor" (p. 26). Thus, the languid form of Adam appears to rise from the blue–grey barren mound beneath him. Beholders of this image cannot help but respond with a sense of rediscovering and reexperiencing some lost moment of their own innocence in the buried past, when there could be complete trust in an all-caring, omnipotent parent.

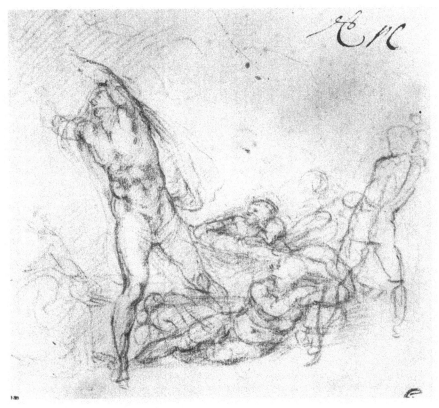

FIG. 7.3. Michelangelo, disegno, *Resurrection*, Louvre, Paris. Alinari/Art Resource, New York.

In 1871, Walter Pater perceptively wrote: "Carrara, those strange grey peaks . . . [Michelangelo] wandering among them month after month, till at last their pale ashen colours seem to have passed into his painting" (p. 87). Indeed, from the jagged, bare rock of the Doni Tondo and the *Battle of Cascina*, to the *Noah* and *Adam* and *Eve* histories of the Sistine ceiling (where even *Paradise* is barren rock except for the Tree of Knowledge), through the *Last Judgment* and the final Pauline Chapel frescoes of the *Conversion of Paul* and the *Crucifixion of Peter* (Fig. 7.5), even the smallest signs of vegetation are virtually nonexistent. Rather, Michelangelo's legion inhabit an earth paved with stone. Flesh and stone are the timeless dialectic of his art. Carrara not only provided him with marble for his sculpture; it also served as the model, only slightly modified, for the landscape we see in many of his paintings.

The constant presence of stone during his stays at the quarries may have functioned as the equivalent of *transitional phenomena* for Michelangelo; that is, just as a "security blanket" or other material object serves

FIG. 7.4. Michelangelo, Sistine Chapel ceiling: *The Creation of Adam* (1508–1512). Alinari/Art Resource.

FIG. 7.5. Michelangelo, *St. Peter's Crucifixion*, Pauline Chapel, Vatican. Alinari/Art Resource.

as a comforting substitute for the absent mother to the toddler and young child, a symbolic substitute until the child is cognitively able to achieve *object constancy* (the capacity to maintain an internalized mental concept of the mother even if she is not physically present), so I believe that the masses of marble at the quarries were comforting companions and representations of the sculptor's repressed or unremembered early childhood with the stonecutter foster family and wet nurse.

A question inevitably emerges from these considerations of Michelangelo's relationship to stone and the quarries: What was he trying to find, or refind, in transforming stone to life? I return to this question shortly when exploring the Florence and Rondanini *Pietas*, which occupied him in his old age.

In the present context, however, we may consider a striking fact about Michelangelo's work: Two thirds of his statues were never completed. The problem of non-finito bears on the present question of the meaning of his relation to stone. Whereas some of these works were left uncompleted for practical or external reasons (as in the case of the *St. Matthew*, abandoned because Michelangelo had to leave Florence for Rome at the summons of the pope), I believe that most were left undone for more complex internal reasons. A central factor was that, for Michelangelo, to complete a statue was also to sever his bond with the block of stone. After so long and intense an involvement with the material substance as well as the idea of a statue, to bring this active relationship to an end held the prospect of evoking echoes of his early, profound separation anxieties. Moreover, the figure that emerged from the husk of marble could never really be the object of his relentless unconscious search. It was simply what it was—lifeless and unresponsive to him. Therefore, more often than not, Michelangelo avoided the pain associated with that stark end. He turned instead to the next project, and the next, and finally, in the last 15 years of his life, to one theme, the union of Son and Mother in the Pietas.

THE LATE PERIOD

In Michelangelo's art of his last period, from 1547 until his death in 1564—the Florence Cathedral *Pieta*, the Rondanini *Pieta*, and his drawings of the Crucifixion—the concerns at the core of his soul are revealed.

Our understanding of Michelangelo is deepened if we consider these last two Pietas as one continuous artistic effort. We consider the Florence *Pieta* (Fig. 7.6) first. It has been generally assumed that he began work on the Florence *Pieta* in 1547, shortly after the death of Vittoria Colonna. Vittoria was the only woman with whom Michelangelo had a significant relationship during his entire adult life. They met 11 years earlier. She came from one of the most noble families in Italy. A widow, she devoted her life to service to Christ. She was an accomplished poet and at the center of a group who, although pressing for reform, remained loyal to the Apostolic Church. Their correspondence, the lyrics that he dedicated to her, and his presentation drawings, all reveal an unwavering, austere Christian character to their relationship. Michelangelo was at the time in the middle phase of painting the Pauline Chapel *Crucifixion of Peter*. The *Pietà* was uncommissioned and, significantly, was intended for his own tomb.

The group consists of the dead Christ sinking in a rhythmic serpentinata pose and supported from behind by the hooded figure of Nicodemus and by the Virgin on his left side and the Magdalene on his right. Christ's head falls to his left, not simply meeting but fusing with the barely carved face of his Mother. His face, after his torment, is serene. Earthly pain in Son and Mother has been transformed into a timeless, beatific union. It is the triumph of sacred love. Few images in art can approach the poignant intimacy of these heads of Christ and Mary.

The *Pietà* in Florence is unique in that it is the only work that Michelangelo actually tried to destroy and then abandoned. After years of work he mutilated the group, apparently beginning in the right lower frontal section, from which Christ's left lower extremity is now missing. His left forearm and hand and right forearm were also broken and subsequently repaired by Michelangelo's young follower, Tiberio Calcagni. As the story comes down to us, it appears that Michelangelo would have completed the destruction had he not been dissuaded.

Why would the 80-year-old master try to destroy this particular creation in such a frenzied way? To understand why he indulged in such strange behavior at that time and not some other, and in that form rather than another, we must probe into the unconscious meaning of the image for Michelangelo. Inasmuch as this group had a deeply personal meaning and purpose (to be part of his own tomb), my inquiry into the latent meaning of the group does, I hope, illuminate the central motifs in his unconscious thought.

Vasari (1598/1967) gives us Michelangelo's curious and personal explanation for the mutilation. One day at Michelangelo's house, where the broken statue remained, Tiberio asked Michelangelo why he had smashed the *Pietà*. The artist replied "that he had been moved thereto by the importunities of Urbino, his servant, who was daily entreating him to finish the work" (Vol. 2, p. 176).

A psychoanalytic inquiry into Michelangelo's destruction of the *Pietà* must focus on two specific issues: first, why the mutilation occurred at the time it did; and second, how to regard Michelangelo's own

FIG. 7.6. Michelangelo, *Pietà*, Florence Cathedral. Scala/Art Resource.

explanation of the act—that he was so vexed by his servant Urbino's nagging that he attempted to destroy a group for his own tomb.

It is often assumed that the mutilation took place late in 1555 but before December 3, the date of Urbino's death, because Michelangelo's explanation of his destructive act implicates Urbino. Urbino had been Michelangelo's devoted servant and artistic assistant for the previous 26 years, beginning when Urbino was 14 years old. To the question of whether there was any extraordinary circumstance or preoccupying worry in Michelangelo's life during those months, we can respond with considerable certainty on the basis of the artist's letters and a sonnet, Vasari's description, and other documents. For at least 5 months, Urbino had been bedridden and declining as the result of a terminal illness. Vasari (1598/1967) relates that during those months Michelangelo "had loved him so much that, although old, he had nursed him in his sickness, and slept at night in his clothes beside him, the better to watch for his comforts" (Vol. 2, p. 174). When Urbino died, Michelangelo wrote two letters that express a level of grief that exceeds anything he wrote about any other person who died during his lifetime. The day after Urbino died, he wrote to his nephew in Florence (Ramsden, 1963):

> I must tell you that last night . . . Urbino passed from this life to my intense grief, leaving me so stricken and troubled that it would have been more easeful to die with him, because of the love I bore him, which he merited no less . . . so that owing to his death I now seem to be lifeless myself and can find no peace. (Vol. 2, letter 408)

Three months after Urbino's death, Michelangelo wrote to Vasari (Ramsden, 1963):

> You know that Urbino is dead, through whom God has granted me his greatest favour, but to my grievous and infinite sorrow. The favour lay in this—that while living he kept me alive, and in dying he taught me to die, not with regret, but with the desire for death . . . nothing is left to me but the hope of seeing him again in Paradise . . . the greater part of me has gone with him, and nothing but unending wretchedness remains for me. (Vol. 2, letter 410)

Thus, at the time when the mutilation presumably took place, Michelangelo was overwhelmingly preoccupied with the imminent loss of his beloved Urbino and his apprehension regarding his own capacity and will to survive that loss. Considering Michelangelo's anxious concern for Urbino, it is not surprising to learn that the sculptor invoked something about Urbino to explain the destructive act. But how do we make sense of the specific content of the explanation—that it was his exasperation at Urbino's continuous nagging at him to finish it that led him to mutilate the statue? Let us assume that Urbino was saying something like, "Please finish it before I die." This would produce a conflict in Michelangelo because, on the one hand, he would want to gratify the wish of the dying but still live Urbino, whereas, on the other hand, to finish the group would be to acknowledge and accept the imminence of the dreaded event. On a more magical and unconscious level of thought, for Michelangelo to complete the work would make him, in his own mind, an active agent in bringing about Urbino's death.

Returning to the point that the *Pietà* was intended by Michelangelo for his own tomb, we realize that the prospect of completing the work was also loaded with symbolic meaning and feeling in connection with contemplation of his own death. In the letter to Vasari quoted earlier, Michelangelo wrote of having been "taught to die . . . with desire." Yet, for the previous 39 years he had unrelentingly expressed a yearning for death in his poetry as well as in conversation.

There is, nevertheless, much to indicate that Michelangelo was not at all ready to die. Nowhere is this more eloquently communicated than in the *Crucifixion of Peter*. The *Crucifixion* probably occupied Michelangelo from 1545 to 1549. During the last 2 of those years I assume he worked on the Pauline Chapel fresco by day and on his own *Pietà* at night, at home.

Michelangelo's treatment of Saint Peter is a radical departure from the traditional representation of Saint Peter martyred on the Cross in a vertical, upside-down position, in accord with Peter's own request, out of humility and conviction that he was unworthy of sharing the same fate as Christ.

Michelangelo's Peter is a Herculean figure, nailed to a Cross that is yet to be placed in the earth. With extraordinary strength, Peter has elevated his torso some 45° so that, with its foreshortened treatment, he lies on a horizontal axis and projects toward the viewer. His head is turned to the right and upward, so that from its three-quarter presentation Peter's eyes glare at the viewer. His facial expression, contrary to the Christian myth of his acceptance of martyrdom in complete humility, communicates fury and reproach. In this last paroxysm of physical energy and spiritual protest, Peter does not accept his fate but renounces humility and willing sacrifice and cries out against death itself. We can only conclude that this image represents the artist's deeply personal statement, not simply because it is so at variance with traditional iconography but particularly because it contradicts hagiographical tradition.

To link Michelangelo's paradoxical statement about Urbino's nagging and the destructive act itself to Michelangelo's thoughts on death and his artistic treatment of the subject, it is instructive to bring to bear clinical observations of people who have lost objects of their love either recently or earlier in life. Such observations consistently yield evidence of unconscious and unexpressed rage toward the abandoning loved one. Indeed, Freud (1917/1953) elaborated on this mechanism as the central dynamic in mourning reactions. It is in this psychological process that we find the explanation for the irritation and blame, otherwise not easily comprehensible, that Michelangelo directed toward the dying Urbino.

On a deeper level, it is even probable that during the 26 years of his service Urbino increasingly became an unconscious surrogate and external representation of Michelangelo's lost mother, who died when he was 6 years old. This pattern conforms to a general psychological law concerning the ways in which we all reenact our unfulfilled past throughout life, albeit in disguised forms and with disguised actors. Thus, if earlier crucial needs—in this case, for adequate mothering—have not been met, one seeks individuals and situations in which the childhood setting is unconsciously reexperienced, and the other person is unconsciously perceived as replicating the role of the significant figure from childhood. The aging artist feared that he would not survive being abandoned by Urbino. Such a crisis would naturally stir up long-repressed conflicts derived from this mother's premature death. Indeed, these conflicts shaped Michelangelo's most basic relationships. Inasmuch as he apparently avoided relationships with women until his friendship with Vittoria Colonna, we can infer that his feelings toward women were distrustful, fearful, and potentially vengeful, and that Michelangelo defended against these painful feelings by his social pattern of avoidance. In the Florence Pietà, Michelangelo created on the surface a beatific union between the dead Christ and His Mother; but for Michelangelo such an image necessarily carried with it feelings of rage and aggression toward the mother who in his real life had left him frightened and alone.

If my psychoanalytic postulate regarding our ambivalence toward loved ones who have died is true, then we are in a better position to understand why, having created this image of loving union between Christ and Mary, Michelangelo also felt strong destructive impulses. In his identification with Christ, which was so pervasive in those years, he must have reexperienced the range of his conflicting emotions and fantasies associated with his own past. All these reactions, leading to the act of mutilation, were forced to the surface by Urbino's impending death. The Nicodemus in the Florence group is significantly, as Vasari recognized, Michelangelo's self-portrait. Here is an instance in which the image that has been created follows laws that parallel dreams. Dreams are a mental activity in which conflicted and repressed impulses and wishes are allowed relatively anxiety-free expression because of their disguised form. In the Florence Pietà, the explicit first-person presentation of the self as one of the actors in the narrative permits the artist to act out another identification in other characters, as in a dream. He can do this because the direct representation of himself as one of the figures draws the awareness of both the creator and the viewer away from the fact that more latent and conflicted themes are being expressed concurrently by the other figures.

Further, the creation and destruction of the Florence *Pietà* can be viewed as part of a continuous process that took place over the last two decades of Michelangelo's life. During this period his creative preoccupation with the reconciliation of the dead Christ and His Mother in the Florence and Rondanini *Pietàs* and in a series of drawings of the Crucifixion, which we note momentarily, was an effort to resolve the frightening prospect of his own death, with its associated fantasy of recapturing the warmth—however little he actually experienced it—of his mother. Having mutilated and abandoned the first group, he continued the quest for a solution in the Rondanini marble, which he worked on until 6 days before his death.

Before proceeding to the Rondanini *Pietà*, I mention briefly seven drawings of the Crucifixion that survive, drawings that were executed when Michelangelo was in his 80s. In these drawings, the aged master is also possessed by the subject of the reconciliation of the Son and His Mother. In the drawings of Christ himself, the artist's hand is unsteady: Lines are often erased; borders are misty; positions of the head are altered and redrawn; features of the face are undefined. A physical presence fades into a haunting poem to be spoken only in the softest whispers. Here, in the reworking and reconceiving of the Redeemer perhaps more than in any other work, Michelangelo is at one with the Man of Sorrows (Fig. 7.7).

Michelangelo also struggled with the figures of Mary and John the Evangelist, who stand at the feet of Christ. Their positions change from drawing to drawing. On each sheet they are filled with *pentimenti* and left unresolved. Incomplete erasures reveal revisions of their poses. In some cases their heads are bowed and arms crossed in passive acceptance of divine fate. In others, John angrily glares outward, his lips parted in protest. In one, the naked John and Mary march forward, drawn like uncomprehending primeval beings. All the earlier drawings set the stage for the final version (Fig. 7.8), in which Mary and John turn to the limp body of the Son and the faintly and unsteadily drawn Mother embraces and kisses Jesus. Thus, again, the identification with the crucified Christ allows for the unconscious motif of reconciliation between mother and son. Perhaps the fact that this final Mary is so faint and incompletely drawn reflects how lost in memory Michelangelo's own mothering figures were.

Our consideration of the motif of reconciliation between mother and son takes us to Michelangelo's last marble statue.

We do not know when Michelangelo began carving the Rondanini *Pietà*, but it is generally assumed to have been shortly after the mutilation of the Florence *Pietà*, in 1553, when he was 78 years old. The piece we see, in which the slender, unfinished Christ is fused with the incomplete

FIG. 7.7. Michelangelo, drawing of *Christ on the Cross between the Virgin and St. John*, British Museum [w. 81]. Reproduced by courtesy of the Trustees of the British Museum.

FIG. 7.8. Michelangelo, drawing of *Christ on the Cross between the Virgin and St. John*. British Museum [w. 82]. Reproduced by courtesy of the Trustees of the British Museum.

Mary (Fig. 7.9), is the outcome of a series of drastic refinements from the Herculean proportions of the original conception suggested by the sheet with five studies now at Oxford (Fig. 7.10). Tolnay (1934) has persuasively reasoned from the third and fourth studies (from left to right) on the sheet, which in chronology were the first and second, that the Rondanini group was originally intended to be an Entombment. In these sketches

FIG. 7.9. Michelangelo, *Rondanini Pietà*, Milan, Castello Sforzesco. Anderson/Art Resource.

FIG. 7.10. Michelangelo, studies for a Pieta and a Deposition. Oxford, Ashmolean Museum.

Christ is carried to his sepulchre by Mary and Joseph of Arimathea. The statue was then transformed into a vertically composed Pieta, as can be inferred from the chronological sequence of the second, fifth, and first studies (left to right) on the Oxford sheet.

As we look back at the years of labor on the Florence *Pietà*, the series of Crucifixion drawings, and the long period of whittling down the Rondanini to its present skeletal form, we also witness the visual images of this continual process of cycles of artistic creation, dissatisfaction, destruction, and re-creation within the context of the motif of union between mother and son. The ambivalent and tormented struggle in Michelangelo, embodied in his Marys and dead Christs, drove him, in the Rondanini, to his final transcendent image of the fusion of the Son and Mother, each consisting of parts carved out of the other, in which even the forces of gravity are disregarded, boundaries are obliterated, and the two are timelessly reunited.

Michelangelo's identification with Christ was profound and complex, and his almost 20 year chain of doing and undoing, of continuous rethinking of this subject, superseded any specific iconographic associations. The dramatic contrast between the rejecting Virgins in the works with the live Child Jesus and the warm, enveloping Virgins of the Pietàs attests to his unconscious belief that the only condition for comforting union with a woman was death. In life, as in his own experience, love was withheld. Perhaps his conviction that this was true made his departure from life in his 90th year tolerable.

REFERENCES

Condivi, A. (1975). *The life of Michelangelo* (A. S. Wohl, Trans., H. Wohl, Ed.). Baton Rouge: Louisiana State University Press. (Originally published 1553)
Freedberg, S. J. (1970). *Painting in Italy: 1500–1600*. Harmondsworth: Penguin.

Freud, S. (1953). Mourning and melancholia. In J. Strachey (Ed.), *Standard edition of the complete works of Sigmund Freud* (Vol. 14, pp. 243–258). London: Hogarth. (Original work published 1917)

Gilbert, C., & Linscott, R. N. (1963). *Complete poems and selected letters of Michelangelo.* New York: Random House.

Liebert, R. S. (1983). *Michelangelo: A psychoanalytic study of his life and images.* New Haven, CT: Yale University Press.

Pater, W. (1961). *The Renaissance.* New York: World. (Originally published 1871)

Ramsden, E. H. (1963). *The letters of Michelangelo* (2 vols.). London: Peter Owen.

Ross, J. B. (1974). The middle-class child in urban Italy: Fourteenth to early sixteenth century. In L. De Mause (Ed.), *The history of childhood* (pp. 183–228). New York: Harper & Row.

Sterba, R., & Sterba, E. (1978). The personality of Michelangelo Buonarroti: Some reflections. *American Imago, 35,* 156–177.

Tolnay, C. (1934). Michelangelo's Rondanini *Pietà. Burlington Magazine, 65,* 146–157.

Vasari, G. (1967). *The lives of the artists* (2 vols.). (Mrs. J. Foster, Trans.). New York: Hermitage. (Originally published 1598)

8

What Aesthetic Development Is Not: An Inquiry into the Pathologies of Postmodern Creation

Mark Freeman
College of the Holy Cross
Worcester, Massachusetts

THE CONDITIONS OF ARTISTIC ACTIVITY

Judging from the wide variety of contributions to the psychology of artistic creativity in recent years, the field is alive and well. These contributions, which range in perspective from (essentially) cognitive (e.g., Gardner, 1982) to psychoanalytic (e.g., Gedo, 1983) to social (e.g., Amabile, 1983) to experiential (e.g., Getzels & Csikszentmihalyi, 1976), have breathed new life into the attempt to understand and explain what is often considered to be a terrifically complex and elusive process.[1] Moreover, with these new goods in hand, it seems that light is being shed on aesthetic development as well: To the extent that we are able to make strides in understanding and explaining what creativity is all about, then we will also, and necessarily, have said something about development. This is simply because whenever some (consensually regarded) optimal form of human experience is posited, so too are less optimal ones, at least implicitly. The difference between these forms contains the work of development, broadly taken. More is said about this issue later on in this chapter.

---

[1]Since the time this chapter was originally written, a considerable amount of additional work has been done in the area of creativity. For a sampling of this work, see the volumes edited by Runco and Albert (1990), Sternberg (1988), and Wallace and Gruber (1989). Needless to say perhaps, a good deal else has been written as well.

These contributions I have been referring to notwithstanding, however, the problem remains that the optimal forms psychologists and the like often talk about may not actually exist in the context of "real-life" artistic activity. Due to the demands of the public, the art world, the market, and so on, it may well be that creativity, as some have come to know it, is impossible. It must be emphasized here that neither the idea nor the phenomenon of artistic alienation is terribly new; Marx, and a variety of others besides, have had much to say about it. But for many, alienation is bound not so much to the process of creating art itself as it is to the destiny of the work. According to Lucy Lippard (1984), for instance, "the history of a work of art once it gets out of the studio is far more closely entwined with the actions of a discriminatory, martial government and the capitalist system that supports it than it is with the ideas and aims of the artist who made it" (p. 6). Revolutionary politics aside for the time being, what Lippard seems to forget in this context is that the studio, far from being a sanctuary, an oasis, happily immune from the powers that be, may in fact be "entwined" already. And this very fact, of course, puts the very idea of creativity itself—as something fundamentally outside the dynamics of social reality—on somewhat shaky ground. Nevertheless, we shall not completely abandon it. Nor will we abandon the idea of development, no matter how problematic we may find it to be.

The way we will try to move ahead in working through some of these issues is by inquiring into the *conditions* of creativity, a topic about which we still know precious little. Now in some sense, it could be argued that, although this kind of inquiry is certainly worthwhile, because it is always useful to know the origins of things, particularly good things, it is ultimately unrelated to the idea of creativity itself. Creativity may be seen as the "dependent variable" from this point of view, brought about as a function of certain "independent variables" out there in the world. Likewise for the idea of development. My own conviction, however, is that this point of view is untenable. Indeed, I argue that we cannot understand either creativity or development without inquiring into the conditions through which they may be brought about (see Freeman, 1993). They are both varieties of genesis, it must be emphasized, and there simply is no genesis apart from the multiplicity of conditions giving rise to it.

RETHINKING THE DISCOURSE OF PLURALITY

Let me continue with a brief narrative. When I began my work in the psychology of art a number of years ago, my foremost interest was in the idea of aesthetic development, especially as it was manifested in the lives of adult painters and sculptors. It was in pursuing this idea that concerns with psychogenesis as well as personal and cultural creation could be brought together neatly, I had hoped, into a broad and synthetic picture. I was fortunate enough to be able to work with Professors Csikszentmihalyi and Getzels at The University of Chicago, who were in the midst of doing an intensive follow-up study of a group of people who had aspired to be artists during the mid-1960s. Their earlier work, which had begun while these people were still students at The School of the Art Institute of Chicago, had focused mainly on the process of creation itself, its experiential dynamics, and its preferred forms. But in the subsequent study, which took place nearly 20 years later, the focus became, in large part, the texture of these people's lives. Some of them, of course, would have left the world of art, perhaps moving on to different ways of life altogether; but there would also remain a good many who it seemed would be able to provide exactly the kind of information in which I was interested: information about creativity and aesthetic development in the lives—the real lives—of adult painters and sculptors.

As if this wasn't serendipitous enough, though, I had come to believe that the situation of contemporary art at the time was such that I would be provided with a remarkably unusual opportunity to address the issues of concern. And this is because the situation of art seemed to allow for a measure of artistic freedom and artistic spontaneity virtually unparalleled in the history of art. Had I begun this kind of inquiry at some other point in history, the data would surely have been contaminated, so to speak, with a whole slew of artistic fetters: from the demands of bourgeois patrons to the harsh confines of the received wisdom, of tradition. Now, however, there was some evidence that the world of art existed in almost a state of nature, blessedly free from all these civilized impediments to creation and development, and that as a result I would have in hand the largely untouched regions of experience I was looking for. There would be no need to tease out the effects of society and culture to arrive at a "pure" psychological model, for essentially this had already been done.

If we go back just a few decades, say to the work of Barnett Newman or Clyfford Still, we see the conviction that everything is being created anew, the art historical past and European culture more generally having been left behind, the artist having been freed from the bondage of tradition (see Rosenberg, 1972; Tomkins, 1980). There was no small amount of anxiety alongside this conviction because the artist may have felt that he or she had been left with the burden of perpetual choice, but the benefits, many argued, far outweighed the costs. As the existentialists, among others, well knew, living in a world without foundations can be dizzying; it can lead us to "nausea" and other not-so-comfortable states of being. But in the end, of course, there is no other way. "By their mutual indetermination," Rosenberg (1964) writes of De Kooning, who had apparently launched himself into the thick of the new (though without negating the old nearly as much as some of his peers), "art and artist support each other's openness to the multiplicity of experience" (p. 112). Many became pioneers, as it were, exploring uncharted territory in their art and in their selves, and whether they chose to avow or disavow the legacy of the masters, it seemed as if an artistic revolution was in the making.

In part, this ethic of the pioneer, particularly that of the pioneer who opted for disavowal, may simply be a testimony to the American way. Marcel Duchamp (Tompkins, 1980) has said:

> In France, in Europe, the young artists always act as grandsons of some great man—Poussin, for example, or Victor Hugo. They can't help it. Even if they don't believe in that, it gets into their system. And so, when they come to produce something of their own, the tradition is nearly indestructible. This doesn't exist over here. You really don't give a damn about Shakespeare, you're not Shakespeare's grandsons. So it's a better terrain for new developments. (p. 13)

The primary question being posed by the pioneer artist, even as early as the mid-to-late 1940s, throughout the 1950s, and on into the 1960s, was a simple but radical one: Wouldn't it be preferable to have the work of art determine its own rules, each and every time, rather than have the rules laid out beforehand? Who says there has to be some one way, or two, or three—Why not an infinity?

"Never before," as one writer (Adams, 1978) commenting on the art of the 1960s tells us, "had there been such tolerance or such great variation both in style and in what was admissible art practice" (p. 7). And this was seen to extend into the 1970s as well, another writer dubbing the era the "pluralist" era, one in which art had become nonsuccessive, nonheroic, and populist—quite the opposite, for this woman, of what modernism had been all about (Robins, 1984). As still another writer (Smagula, 1983) puts the matter, gazing now into the art of the 1980s: "We face the most pluralistic, complex, and contradictory era the world has ever known" (p. 1), the world of contemporary painting consisting "mainly of individuals embarked on personal journeys of artistic self-discovery and fulfillment" (p. 40). "Progressive art," he writes, "has emerged from the rarefied atmosphere of the museum into the mainstream of life" (p. 1), the result of this emergence being at least an incipient realization of what he refers to as "the dream of artistic freedom" (p. 98). For him, I should note, these trends signified the rebirth of modernism, not its end or its opposite, a resurfacing of the profoundly individualistic vigor that had been witnessed earlier during the heyday of the avant-garde. But the basic premise is nevertheless the same: Things are happening that are new and *different*.

For the sake of convenience of naming the kind of cultural movement being described here, I refer to it in terms of the *postmodern*. Now this, of course, is a very complex term, and to try to offer any pat definition would certainly be a bit ironic, not to mention difficult. But perhaps there are some basic features that might be agreed upon. We have already heard about tolerance, variation, pluralism, and, perhaps most importantly, *freedom*. Play is often a central idea in this context as well: Rather than trying to capture the world, to represent it in some all-encompassing way, which is pretty serious business, we might consider loosening up a bit. The inability to capture the world is no cause for anguish, as the existentialists might have had it, but for celebration: Whether in philosophy or in art, the less we concentrate our energies in that singular goal of finding and expressing the foundation of our being, the more interesting things are going to be.

Jacques Derrida (1978) speaks of this singular goal in terms of what he calls *totalization*. Now people often abandon this kind of project because they may decide that the richness and complexity of the world prevents it from being represented. "There is too much," as he puts it, "more than one can say" (p. 289). The project might also be abandoned, however, "not because the infiniteness of a field cannot be covered by a finite glance or a finite discourse, but because the nature of the field . . . excludes totalization" (p. 289). This is what leads us to the idea of play. We don't become playful because of our never being able to capture the world, to contain it—which wouldn't be much of a cause for celebration at all—but because the world is in essence created anew each time we write or paint or whatever; thus it can't be made steady enough, in a way, to be represented. So this field, says Derrida, "instead of being too large, actually has something missing from it: a center which arrests and grounds the play of substitutions" (p. 289). Rather than totalization, Derrida (1982) insists on what he calls *differance*, that which is precisely "not. It is not a present being, however excellent, unique, principal, or transcendent. It governs nothing, reigns over nothing, and nowhere exercises any authority. It is not announced by any capital letter. Not only is there no kingdom of differance, but differance instigates the subversion of every kingdom" (p. 22). And thus, "There is no maintaining, and no depth to, this bottomless chessboard on which Being is put into play" (p. 22). These kinds of ideas would seem to loosen things up somewhat.

Jean-François Lyotard conveys some similar ideas in his book, *The Postmodern Condition* (1984), which will hopefully help us to further distinguish between the modern and the postmodern. He considers modern aesthetics to be "an aesthetic of the sublime, though a nostalgic one" (p. 81). Modernist works, because of their recognizable consistency, can offer the reader or viewer "solace and pleasure," but these sentiments inevitably fall short of the really sublime, which is unattainable. Once again, the world is simply too large, too great, to be captured, so even the most sublime work will always bring its share of nostalgic desperation as well: There can never be enough.

The postmodern, on the other hand, Lyotard (1984) continues:

> denies itself the solace of good forms, the consensus of a taste which would make it possible to share collectively the nostalgia for the unattainable . . . A postmodern artist or writer is in the position of a philosopher: the text he writes, the work he produces, are not in principle governed by preestablished rules, and they cannot be judged according to a determining judgment, by applying familiar categories to the text or the work. Those rules and categories are what the work of art is looking for . . . We have paid a high enough price for the nostalgia of the whole and . . . of the transparent and the communicable experience . . . and it is time to wage a war on totality. (pp. 81–82)

According to Clifford Geertz (1983), even (some) social scientists have come to think in these terms. "Social scientists have become free to shape their work according to its necessities rather than according to received ideas as to what they ought or ought not to be doing" (p. 21). It is true, of course, that they may not be quite as liberated as artists and philosophers, because institutional demands still tend to dictate what can and cannot be considered legitimate practice, but, nevertheless, we seem to be witnessing history in the making. Given genres are becoming blurred, the lines of disciplinary distinctions erased; knowledge is headed in the direction of becoming a kind of collage, with multiplicity—surely "the hallmark of modern consciousness" (p. 161)—finally having its day.

If there is any common element at all to these different words, it seems that it has something to do with freedom: freedom *from* rules, from totalization, from an illusory and desperate attempt to catch the world and hold it for awhile, from a retrogressive nostalgia, and from a whole host of other things besides. And as for freedom *to*, we can only mean the freedom to *create*: However liberating the modern may have been—we might think of the mythical passions of the Abstract Expressionists, for instance—it had become high time to move still further, to at least conceive of what it might mean to break the stronghold of our slavery to the "received wisdom" altogether. Anyway, to make a long story short, it seemed like this was a pretty good time to study aesthetic development.

In point of fact, I think it *was* a good time for studying aesthetic development, but, ironically enough, not for any of the anticipated reasons I had assumed. And this is because far from finding a collection of life stories blessedly free, as I put it earlier, of all the constraining noise of civilization—rules, injunctions, laws, commands—there were instead stories of repetition and loss, ones that told of a brand of freedom that seemed to freeze people in their artistic tracks and to actually foreclose the possibility of their development. Beneath the surface of the "text" of postmodern creation, therefore—and I use the word "text" here because we are talking about discourse, the language of pluralism, freedom, play, and so on—lay a number of very real and very serious problems: for individuals and their artistic processes, and for culture.

The presence of these problems, some of which I discuss shortly, told me two things. First, the *experience* of postmodern creation, and the possibilities it held out for aesthetic development, was radically different in many cases from the lore that surrounded it. These were difficult times, not easy ones, and it would be important to try to find out why such a profound disjunction existed between the discourse and the experience. And so, what had begun mainly as an inquiry into the psychology of art became an exercise in cultural analysis and criticism. I should emphasize that my aim here is in no way to knock the postmodern, as often gets done, for its supposed irresponsibility, disrespect for tradition, nihilism, and so on, but rather to try to rethink it through an exploration of some of its practical consequences. By looking beneath the surface, beneath the manifest, perhaps we can begin to draw out some of its latent thoughts and wishes.

The second thing the presence of these problems told me was that even though there might conceivably remain a way of talking about creativity and aesthetic development *outside* the sociocultural context in which artists live and work, this is no easy task. For it appeared that the artistic processes people were describing were not merely *affected* by existing sociocultural conditions (i.e., the artistic process is right here, in the studio, whereas the sociocultural conditions are somewhere out there, in the world); these processes were *constituted* by these conditions, thus contingent upon their very nature. This does not mean that the process of artistic creation is to be considered as *nothing but* the helpless pawn of scheming social forces, only that the alleged inner sanctum of the studio and of the artist him or herself is in no way independent of them. "Individuals," Durkheim (1951) reminds us, "share too deeply in the life of society for it to be diseased without their suffering infection" (p. 213).

What this means is that however universal the idea of creativity or development might be, and however much we may want to refer to these ideas in terms of standards or ideals against which to compare the decidedly more various processes observed in real life, it is also clear that the parameters of creative or developmental possibility "allowed" at specific times and places very much change. Sometimes the supposedly

more optimal processes we often hear about are possible, but other times
apparently not. With this in mind, it seems important to begin to consider
what some of the more positive conditions, both psychological and
sociocultural, might be. It is these very conditions that I address,
somewhat obliquely, throughout the remainder of this chapter.

I say obliquely here because I address not positive conditions per se,
but negative ones, pathologies; not what aesthetic development is, but
what it is not. This doesn't spare us from certain value commitments, of
course: To speak of the nondevelopmental is to imply a *telos* of sorts, an
end. But it may still be more prudent to work toward articulating this
telos in the negative manner just suggested. In a quite broad sense, then,
the task at hand is one of *reconstruction*: On the basis of some of the
apparent pathologies, we will try to work toward the idea of normality
and what it could possibly be about. Let me turn now to an artist whom
I have been studying so we can put some flesh on these ideas.

THE MARKETING OF "DEVELOPMENT"

The man is a painter in his mid-40s, who divides his time between New
York City and his home in the Hamptons on Long Island, which is where
we met.[2] It was very nice. He is well known but is not quite a "superstar,"
if you will, the idea of which he will operationalize for us later on. The
works with which I became most familiar "look like flimsy approxima-
tions of oil paintings," as one critic puts it. "Their surface," he writes,
"mimics and mocks a 'rich surface.' The paintings are, to a degree,
parodies of the paintings that you win at a booth at a carnival if you hit
the duck." His entire body of work, this critic suggests, "is about kinds
of fakeness, of simulation." Many "unlikely elements" go into his
paintings, and as the artist himself acknowledges, the images employed
are essentially arbitrary. Put his work alongside that of other prominent
contemporary artists, this critic continues, and "one sees American art of
the past twenty-five years as an ongoing tale about irony and fakery,
about feeding off popular art, about the worship of formalism and craft."
His art is playful, to use a term we discussed earlier, as well as subversive.

Another critic describes this man's painting as encompassing

> an expansive contradiction, straddling that deep dichotomy between the
> woolly, uncivilized imagination that we associate with his hometown of
> Chicago and the theorizing, formalist sensibility associated with New York.

---

[2]The case history information used in this chapter was gathered as part of a research
project conducted at the University of Chicago, funded by the Spencer Foundation and the
MacArthur Foundation.

(He) has never resolved that contradiction into an art of seamlessly unified wholeness. He has, rather, thrived on the contradiction, gathering out of it an exuberantly impure art that indiscriminately gathers together the form and the theory of modernism with that which the modern traditionally abhors.

His latest work, this critic adds, "offers a combination of arrestingly perverse technique and highly abstracted, vacantly illustrative and vaguely comic imagery . . . (an) intricate parody of Modernist reflexivity." His art "defies known pigeonholes," the works' "real center of aesthetic gravity" being "the absurd process of painting." There is "that strong, genuinely populist impulse to welcome aboard the unruly, heterogeneous liveliness of the world that modernism rejected." Now these, of course, are other people's words, not the artist's, and not my own, but they may still help us to place the discourse within which his work is located. Needless to say, there are some striking similarities between these ideas and those we encountered earlier in conjunction with the idea of the postmodern.

Since around 1974, this man has survived on the sale of his work. Occasionally, he will do a stint as a visiting artist, but mostly, he paints. Over the years, he says, he has been involved with "relating certain kinds of images to the surface of the painting . . . trying to correlate certain images to a certain type of physicality," an aim that continues to find its way into his work. To give you a sense of what he is doing, a fairly recent series deals with Ponce de León, which he speaks of in terms of the "irony about the search for the elusive fountain of youth . . . an idea about problems of style, and style for style's sake, the very problem of doing something new all the time."

We are in a period of provincialism, he believes, which he also refers to as a "pluralistic time in the art world. People wanted a pluralistic art world," he says, "because philosophically it exists." But the problem, he explains, "is that once you get a pluralistic art world, although it exists philosophically in reality, it makes marketing difficult. So I think what we're in now is a period of high marketing: You need to have a monotheistic thing on the surface for business reasons." Somehow provincialism, pluralism, and monotheism find a home here.

> Trouble is you can't even make judgments . . . You reach a certain point and you're trying to figure out what you're doing . . . I think that the problem of painting, the dilemma of survival in painting, is that paintings, like people, have skins. Painting is like your handprints, this record of your life being different than mine . . . I think that one of the challenges in this time has been to establish a concrete abstract reality of the painting. This must go out in the world as this *thing* that has this face to it . . . You measure in degrees why one travels and another one doesn't. It's like Sebastian Coe and Steve Ovett running in the 1500 meters: The difference

between the winner and the loser is measured in milliseconds. And I think that that's a lot of what the dilemma of being an artist is. You're fighting for a very limited attention span with a highly jaded, super critical, fickle audience and you have to "curate" those decisions. You look back on what you've done and you want to make a move in your work, you try to maintain some sort of linear relationship . . . The older you get in terms of your life isn't so good necessarily, but the advantages of it as an artist is hindsight. Having a career of even semihistorical validity is a terrific advantage, because you can take from your past to make the future. I think that's why Ponce de León is an interesting metaphor for me, because it's a suspension of time. This notion of the quest, this kind of exoticness of art, the childish life that at times one leads, the notion of being a young artist when you're 40, but if you're a baseball player they call you an old man . . . I don't know what you call it. It's a different set of marks; it's out of kilter with the rest of the world.

I once had a notion I wanted to do a painting of myself where I'd put the paint on the bathroom scale for structure, and then I'd paint on it until it weighed as much as I did; and then I was stuck with this damn thing until the day I died . . . the dilemma of either painting it heavier or reducing it somehow . . . so there was a lifelong commitment to a single problem, where it's you but not you, where all of those things are in balance.

This project would allow for continuity, for a revelation of who he was, without really disclosing anything at all about himself, and would be an easy forum for making artistic decisions; he would always know, ahead of time, what the next move was, and the next after that too. For the time being, though, "I just try to have the things make some sort of connection from one group of objects to the next . . . Everything's in transition, art mirrors that transition, and you know, sometimes I think that's all I make is transitional work." His work is without a center, except for the skin it possesses, which identifies it as his alone; it is the work's transitional, differential quality, with each painting playing off what has preceded it, that allows for it to be named as *his*.

He knows all about freedom, but in a time like the present, appearances notwithstanding, there are very, very few who have it. "The people from the art world don't like artists that have freedom. Jasper Johns or De Kooning, these people are phenomenal ones because they have more power, and with power comes that kind of freedom for an artist." And this can only exist, he believes, when your wealth exceeds that of the people who market your work. This is what it means to be a "superstar." What freedom requires, in short, is money, which in turn requires constructing an identity through linearity, constructing sameness through difference. This, in part, is why it is so difficult to avoid becoming a "business partner" in the art world, as he puts it.

"New York has no memory," he reiterates; it is "the most vicious, fickle place in the world; they'll forget you in 2 years": unless, of course, you take measures, serious measures, to ensure that you will have a chance to endure. "I feel highly manipulated and I feel it's a very, very dangerous business . . . it fluctuates between fear and shame and gloating and power . . . This is a life for somebody that has to go from being a saint to a salesman, from a priest to a pimp; it's a quick change act."

I bring together these words by saying, for now, that the idea of development can assume a quite different form, for some artists, than most of us are probably used to, the past being seen here as an "advantage" drawn upon so as to decide upon an appropriate next move, a future. It is necessary to think in this way apparently to ensure that you will continue to "win" and thus be able to continue the process, even while recognizing that as you move through time there may still be a certain childish quality to the whole thing. He finds this strange. But a good part of this strangeness, of course, seems to have to do with that audience out there, hungry for prey. It seems to be this audience, in fact, above all else, that leads to the necessity of his maintaining a linear relationship in his work, a kind of *mock* development designed to provide for his own—and his audience's own—continuity. They *want* him to develop; they want to see signs of his own organic growth as a painter; they want to see a history that looks like it's going somewhere. And he has been able to meet these demands. But as he is coming to realize, as he gazes out over the terrain of his past, he may be doing this at his own peril.

THE FRAGILITY OF POSTMODERN CREATION

Things haven't always been so linear and continuous. Back in 1969, he made a painting that had in it a multiplicity of different styles, like a Sears catalog, as he puts it, from which he continues to draw ideas for his present work. But ultimately, he sees this painting as "an existential problem that failed," and this is because "the notion of painting every day a different style is ultimately as confining as trying to develop one style: because the limitation is you. So the only way you could beat that problem is you become a stylistic entrepreneur, and the only way to create that is to hire people to paint for you, thus becoming, in a sense, a patron of your own art." This idea interests him. But at the same time, he acknowledges that ideas like these represent a nihilistic attitude toward society. He finds a tendency in himself to go back and forth between philosophical beliefs, between what is meaningless and what is meaningful. Like a number of others, he finds himself suspended in this between space, "balancing the tightrope between nonobjective art, conceptual art, and figuration . . . like the Walendas, all on this thing."

He continues:

> I sometimes think that with the death of modernism, in a sense, what I'm doing is *performing* the notion of painting, that all of this is a highly realistic theater that comes with real painting and real pleasure, but possibly that's what some of us are doing: talking about the end and not the beginning of an art form.

This simply does not sound like play at all. His work may look like play, just as his own self-designed linearity may look like development. And philosophically speaking, there are no grounds for lamenting this state of affairs, because simulation seems, in many ways, to be what his art is all about. But at the very same time that he can affirm the idea of simulation, he is also haunted by the death of those very ideas that he himself is dedicated to killing. People on tightropes, we can probably assume, even if they are professionals through and through, fear what lurks beneath them; they are probably all too aware that their performance can suddenly be brought to an abrupt halt.

This man is not quite sure what he is doing, but what he fears, perhaps in more reflective moments, is that somehow simulation and death go together: This theater that comes with real painting and real pleasure may well be about to shut down. Right now, there remains a connection to the real, and it is a fragile and tenuous one, a mocking one, but even this may be severed, hurtling him into that bottomless chessboard Derrida was talking about. He is more than uncomfortable at the prospect of this. There is a sense in which he seems to be ashamed that he has been an accomplice, an actor, in this performance.

We might just ask in this context where exactly the ideas of real painting and real pleasure come from. Maybe they signal a nostalgia for something that once existed: a feeling of oneness and wholeness, dating back to the nether reaches of his childhood, or a sense of awe before the massive presence of the world. They may also signal a nostalgia for something that never did exist: a fantasy, a wish that things could be as real as they seem. It is sometimes difficult to reconcile the idea of the ultimate plurality of things and the ultimate arbitrariness of the way we regard them—paintings, works of literature, people—with the command they often hold over us. It is easy to be perplexed by the idea that all these experiences can seem as if they issue straight from the heart. We might also ask whether this nostalgia can ever fully be erased, or whether it is destined, or better, doomed, to persist as a tragic reminder of what once was, real or imagined. Whatever the origins of the idea of the real, and whatever its fate, it is extremely difficult to see how this painter could *develop*, whatever this might mean, after recognizing, or at least suspecting, that his own artistic process may be something of a sham: mock creation, like mock development.

He swings in another, but related, direction. "I try to make paintings that border on expressionism but are controlled." He refers to these paintings in terms of "repressionism," and they have to do with repressing certain images, "never getting too loose with the paint, but understanding what paint can do. A lot of people never learn anything from the paint because they're so involved with a didactic idea about history or philosophy." But the problem is that without this knowledge of what paint can do, without attention to the "skin" of the work, the "magic" that paintings can hold cannot be "released." He talks, for instance, about Magritte and Rousseau in this context and feels that even though the content these painters chose to work with may leave something to be desired, certain of their works remain, for him, "very intense abstract realities."

Other paintings do this too, "in an existential sense of, like, a *thing*." From simulation, then, from painting one step removed from the real, he can still speak, cogently, about magic, intensity, and the thing-ness of objects. He feels that he, unlike many others, recognizes "the importance of trying to control the paint and understand what it does."

He cannot find much solace in this and needs to return to the question of why, despite his avowed connectedness to the medium, his life and work are so uncomfortable. He is suspicious, even of his own commitments. "Maybe it's that artists can only make these . . . fake careers, that painting is so bankrupt that your whole career becomes an intellectual construction. It's such an unmeaningful art in this century that what you're doing is constructing a life that has documentation." This gets us back to that linearity, all those moves that were being devised to convey, for his audience and perhaps, on occasion, for himself, an illusory image of order, continuity, and coherence. It may be somewhat ironic to think of one's artistic history in terms of a linear series of works that pride themselves on their heterogeneity and disconnectedness. And we can be sure, I think, that this irony hasn't escaped him either. Painting doesn't look too good, he feels; its virtue seems to be its stupidity. "I guess the only things that's interesting about it (are) the intellectual arguments that people who are equipped can make about its death; not its death, its existence as a vehicle for criticism and writing." So maybe what he is doing is only a means to the destructive ends of others, these parasites who feed off his own dilemmas and the pain and anxiety they entail.

He does not and cannot really believe these things. He did a painting around 1975 that was in a major museum, a commission. The way he describes it, it was a giant painting of these dinosaurs, elegant and colorful, the scene of a time "before man existed ... about almost a perfect world ... it was perfect. The painting rejoiced in its big, dumb shapes ... 20-foot-long brontosaurus painted light pink, a kind of ... lesson about ourselves." He talks about this work in terms of the "language of the dumb shape ... the language of visual stupidity. But elegant, I mean beautiful looking." It may have been my own imagination, but his voice seemed to be cracking as he spoke, wavering, over this stupid beauty that he knew was somehow both possible and impossible. There was both wonder in his voice and a great sense of loss, together, in the same words.

A QUESTION OF BEING

I have spoken of only a single painter in this chapter and, as such, I refrain from making any coarse generalizations about the plight of the contemporary artist and of contemporary art. There is also the further methodological problem bound up with the fact that I have relied on this man's own narrative account of his life and work; there exists the possibility that maybe things had been especially difficult for him as of late, and that this difficulty cast a shadow over his past and its validity. But I assure you that he is not alone in many of his sentiments. Many other artists with whom I and other members of our research project have spoken reveal the very same themes.

In the midst of what would seem to be a pluralistic art world, free of the dogmas of tradition—although of course not in any way exempt from its own dogmas, such as the need for displaying this freedom in some way—there was often the need for people to establish an unequivocal front, a brand image, so that they might differentiate themselves from the field and be able to enter the race with a chance of winning. Many, I should note, thought that once they were in fact in the race, maybe by having gained some measure of notoriety from their work, they would be able to become somewhat freer in their artistic processes. They could even become modernists again if they wanted, letting out all that angst that had been building up through the years. Linearity, serial thinking, whatever we wish to call it, was seen as a prerequisite for entry, but once they were in, there was the assumption that all these constraints would be stripped away. And it simply was not so. Indeed, notoriety may actually have served to further the need for repetition, for devising variations on a theme, to ensure their own continuity: You go with what works.

Now I wouldn't be so crass as to suggest that none of these artists was able to develop—if we regard development, tentatively, as something having to do with more closely approximating what one sees and feels art to be about—but it has also become clear to me that the frequent mistrust and suspicion of the artistic paths many have created leaves the idea of development very problematic. From an outside perspective, of course, a given artist's body of work may bear within it signs of development; we can establish connections and see how earlier problems were progressively articulated and elaborated upon. From the inside, however, from the perspective of the artist him or herself, these connections may sometimes be seen as little more than a mocking reminder of the ultimate uncertainty of one's history. Looking back on his own history, the man we have been considering cannot disentangle his own artistic movement from the sociocultural conditions in which it has taken place, for these conditions have been constitutive, in one way or another, of everything he has done. And whereas it would be naive to argue on behalf of eliminating sociocultural forces in the constitution of aesthetic development—because it would not only be impossible but undesirable—we may want to think of ways in which they could be rendered less oppressive and alienating. Note here that there is more at stake in all of this than individual artists and their creative processes and possibilities; we are talking about culture as well.

As for the specific kind of work this man has been doing, it is again the case that from the outside, in the eyes of critics for instance, his art appears to be one of liberation, a kind of joyous, madcap dance through the heterogeneous sensibility of the postmodern way, with its refusal to get too hung up on all those pressing questions about the real and the true. His is an art about simulation and fakery, as we have seen, and as such is very much an affirmation of that kind of discourse that would seek to loosen the hold of the somber, self-involved passions tied to what we had formerly assumed to be real art. In lighter moments, I would guess that this painter himself can experience this loosening; he can see in his work some evidence for a new and compelling way of looking at things and thinking about them. But as is the case with his career more generally, there is something about the specific work he has chosen to do that simply is not quite right: Something, somewhere, is being denied in his own performance of painting. The discourse, which, as a philosopher of sorts he can accept, simply doesn't mesh with his experience, his sense, however dim, of what painting can be. Nostalgia here appears as a return of the repressed, and the real, even the beautifully real, rears its ugly head; it cannot be put to rest—not yet, at any rate.

This idea may be framed by saying that, although this painter can think in a postmodern way about philosophy and about art, he finds that he cannot think that way about himself; he cannot think of his own being without a center, a foundation. The surfaces of his paintings, the skins he talks so much about, remain very real to him and important, but he cannot reconcile the fact that his primary connection is to surfaces alone. What this means, I suggest, is that to the extent that painting—even if only in a marginal way—is an expression of his own being, his own center, then his work cannot wholly be decentered or deconstructed, if you will, either.

There is a contradiction at work here, then, and it can be resolved in one of two ways: He can either embrace the idea of simulation more fully and move still further into its emptiness, or he can recollect that aspect of his own being that has been denied in and through his work. If he opts for the latter—and it seems to me we have good reason to hope he does—then perhaps he can restart the process of development and, in this process, lessen some of the burdens of his life.

TOWARD DEVELOPMENT

Although development is, in the end, an eminently individual process, it is also clear that it very much relies on the social fabric for its nourishment. Admittedly, there are some individuals who seem able—in some sense—to transcend certain features of the social fabric, no matter how difficult things are; they may even gain some of their own developmental momentum through their adversarial relationship with it. Along these lines, some of the other artists with whom I have spoken, experiencing many of the same difficulties as the man I have discussed here, have decided to call a sudden halt to the way they operate in relation to the art world and to adopt new strategies for freeing their creative energies. Rather than continuing to sow the seeds of what they came to feel might be their own self-destruction, they began to move in a direction they believed to be more true to the mission of art, even if this meant challenging the new tradition and the power structure that legitimated it. In part, this is how the art world changes and how culture itself, on occasion, develops.

And so, if we were punitive types or, alternatively, people possessing an unwavering belief in the capacity of the individual to freely choose his or her own attitude toward the world, we may well conclude that the artist of whom I have spoken is guilty of abdicating responsibility, of forfeiting his own human capacity to take a stand in the face of the countless obstacles in his way. After all, the social world, although unquestionably serving as a weighty *influence* on the workings of individuals, surely is not strictly *determinative* of them. Indeed, the simple fact that others have put a stop to some of the madness is good evidence of this. Some even speak in terms of having carried out their lives *as if* they were determined, only to realize that it wasn't so.

Although this perspective has its merits, I do not think it is the most profitable way to deal with the present issues. For one thing, there may be the tendency to sneak the putatively "autonomous process of artistic creation" in through the back door, so to speak. The social world will come to be seen as so much "noise," to be confronted and managed to let the pure process emerge. Second, and more importantly, if the individual, alone, is deemed to be the primary locus of responsibility for his or her various ills, there may also be the tendency—even if it is an unwitting one—to exonerate what may quite objectively be very problematic conditions. What this means, of course, is that those interested in development, whether aesthetic or otherwise, must also be concerned with the dynamic forces present in society and culture; there is simply no way around it.

To return to an earlier point, the process of artistic creation and the movement of aesthetic development are constituted by existing sociocultural conditions; their "space" of possibility is a function, again, of what is "allowed" at specific times and places. If one is exceptionally hardy, then maybe he or she will be able to extend the boundaries of this space, maybe even burst them in a way, but I am not sure we ought to expect this hardiness as a general rule.

As concerns the situation of postmodern art, at least as experienced by a segment of those who aspire to create it, it appears that the space of creativity and development has become somewhat constricted. Echoing a theme we have already encountered, many contemporary artists, says one critic (Owens, 1983), "are able at best to *simulate* signs of mastery, to manipulate its signs" (p. 67), and this, he says, can only point to its loss. Butler (1980) says, "Aesthetic subversion has thus become revolutionary pantomime" (p. 122). Or, Habermas (1983) comments, "The new value placed on the transitory, the elusive, the ephemeral, the very celebration of dynamism, discloses a longing for an undefiled, immaculate, and stable present" (p. 5). From this point of view, it is almost as if certain processes and forms of postmodern art are defensive maneuvers, designed to ward off some of the pain of living in a world where meaning has somehow run dry. There is even a sense in which this longing Habermas refers to is already contained in the flux: Perpetual change becomes tantamount to a kind of stasis (see Jameson, 1983, for his discussion of this idea as well as his attempt to establish the relationship among postmodernism, consumer society, and multinational capitalism).

As for the idea of pluralism, it is evident that we need to be very cautious about proclaiming its virtues. Suzi Gablik's (1984) work is instructive in this context. "As long as we are to consider *anything* as art," she writes, "innovation no longer seems possible, or even desirable" (p. 11); pluralism has become "impenetrable," as she puts it. Once again, we need to recognize how broader social and economic forces enter into this picture. "Posed as a freedom to choose," says Hal Foster (1985), "the pluralist position plays right into the ideology of the 'free market'" (p. 15), and the end result is that it leads "not to a sharpened awareness of difference, but to a stagnant condition of indiscrimination—not to resistance, but to retrenchment" (p. 31). Ironically enough, pluralism seems to eventuate in what Edward Said (1983) has called the "neutralization of dissent" (p. 154). Difference becomes a guise, a pretext, for repetition of the same, leaving us with the mere illusion that things are changing for the better (i.e., developing).

The question remains, then, as to how development, both individually and culturally, may be "restarted," as I put it earlier, and I think that two plausible answers present themselves. The first of these can be gleaned from the artist we have been considering, and it has to do with the dialectical dimension of development. For what we began to see in some of this artist's meditations on his own situation in relation to the world of art was a perceptible "rift" between the given and the possible, between what was and what could be (see Freeman & Robinson, 1990). He had become haunted by images of the real and the true, and these, juxtaposed against the possibility of his own charade, seemed to serve as a provocation for him to at least consider ways of resolving this tragic contradiction. Occasionally, if the strain of the dialectic becomes palpable enough and desire manages to break through, into consciousness, development solves its own problems; the anxiety of the liminal projects itself forward, in the direction of its dispersion.

The second answer has more to do with the social world than with the individual him or herself. In line with all that has been said in this chapter regarding the social constitution of development, it follows that another way of restarting the process of development in cases where it has become halted is through trying to rethink and perhaps rework the "facts" of society and culture. Needless to say, this is easier said than done, and I do not pretend to offer any easy solutions to the problems that have been raised here. But unless we, as students of development, begin to think more critically and dialectically about the conditions through which this process may be facilitated, we may not get to see it in action very often. Or, worse still, we may wind up mistaking the nondevelopmental for the developmental and thereby serve as accessories in the maintenance of the status quo. Writing is a kind of political action, and even if its effects extend only as far as academic psychology, they are effects nonetheless.

I also realize that I have made only fleeting references to what development might conceivably be about. It seems to have something to do with expanding one's own being-in and relatedness-to the world in such a way that it is possible to genuinely believe that one's life and the various actions that compose it are not only valuable and worthwhile but become even more valuable and worthwhile as time marches on. As for a specific *telos*, some final end to which all these actions ultimately point, I am not quite sure what we can say right now. Maybe when the conditions are a bit more ripe, we will be in a better position to know.

ACKNOWLEDGMENTS

I wish to thank Mihaly Csikzentmihalyi, Jacob W. Getzels, and Stephen P. Kahn for their direction in carrying out this project, as well as Rick Robinson and Daniel Schouela, both of whom provided useful comments on this chapter.

REFERENCES

Adams, H. (1978). *Art of the sixties*. Oxford: Phaidon.
Amabile, T. (1983). *The social psychology of creativity*. New York: Springer–Verlag.
Butler, C. (1980). *After the wake: An essay on the contemporary avant-garde*. Oxford: Clarendon.
Derrida, J. (1978). *Writing and difference*. Chicago: The University of Chicago Press.
Derrida, J. (1982). *Margins of philosophy*. Chicago: The University of Chicago Press.
Durkheim, E. (1951). *Suicide*. New York: The Free Press.
Foster, H. (1985). *Recodings*. Seattle, WA: The Bay Press.
Freeman, M. (1993). *Finding the muse: A sociopsychological inquiry into the conditions of artistic creativity*. New York: Cambridge University Press.
Freeman, M., & Robinson, R. R. (1990). The development within: An alternative approach to the study of lives. *New Ideas in Psychology, 9*, 53–72.
Gablik, S. (1984). *Has modernism failed?* New York: Thames & Hudson.
Gardner, H. (1982). *Art, mind, and brain*. Cambridge, MA: Harvard University Press.
Gedo, J. (1983). *Portraits of the artist*. New York: Guilford.
Geertz, C. (1983). *Local knowledge*. New York: Basic.
Getzels, J. W., & Csikszentmihalyi, M. (1976). *The creative vision*. New York: Wiley.
Habermas, J. (1983). Modernity: An incomplete project. In H. Foster (Ed.), *The anti-aesthetic: Essays on postmodern culture* (pp. 3–15). Port Townsend, WA: The Bay Press.
Jameson, F. (1983). Postmodernism and consumer society. In H. Foster (Ed.), *The anti-aesthetic: Essays on postmodern culture* (pp. 111–125). Port Townsend, WA: The Bay Press.
Lippard, L. (1984). *Get the message? A decade of art for social change*. New York: Dutton.
Lyotard, J. F. (1984). *The postmodern condition: A report on knowledge*. Minneapolis: University of Minnesota Press.

Owens, C. (1983). The discourse of others: Feminists and postmoderism. In H. Foster (Ed.), *The anti-aesthetic: Essays on postmodern culture* (pp. 57–82). Port Townsend, WA: The Bay Press.

Robins, C. (1984). *The pluralist era: American art, 1968–1981.* New York: Harper & Row.

Rosenberg, H. (1964). *The anxious object.* New York: Collier.

Rosenberg, H. (1972). *The de-definition of art.* New York: Macmillan.

Runco, M. A., & Albert, R. S. (Eds.). (1990). *Theories of creativity.* Beverly Hills, CA: Sage.

Said, E. (1983). Opponents, audiences, constituencies, and communities. In H. Foster (Ed.), *The anti-aesthetic: Essays on postmodern culture* (pp. 135–159). Port Townsend, WA: The Bay Press.

Smagula, H. (1983). *Currents: Contemporary directions in the visual arts.* Englewood Cliffs, NJ: Prentice-Hall.

Sternberg, R. J. (Ed.). (1988). *The nature of creativity.* Cambridge: Cambridge University Press.

Tomkins, C. (1980). *Off the wall: Robert Rauschenberg and the art world of our time.* Garden City, NY: Doubleday.

Wallace, D. B., & Gruber, H. E. (Eds.). (1989). *Creative people at work.* New York: Oxford University Press.

9

Narratives of Change and Continuity: Women Artists Reflect on Their Work

Margery B. Franklin
Sarah Lawrence College

Most discussions of change in art work, whether centered on the individual artist or the course of history, rest on formulations familiar to students of developmental psychology. Constructed on the model of a biologically grounded sequence that aligns earlier with "less developed," these discussions assume that later forms "grow out of" or build on preceding forms in rational if not always predictable ways. Some analyses of artistic development emphasize continuous incremental change, whereas others—including many artists' accounts—are constructed in terms of a linear sequence of phases or periods marked by changes in style or subject matter.

The hegemony of traditional developmental models leads to smoothing over, recasting, or neglecting phenomena that do not fit the template of gradual or stepwise orderly progression toward an endpoint. Thus, for example, phenomena of radical change or "emergence" in artistic work too often remain unanalyzed or are construed in terms of underlying continuities. But possibilities for conceptualizing radical change exist within developmental theory, *albeit* in developmental theory outside the mainstream. Attempting to understand a dramatic shift in one artist's work, I turned to Werner and Kaplan's (1963/1984) model of the emergence of language in the child, a model that proposes that the beginnings of language issue from the convergence of two distinct streams.[1] The notion of *convergence of streams* served to schematize the artist's sense of how her new work came into being (Franklin, 1989). Similarly, Wolf (this volume) draws selectively from Werner and Kaplan's theory, as well as others. In these cases, themes or principles are disembedded from a larger theoretical matrix but not torn from their roots. Nonetheless, if theories are regarded as whole structures resting on root metaphors and embodying world views (Pepper, 1942/1957), then using one or two principles without buying the whole apparatus might mark a fatal step toward eclecticism, a move toward using formulations from different world views without regard to consonance among underlying assumptions. Eclecticism in theory building, Pepper argued, is "almost invariably sterile and confusing" (p. 106). Further, as Hein (this volume) suggests, major tenets of theories are complexly interwoven. So, in Hein's view, Gilligan (1983) rejects a central theme of standard models of moral development but perhaps inadvertently adheres to others; Gilligan's proposed alternative to the standard model suffers from the "phallocratic bias" of all progressivist, hierarchically ordered developmental theories.

Considering the uses of developmental theory in relation to understanding artistic work, we find ourselves poised among three possibilities: First, staying with, or returning to, the security (and, for some, the strength) of one or another standard developmental model; second, rejecting all developmental formulations tied to theories that assume gradual or stepwise progression from "lower" to "higher," toward an endpoint; third, drawing selectively on formulations in existing developmental theory, and perhaps improvising others, with the aim of developing schematizations and interpretive frameworks for understanding sets of phenomena. The study discussed in this chapter is grounded in the third possibility, as becomes clear later.

Questioning constructions of artistic development provided by current theory, I wanted to find out how artists themselves experience and conceptualize the development of their work over time. From the start, I was interested in talking with women artists. In spite of countercurrents, women artists remain seriously underrepresented in the literature—in the Oral History Collection of the Archives of American Art, in published collections of interviews, and in studies of artistic development. The greater availability of material about male artists can only contribute to the propensity, within psychology and beyond its borders, to take men's development as the norm.

In this chapter, I present some ideas emerging in the first phase of an ongoing study focused on how women artists see the development of

---

[1]Conceptualizing the shift in Zink's work in terms of "emergence" is also grounded in Werner's (1978) theorizing (pp. 117–118).

their work. I begin by discussing aspects of the method and then turn to discussion of four themes: *points of origin* of the developing sense of identity as an artist, *modes of change* characterizing transitions, *images of development*, and tensions between *continuity and change*.

THE PARTICIPANTS

For the first phase of this study, I selected seven women artists: Susan Crile, Louise Fishman, Harriet Shorr, and Pat Steir (painters); Donna Dennis and Melissa Zink (sculptors); and Joanne Leonard (a photographer). With the exception of one who was born in 1932, these seven artists were born in the 4-year period between 1938 and 1942 in the United States and so grew up and lived their lives in the same period of American history. They were born in different parts of the United States, into different circumstances, had differing school experiences, and so forth. These artists are accomplished, well-established professionals: Their work is shown regularly in first-run galleries; they have been written about, some extensively; all have works in museum collections; three have been included in Whitney Museum Biennials; and most teach at colleges or universities.

ASPECTS OF METHOD

Prior to interviewing each artist, I examined her work in the original or reproduction, read reviews of her shows and related writings, and, in two cases, read writings by the artist. With one exception, I interviewed each artist for 4 to 5 hours, in two or three sessions, in her studio. In the interviews, I asked about phases of the artist's work and points of transition, always with reference to specific works. Other questions—concerning background, commitment to becoming an artist, major influences, and ways of working—were also discussed.

My focus on the individual's work in the context of the life, and the use of first-person materials in conjunction with intensive study of work objects, is consonant with the *cognitive case study* approach formulated by Gruber (1980) and Wallace (1989). Focusing on the *work stream* assumes it is appropriate to delineate such a stream as distinct from other streams of the life course, an assumption that is culturally grounded. In societies that do not separate work and domestic life as we do, or for the period of childhood in our culture, it would be bizarre to focus on a person's work as distinguished from other aspects of the life. For participants in this study, it was natural and comfortable to do so.

The use of first-person materials is an inherent part of a phenomenological orientation, indispensable to constructing the "view from within." Although Gruber (1980) sometimes privileges the interpreter, he urges that "[w]e have the double task of reconstructing events from the subject's point of view and then understanding them from our own" (p. 277). Wallace (1989) conceptualizes this duality in terms of two roles the investigator assumes: the phenomenological role in which the investigator attempts to reconstruct the meaning of experience from the person's point of view, and the critical role in which the investigator "stands outside the subject to appraise the data of the case and to explain and interpret them" (p. 31). This distinction is crucial but does not accord the "subject" a sufficiently independent voice. Working with living people, and using an interview methodology, I attempt to maintain a clear distinction between the person's account of her experience and my version. The aim is to acknowledge both versions and to avoid privileging one over the other.

Differences among kinds of first-person accounts must be recognized. Letters and interviews involve an explicit other, but only interviews involve an actual other, a potential partner in dialogue. Diaries, journals, and memoirs may be addressed primarily to the self or intended for a wider audience. The fluid nature of open-ended interviews brings forth material in a form not readily available in written records and provides opportunity to pose questions as they occur.

Until relatively recently, academic research psychologists tended to see the interview in terms of extracting information or gaining access to material—processes often conceptualized in terms of metaphors of *laying bare*, *uncovering*, or *penetrating*. Some discussions (e.g., Mishler, 1986) counter the traditional view not only by examining the interview as situated discourse but by emphasizing that meaning is created rather than simply brought forth in the interview process. Kvale (1983) argues for the importance of holding specific hypotheses and presuppositions in abeyance, conducting the interview in an open-ended fashion, and corroborating interpretations with the interviewee. My approach to interviewing follows Kvale's in form. However, Kvale seems directed toward reaching agreement with the interviewee, not only on matters of fact but on interpretation, whereas I am interested in maintaining two voices, two perspectives: the artist's and the interpreter's.[2]

The artists participating in this study knew that they would be referred to by their names; this may have affected what they said. Further, because successful artists are called upon to talk about their work "in public," it

---

[2]Elsewhere (Franklin, 1992), I have distinguished three models of the interview—the traditional, the phenomenological (represented by Kvale), and the discourse or postmodernist model.

is likely that in the interview situation they drew to some extent on previously constructed narratives. This need not be seen as a drawback: We are hearing the person's narrative of her work life. Moreover, as several artists remarked, the interview situation provided an opportunity for reflection; new ideas or formulations occurred with fair frequency in the interviews and in the period between first and second sessions. Thus, for some, the interview was an occasion for newly articulating the work stream narrative, and for others, an occasion for elaborating or revising.

I began by considering each artist individually. However, working with a number of people who have some things in common—profession, gender, level of accomplishment, generation—provided a basis for thinking about themes or patterns that might transcend the individual case and, equally important, an opportunity to discern contrasts. This, then, is a *comparative case study.*

Initially directed toward phenomena of change, I began with a close focus on artists' views of phases and transitions. Listening to the artists and working with the interview material, I became interested in references to childhood and student days as embodying a sense of "beginnings" as an artist, and in metaphors used to describe patterns of work over time. The artists' references to recurring themes and concerns in their work impelled me to consider continuities as well as change.

POINTS OF ORIGIN

All narratives of development have a beginning. For life narratives, at least in our culture, it is generally the moment of birth or the beginnings of consciousness as represented in first memories. As far as I know, there is no conventional beginning point for narratives that center on the development of one's work, oneself as a professional. As I talked with artists about the development of their work, it seemed that rather than one beginning there were several. The interview material suggests three *points of origin* for the sense of artistic identity or self-definition.

The first point of origin is in childhood, centered (perhaps symbolized) in memories of intense interest in the visual world, and making drawings or other artworks. Most of the references to childhood experience occurred spontaneously, in the context of other discussion. Harriet Shorr said:

> It turns out that I always painted and drew. Since I was a little kid . . . I think there's a basic underlying aesthetic that you develop in your childhood, that informs a lot of your choices . . . I know that my aesthetic was probably influenced by growing up near a beach . . . lots of light, space, water . . . I always wanted to have a lot of room . . . sort of the emptiness

of my paintings . . . All these ideas about arranging and placing things in the right place and having enough space . . . I want to re-create that sense of expansiveness and light.

Here, we have not only the memories of making art and of physical surroundings—the sensuous, and more particularly, the visual world—but the suggestion that aspects of early experience are a source of later imagery (see Fig. 9.1). Several artists also made reference to childhood play as linked to aspects of their work, sometimes in terms of feeling rather than content.

FIG. 9.1. Harriet Shorr, *Forgetting Fantin*. 66 × 56", oil on canvas, 1991. Courtesy of the artist.

In this context, "childhood" is the psychological period that precedes being "grown up" and may include the years of adolescence.

The second point of origin is located in the years of college and/or art school and slightly beyond. For most of the artists I talked with, this is when they made the explicit commitment to being an artist—sometimes with their parents' approval and support, sometimes in defiance of parental wishes. The self-definition as artist that occurs in this student period centers on commitment to being an artist, acquiring professional-level skills, studying with accomplished artists who may be seen as significant influences, and locating oneself in relation to the art scene—for example, in relation to abstract expressionism, which was the dominating force when these artists were in school. Some of the artists described the work of their student days as if it were prehistory. Reflecting on the particular concerns that shaped her early work and were subsequently superseded, Pat Steir remarked on her strong interest in the figure, Jungian symbolism, and self-representation (what she later called her "autobiographical obsessions"). Of this work she said, "That work was too influenced . . . it is real student work. I don't even count it." Other artists see threads of imagery, or concerns, that connect directly to later work. This becomes most interesting in instances where the observer could not discern such a connection. For example, describing a painting of her student days, Donna Dennis said:

> When I look back on this painting, in a way it has some of the elements that the sculpture later had . . . It has an opening which is sort of a door in the center.

The third point of origin centers on having artistic ideas and ways of working with materials that are felt as uniquely one's own—finding one's own voice, as writers say—independence from the influences of student days, a new sense of autonomy. This is the beginning of what artists call their "professional work." Pat Steir (1986) refers to her painting, *Bird*, done in 1969, as her "first painting"—meaning, of course, that it marked a significant new beginning (p. 14).

Several artists linked the sense of finding their voice—which doesn't necessarily mean a signature style—to the liberating force of the women's movement and others referred to their participation in the women's movement as contributing to changes at later points. In any case, for these women, the sense of themselves as professional artists concerned feelings about the development of the work itself rather than external markers, although there is no question that the first one-person show in an established gallery is a very significant event.

These narratives suggest that different aspects of the artistic self are seen as rooted in different periods of one's own history, and in some cases, as carrying forward rather than being left behind. The notion of points of origin is consonant with the idea that the self can be thought of as a narrative constructed and revised over time (Polkinghorne, 1991), and as comprised of more than one "voice" or self (Watkins, 1986). In self- narratives, certain moments or periods may be identified as originating points for different selves (e.g., my professional self as contrasted with myself as mother). Further, as with the *artistic self*, each may have several aspects with different points of origin. How many such points are identified and where they are placed is a basic structural feature of life narratives, varying within and across culture. One wonders, for example, whether women artists, more frequently than male artists, tend to locate a point of origin for the artistic self in childhood.

TRANSITIONS AND MODES OF CHANGE

Change goes on all the time—in life and in work. *Transitions* are moments or more extended periods of intensified change. Prior to the interviews, I had told each artist that I was interested in whether she conceptualized her work in terms of phases, and how she experienced transitions. Rather than posing these questions in general terms, I asked them in the context of talking about particular pieces of work and series of works. Going over the interview material, I identified three modes of change: *generative problem solving, focused exploration*, and *converging streams*.

For a number of years, Melissa Zink had been working in various ways to integrate language, sculpture, and painting. Titles, often with double meanings ("Table of Contents") or metaphoric ("Museum of the Mind"), played an important role from the beginnings of her figurative work in sculpture in the late 1970s. Two shows of works in the mid-1980s were built around legends written by Zink, one about the land of the mystic garden (an imagined place, with an imagined religion, customs, and so forth) and the other about the travels of a character named Gypsy Dog and her friend M. Hattie Maxwilliam. Speaking later of the relation of words to sculptures in these works, Zink said:

> There was a story, and a series of objects. The objects were illustrations of an event or thing in the story. When I realized I was using the objects as illustrations, I realized that wasn't what I wanted. I wanted some other kind of integration. But then I put it on hold, and went back to thinking about two and three dimensions, how to get painting and sculpture together.

In a 1986 work, *The Opening & Concluding Chapters of an Oriental Tale* (see Fig. 9.2), figures were placed in a stage-like setting and the walls

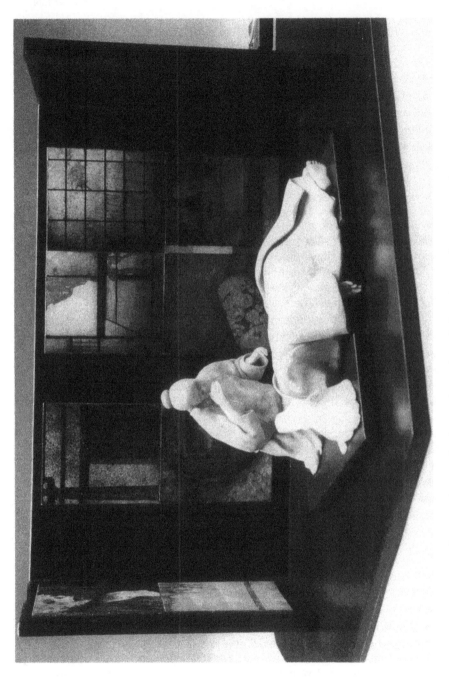

FIG. 9.2 Melissa Zink, *The Opening and Concluding Chapters of an Oriental Tale*. 12 × 26 × 18″, mixed media, 1986. Collection of Gayle Maxon.

painted with oriental motifs. Other works of this phase, quite different in theme, also have figures placed in settings with painted "backdrops." Zink contrasts *Oriental Tale* with a later piece, saying "I struggled for a long time to figure out a way that the painting wouldn't be a background, like a set design." For example, in a sculpture entitled *The Arnolfinis at Home* (based, of course, on van Eyck's double portrait), a large cube with paintings on it was centrally located in the sculpture. A few months later, Zink was dissatisfied with this attempt to integrate two and three dimensions.

> There is something about an object . . . Three dimensional objects occupy real space—in a gallery, in someone's house. I think you experience things on the wall differently. Pictures somehow have more magic for me. So I felt dissatisfied with what I was doing. I wanted to combine the two kinds of experience—two-dimensional and three-dimensional. And I wanted to challenge the convention of how things have been represented—in two dimensions *or* three dimensions. So I decided to do it, and to let myself work with language at the same time.

Until this time, Zink had attempted, on the one hand, to work with language in relation to sculptural forms and, on the other hand, to integrate painting with sculpture. The new works (1988–1989), designed to hang on the wall, had fully developed paintings on the two-dimensional surface and sculptural elements as an integral part. Thus, in a work titled *The Relationship between Word and Object*, paintings of chairs, and two of men seated in chairs, are on the two-dimensional surface, whereas a three-dimensional representation of a man-fused-with-chair emerges from the surface. The word *chair* (meaning *flesh* in French) is inscribed in block letters on the lower portion of the work, overlapping with the phrase, in script, "The word was made flesh and dwelt among us" (see *Dimensional Paintings*, 1989). The works of this series included words or phrases intended to complement the images, to resonate with them and create new meanings. But the writing on the surface of the paintings was dim, veiled, aesthetic. In a work of the next year, *W* (1990), Zink allowed herself to write much more. However, in the interview she said of this piece:

> The words are not there necessarily to read. They look like part of the design, part of the surface. I looked at it and felt, the tail is wagging the dog—meaning that the words were getting too important. Then I realized what I wanted to do—I wanted to change the emphasis entirely, to make the words central and the images peripheral. I look back and see that language is a whole strand in my work. But, for me, making the text central and legible is a major break.

In the next series of works, also working with two and three dimensions, Zink wrote text of a page or more and gave it central position on a "dimensional painting" that included figurative painting and sculptural elements.

As can be seen from the interview excerpts, the identification of problems—the integration of two- and three-dimensional representation, and of visual representation with word meaning—came from the artist herself. The sequence was more complex than represented here, involving different kinds of works, change of themes, and other concerns. However, working concurrently with two problems of integration defines this phase of Zink's work. In each subphase, the "problem" may have come through affectively rather than cognitively, at first—as a tension within the work that required a new integration. In such instances, the problem emerges from the previous work and sets the parameters for the solution; the solution is more a beginning than an ending. The process can be characterized as *generative problem solving*.

Discontent or dissatisfaction, ranging from mild to acute, is not uncommon in artists' narratives of their work. In some instances, discontent is followed by a kind of turning away from ongoing work, followed by an opening up that centers on active exploration of new possibilities. This second mode of change is *focused exploration*.

Speaking about the end of the series she calls her "rug paintings," Susan Crile said:

> After making perhaps 20 of these [the "rug paintings"], I started a painting that I never finished, in which I just couldn't go any further. This happens to me—it's a strange phenomenon. I don't technically know how to do it any more. I simply cannot do it any longer . . . If the interest and the involvement aren't there, the skill to do it disappears.

At that point, feeling herself at a juncture, Crile found herself looking at maps:

> I remember around that time, I had been in Venice, and I'd gone to the city museum which has some beautiful maps, and I became extremely interested in all this. I had no idea why. I just noticed that this was happening.

While traveling, she did some sketches from airplane windows, "nothing terribly serious" in her words.

> I decided that since I didn't know what I was going to do, I had to start with something I knew about and that was my own life. So I started a series of pastel drawings which I call my psychological maps . . . These

were of places that had been important to me at one time or another in
my life, as I imagined them from the air. And I did this for about six months
or maybe it was a year.

Sometimes, after completing a "psychological map," Crile would study
a topographical map of the area. This gave her the idea of using
topographical maps more systematically.

> When I started the mapping series . . . I wanted to work with the specificity
> of the topographical map that gave me a kind of formal layout and a lot
> of information, but then I wanted it overlaid with actual concrete experience,
> what it was like to see the land from above and to be in it. So I was dealing
> with three levels, at least . . . the concrete aspect of the topographical maps,
> the experiential part of being in the landscape . . . and the more distant
> overview.

The initial explorations with maps and mapping became progressively
focused, evolving into a series of works including *Lake Dancers* (1975),
which is on two six-panel folding screens (see *Susan Crile: Paintings*, 1984,
p. 12).

The third pattern of change illustrated here is *convergence of streams*
(see Franklin, 1989). Four years out of college, having spent some years
painting, Donna Dennis was making large (c. 7 by 10 feet), two-dimensional works that stood on the floor and were constructed of contact
paper laid on wood, mirror strips, enlarged photographs, and some
painted areas. She explains:

> I was getting really dissatisfied with those big pieces because in a way, I
> was trying to make minimal art . . . Actually, I was interested in surrealism
> . . . and I liked to paint. These things hadn't allowed me to paint much . . .
> It's really a big collage. In the end, I just didn't feel great about these. I
> never showed them.

At about this time, several things happened: A close relationship broke
up; Dennis moved to a new loft; she became involved with the women's
movement and, shortly thereafter, with a consciousness-raising group.
She read Virginia Woolf's *A Room of One's Own*, and—in her words—
"decided to really change the work."

> I didn't know why I was working so big. I decided I would just work small
> and sort of start all over again. I wanted to make work that had to do with
> women's experience. A lot of the women who were showing then as
> feminists were concerned with making stuff that looked kind of macho, as
> good as the boys. And I thought, why as good as the boys? Why not better?
> Why not celebrate the differences?

One of the works that Dennis did at this time (1970) is a small collage (overall dimensions, 8 by 11 inches) in which a series of self-portraits from a 5 & 10 photo machine are centered within a painted border. Another small collage included sofa, lamp, and other objects of the intimate domestic world. Dennis refers to these as "self-portraits."

During this difficult time, Dennis thought about how she had wanted to be an artist since she was 5, and about the way she was then: "Making art had been almost as natural as breathing when I was a child, so I wanted to tap into it and find it . . . What I was trying to remember was a feeling, the most exciting thing that stirred me." She recalled the games she played when she was little—making structures that one could get into—a blanket over a card table, shelters made of raked leaves. She also remembered, from later childhood or early adolescence, having seen the mastaba at the Metropolitan Museum of Art in New York, and entering it:

> This very mysterious and sort of narrow doorway, and you go down and there's a corridor that goes to the left, and then it turns to the right, and it made you feel as if you were getting to the heart of the matter, the heart of the mystery, but then you end up in front of a false door.

Dennis went to her parents' home and retrieved the blocks she had played with as a child. She looked at old buildings in New York City where she lived, she thought about ziggurat structures, and more. She started keeping a journal that included observations, reflections, and sketches—"whatever came to mind." Finally, she did a drawing of several versions of an imagined structure with ziggurat shaped sides and a black-and-white checkered surface.

> Until now, I felt as if I'd been looking and I'd been finding clues. When I did this drawing, I felt that I'd found it. There was this false-front thing, with a mirror down the center—so there's some connection to things before—but the doorway in the center sort of opens up into the mirror; it could be the sky, it could be deep space. So I felt great, I had found it. Then it was like I remembered when I was little. I did several drawings every day . . . I just tapped into something. And then I decided to build one, so I built one. I'd never built anything before, but I realized that for a long time I had wanted to get things off the canvas. I wanted to make things that would have an impact.

Dennis' first sculpture, entitled "False Front" (1972), was several shaped canvases one behind the other, with a narrow opening in the front, and a narrow strip of mirror reflecting the light. The "False Front" evolved into "hotels"—*Hotel Pacifica* (1972) and others. Here, as in her later structures, the lintel is at Dennis' eye level; Dennis refers to all these works as "self-portraits," acknowledging a connection with the body, and embeddedness in personal associations. Equally important, the designation of "self-portrait" suggests a link to the small collages that preceded the first "false front" drawing. And then other kinds of structures came—tourist cabins, towers, subways, *Skowhegan Stairway* (see Fig. 9.3), and most recently, bridges—all with multilayered meanings (for some illustrations, see *Developments in Recent Sculpture*, 1980).

The beginnings of Dennis' work with three-dimensional structures, coming after struggles and explorations of almost 2 years, marks the beginning of the work she identifies with and is known for. I suggest that it issued from a *convergence of streams* that occurred in a context of dissatisfaction with the previous work and changing life circumstances. The streams—memories of making shelters in childhood, feelings about the Egyptian structure at the Metropolitan Museum, images of other buildings, valuing autobiographical experience (as a result of involvement with the women's movement), journal explorations of personal experience and of metaphors (hidden/visible, inside/outside, seen/reflected), free drawing ("whatever came to mind")—these streams, previously outside the work stream, came together with some threads carried forward from earlier work. A fundamental reorganization occurred, a reorganization that was deeply generative for the artist.

I've now illustrated three modes of change—generative problem solving, focused exploration, and converging streams. I must emphasize that the transitions in an artist's work are not all of a kind: convergence of streams might capture the dynamics of one transition, whereas generative problem solving better describes the next. Further, more than one mode of change may be operative in a particular transition: Focused exploration, or a converging stream or two, might enter into an instance of generative problem solving.

IMAGES OF DEVELOPMENT

Let me turn now to the more encompassing question: How do artists see the pattern of their work over time? (By "work," I mean not only tangible artworks produced, but the stream of ideas and technical concerns that are part of the artist's project). What *images of development* are contained in their narratives?

Before going on, one word. In much of the now voluminous literature on retrospective narratives, it sounds as if narrators are unaware that life narratives are not simply reruns of lived experience. Here is an artist reflecting on the process:

FIG. 9.3. Donna Dennis, *Skowhegan Stairway*. 138 × 140 × 37", mixed media, with sound, 1983. Courtesy of the artist.

It's one thing how you feel when you're in the middle of it, and another, looking back on it. When I'm in a transition, I don't really know what's happening . . . I feel the dissatisfaction and the need to do something different, but I don't necessarily know where I'm going. But from the outside, looking back in time, the transitions are very straightforward, there's a logical connection . . .

As mentioned earlier, most of the artists identified a time when their professional work began. For some, there was a period of professional work—sometimes as long as 10 years—that preceded what they regard as their "mature work." For example, Harriet Shorr (1990) identifies her painting, *Magnolias* (1976), as a "turning point," the beginning of a new direction (p. 79). This painting was done when Shorr was well into her professional career, having participated in many group shows and having had a series of one-person shows. The changes had to do with scale, working with only two objects and the space between them, and other formal concerns.

Most (but not all) of the artists not only identify an early professional stage but describe the extended period of their mature work in terms of several phases. Phases are defined by changes in subject matter or themes, formal concerns, modes of working, materials and techniques. The changes come from several sources, both within the work and outside it, as illustrated in the preceding discussion of modes of change. For some of the artists, specific life experiences mark the beginning of a new phase or subphase and are identified as significant sources of subject matter or technical innovation.

Joanne Leonard related a significant change in her work to a change in her personal life:

Then my marriage fell apart, and I did a series of collages based on my own difficult life . . . the series called 'Dreams and Nightmares' . . . and that's when the collages took a different turn, where they became more about fantasy and inner feelings . . . and in a way, I've continued that, with the photographs signifying what's out there and the collage being the fantasy, the interior world . . . or at least they played around that issue, of real and not real, how to suggest what one thinks and feels together with what one sees. I wasn't satisfied with taking a photograph and pasting things on top of it as a collage idea . . . I found out how to print a photograph on something transparent . . . that added another dimension, transparency became part of it.

Louise Fishman described the beginning of a series of works as follows (see *Louise Fishman: Paintings 1987–1989*):

Some events have affected my work dramatically . . . A very important event that took place in my life was a trip to Eastern Europe and to several concentration camps, including Auschwitz. I came back with a series of black and white photographs that I took there. I went with a friend of mine who was a survivor of Auschwitz, and it was a terrifying experience. I became a kind of witness . . . I came back with a handful of soil that has some ashes in it . . . I was having a terrible time working, I found it almost impossible to think about making art after having witnessed what I had seen . . . I mixed these ashes in with some beeswax and mixed it in with all my paints, and each of the paintings I did in that series had a little bit of ashes in it . . . All these paintings have Yiddish titles, and they all have to do with the holiday of Passover.

Interestingly, artists who talk about their work in terms of clearly demarcated phases tend to identify qualitative shifts that involve more than one of the markers mentioned previously: subject matter or themes, formal concerns, modes of working, materials and techniques.

Are these artists talking about development? That depends, of course, on what you mean by *development*. As Wartofsky points out (this volume), in its weakest version, *development* refers simply to a series of occurrences arranged sequentially in time. So it applies to virtually any chronologically ordered series, including artists' accounts of the sequence of their work. But that's not very interesting because it doesn't say much. In a stronger and thicker meaning, very familiar to developmental psychologists, *development* means that there is *something* that changes from one state to another; the change is *directional* and it is *cumulative*: Later states *build on* and perhaps incorporate what went before. There is a *necessary sequence*: A leads to B, B to C, and so on; one cannot get from A to C without going through B. Some theorists argue that the notion of *direction* involves the notion of *telos*—an endpoint or goal toward which development tends (see Kaplan, 1986).[3]

On the whole, the artists' narratives contain elements of this stronger version of development—most clearly, the idea that there is a kind of naturalness in the sequence, that one kind of work *grows out of* and *builds on* what went before, and that phases—if they exist—cannot be skipped. Some narratives even indicate an implicit *telos*: the progressive integration of personal experience with changing, expanding artistic concerns (explorations and reconstructions of the medium).

For example, Joanne Leonard sees her recent works, *Moments of Being I* (1990) and *Moments of Being II* (1990), as embodying a higher level integration of evolving themes and inventions in the medium than achieved in the earlier work (see Golden & Leonard, 1981). The themes

---

[3]I have here collapsed some important distinctions, particularly with reference to the concept of *stages* that Wartofsky (this volume) makes clear in discussing different meanings of *development*.

to which Leonard referred are her use of autobiographical material with
its theme of memory, and the commentary on photography itself. The
medium inventions have to do with the use of collage, waxing photographic prints, and printing on transparent material—techniques that
allow the layering of images (see Fig. 9.4).

Leonard explained:

> Making these works [*Moments of Being I and II*], I used photo collage
> strategies of associating, specifying, blending, contrasting, layering and
> stretching out in time and space . . . In *Moments of Being*, Virginia Woolf
> suggested that memory is like little corks that float in a sunken net, its
> contents all unsorted. My use of collage places photographs and collage
> fragments within a relatively open space, not organized by any sense of
> linear time or narrative, with the idea that these fragments will rise to the
> surface (they are sometimes literally submerged under semitransparent
> layers) and offer up associations with the sunken past.

So, aspects of some artists' narratives exemplify the successive
integrations and reorganizations that some developmental theorists—
most notably, Heinz Werner—identify with developmental progression.
In fact, a number of concepts embedded in Werner's (1978) writings and
his work with Kaplan (Werner & Kaplan, 1963/1984) seem particularly
apt for schematizing artistic development. But the pattern of "progression" from "lower" to "higher" forms (albeit not unilinear and perhaps
spiraling rather than straight-line) fit only some portions of the narratives;
in many instances, its application would have yielded a distorted
picture—not only in how events were ordered but in what was left out.
I resolved to take my original question seriously: How do artists construe
the "development" of their work?

Harriet Shorr resisted my suggestion that over a period of some years
her interest in associations and metaphors had grown, whereas purely
formal concerns receded somewhat. She said:

> Themes are cyclical in my work. They've always been there and they keep
> spinning around and coming back. Sometimes they're formal concerns, say
> light and color; sometimes they're more about resonant objects, associations.
> I see it as a kind of wheel that's turning around.

Susan Crile describes her past work in terms of different phases, but
not on a linear model:

> My work is additive. I think of myself as being Proustian in that sense, in
> the sense that things get absorbed into the body; they become integrated
> into it and then become part of the general matrix out of which everything
> else rises and rebuilds and re-invents itself, so to speak . . . What's been

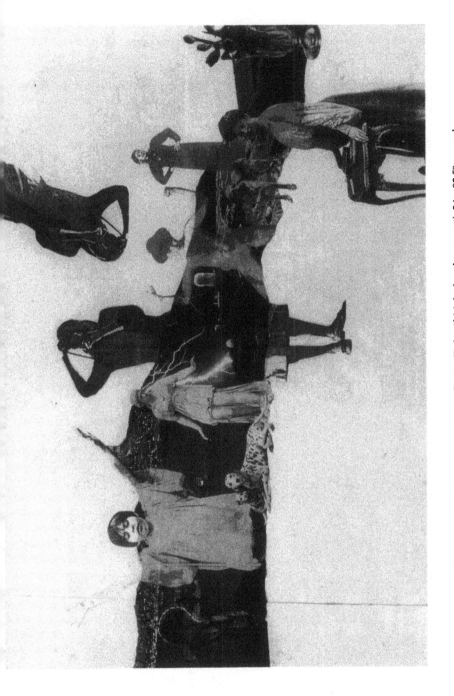

FIG. 9.4. Joanne Leonard, *Moments of Being II*, detail (right-hand segment). 24 × 92.5"; waxed gelatin silver photographic prints, waxed photocopies, glassine, collage, gouache, cream colored support paper, text. Courtesy of the artist.

done is there as a deep part of my memory and the memory of the work. It's not as if I leave the maps behind or I leave the rugs behind, or I leave the architectural sense behind, or the issues of perception. They may take on another form, they may go underground; they may get condensed or abbreviated or alluded to symbolically. But they don't disappear . . . nothing is ever left behind, everything resurfaces. (See Fig. 9.5.)

Here there is an image of accumulation, of stuff gathering into an organic whole—a whole that is deeply generative.

Speaking of the beginnings of her new work, Donna Dennis explained:

Usually, when I've made a change, I go way out, far away from what I've done before, and imagine things that are a huge departure, whole new materials—very, very different. And then when I finally get started, what

FIG. 9.5. Susan Crile, *Liaison Dangereuse*. 34 x 30", Charcoal, pastel and oil pastel on paper, 1990. Courtesy of the artist.

seems to work is right next door. To make that step, I had to go way out, far afield, way out in the solar system . . . But I don't think anything has ever been lost. Those side trips might have felt like dead ends at one point, but they all add up in the end.

The image here is different—there is a path, but the side trips are not minor excursions. Also, there is again the sense that nothing is left behind or lost—the excursions are not relinquished to the realm of bygone days but exist as living material for ongoing work.

These images of development, by no means uniform, all have an aspect of *gathering—of bringing things together, including the past and the present.* Wheels, matrices, paths with looping side roads—such images do not fit the images of canonical models. Theorists such as Freud and Piaget would not be disturbed by this lack of consonance between their models and the artists' images: Their theories were not designed to "fit" the *manifest* content of psychological experience and action but to provide an explanation of surface phenomena via appeal to *underlying* structures and processes. Bu⁺ some of us believe that psychological theories should give more weight to people's experience of their own lives.

It is not only those with phenomenological leanings who challenge the hegemony of canonical theory. Another critique comes from theorists who do not necessarily reject developmental stage theory but question its application to phenomena of creative lives. Gruber (1989), for example, argues that notions of "uniform stages" and "unilinear developmental pathways" are off the mark as characterizations of creative lives. Taking Picasso's work as an exemplar of artistic development, Bornstein (1984) examines the applicability of principles of maturation, equilibration, learning through reinforcement, learning through imitation, and adaptation. He concludes that, whereas each of these can account for some aspects of change in the work of particular artists, there does not appear to be a "monistic or even prevailing perspective available from developmental psychology that could account for artistic evolution in the individual" (p. 141). Others take exception to traditional concepts of development not only with respect to art, but more generally. Some argue for radical revision of the concept of development; they see the individual as "co-producer of his development" (Brandtstädter, 1990) and reconceptualize *development* in terms of the progressive transformation of ends, as a movement toward optimizing experience in one or another of many possible forms (Freeman & Robinson, 1990). More extremely, theorists such as Hein (this volume) and Kessen (1991) seem skeptical about the project of revamping the concept of development, a concept that is historically tied to notions of progress, hierarchy, and telos—that is, to a family of value-laden assumptions that have to do with things moving in a given direction and getting better and better. I take Hein to suggest that, rather than using (and overusing) a concept of development, we bracket it and try to think in a more differentiated way about various kinds of change.

CHANGE AND CONTINUITY

As I spoke with artists about changes in their work, about phases and points of transition, they also told me about continuities. Because I was focused on change rather than continuity, it took me a while to hear this theme—but reading and rereading the transcripts, I finally listened.

One way of articulating continuity is to talk about themes or concerns that run through time, *connecting work of different periods by identifying what is the same in disparate appearances.*

Louise Fishman responded as follows to a question about phases of her work:

> I'm more conscious of phases, from one to the next, than I used to be, but what I've noticed is a line of thinking, a line of identity that runs through all the work. And maybe change is less important than what's constant. I've been painting abstract paintings, without a break, since art school. And they've change a lot . . . But what seems to run through is that my paintings have to do with balance in the body . . . The physicality of the painting is connected with my body, how I experience my body and the space I live in. (See Fig. 9.6.)

Continuity is expressed differently by Pat Steir. She emphasizes the *ongoing flow,* even as she refers to different phases of her work:

> I finished the Breughel painting [see Steir, 1986] . . . As a result of that study, I decided to pick up again at early modernism, so I picked up with Courbet . . . and so I did the wave paintings . . . and from waves to waterfalls, the step was small . . . There are never big moments of change in the work, work moves slowly toward something else . . . In a way I see there are no changes in my work at all; it is all one work; there are no separations between this painting and that—it is all one piece of work and there are no changes, there is never a dramatic change. It *looks like* a dramatic change . . . It's an organic growth . . . You allow it to change, and allow yourself to change. (See Fig. 9.7.)

This way of establishing continuity or connectedness—centering on how one kind of work evolves organically into the next—differs from *identifying similarities underlying different appearances,* as in Fishman's description. Both ways of connecting things appear in other artists'

FIG. 9.6. Louise Fishman, *Lander*. 40 x 32", oil on linen, 1989. Private collection. Courtesy Robert Miller Gallery, New York.

accounts as well, suggesting that the *tension between continuity and change* is a central theme of artists' life/work narratives.

Although the theme of continuity and change is fundamental to issues of identity and "self-realization" in the dominant culture, it may have special meaning for artists working in this milieu. The sense of oneself as a centered, creative, productive artist involves seeing one's work over time as changing, generative—and at the same time as a unified body,

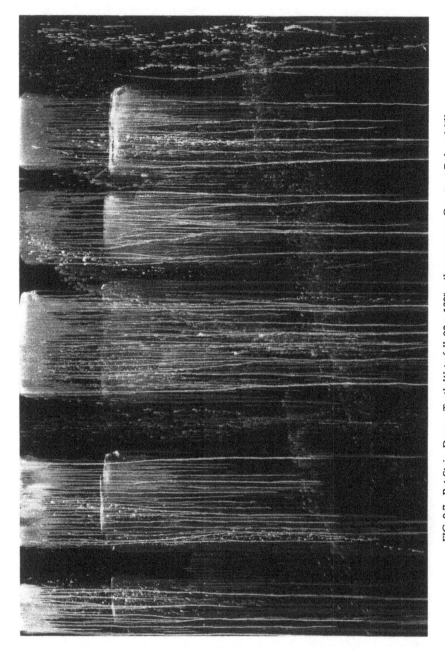

FIG. 9.7. Pat Steir, *Dragon Tooth Waterfall*. 92 x 132", oil on canvas. Courtesy Robert Miller Gallery, New York.

188

all of a piece, different parts connected to each other in one way or another. Market pressures resonate with these more personal inclinations: It is important to have a recognizable style and, at the same time, to produce work that critics and other gatekeepers see as indicating "growth" and perhaps "progress."

CONCLUDING COMMENTS

I agree with those who emphasize the importance of recognizing that artists and other creative people, like the rest of us, live and think and formulate their experience in a sociocultural matrix. Artists' shared concerns and, to some extent at least, the way they structure their narratives no doubt reflect their participation in a particular professional milieu, a subculture. Further, women artists probably share some concerns, or ways of organizing their life/work narratives, that are less frequently found among male artists. But if subcultural membership were the sole source of themes for life/work narratives, there would be much more uniformity than there is. In this chapter, I tried to show that even within a relatively "homogeneous" group variation abounds. It seems clear, then, that significant aspects of these life/work narratives have their origins in the individual artists' particular experiences, interests, passions, and proclivities—in the way that the artist, as active agent, structures her lifeworld.

If we want to do something other than tell or retell the story of an individual's life and work, we begin to theorize. In this chapter, I resisted "high theory" and attempted to provide schematizations that are relatively close to the phenomena as I see them. These schematizations— notions such as *points of origin, generative problem solving*, and *converging streams*—are generated within a narrative perspective that assumes that constructing narrative accounts, on both personal and theoretical levels, is a prime way of rendering and understanding the meanings of human life. Two dimensions must be considered: The chronological or "episodic" dimension involves temporal ordering of events and experiences; the other dimension centers on constructing meaningful wholes from "scattered events" (Ricoeur, 1981); that is, configuring parts to display relationships in addition to sequential order.

This kind of approach, which might be characterized as "local theorizing," may draw on concepts from different theories *if* the concepts do not rest on incompatible underlying assumptions. For example, the idea of generative problem solving, rooted in classical Gestalt theory, and the concept of converging streams, exemplified not only in Werner and Kaplan's view of the emergence of language but in Vygotsky's, are not in conflict. The incoherence engendered by eclecticism is avoided through attention to underlying assumptions.

Any schematization is necessarily interpretive, not merely a representation of some set of "facts." However, in the postmodern era, there is some danger that heightened awareness of our interpretive standpoint leads to abandoning attempts to see beyond our initial vision, to hear voices other than our own. In this study, I have tried to hear, and to learn from, the artists' articulation of changes and continuities in their work.

REFERENCES

Bornstein, M. (1984). Developmental psychology and the problem of artistic change. *Journal of Aesthetics and Art Criticism, 43*, 131–145.

Brandtstädter, J. (1990). Development as a personal and cultural construction (pp. 83–107). In G. R. Semin & K. J. Gergen (Eds.), *Everyday understanding*. London: Sage.

Developments in recent sculpture (1980). New York: The Whitney Museum of American Art.

Dimensional paintings (1989). Santa Fe, NM: Gerald Peters Gallery.

Franklin, M. B. (1989). A convergence of streams: Dramatic change in the artistic work of Melissa Zink. In D. B. Wallace & H. E. Gruber (Eds.), *Creative people at work* (pp. 255–277). New York: Oxford University Press.

Franklin, M. B. (1992). Making sense: Interviewing and the narrative representation of artists' work. In R. Albert (Chair.), *Future directions in creativity research*. Symposium conducted at the meetings of the American Psychological Association, Washington, DC.

Freeman, M., & Robinson, R. R. (1990). The development within: An alternative approach to the study of lives. *New Ideas in Psychology, 9*, 53–72.

Gilligan, C. (1983). *In a different voice*. Cambridge, MA: Harvard University Press.

Golden, J., & Leonard, J. (1981). *Photo/Trans/Forms*. San Francisco: San Francisco Museum of Modern Art.

Gruber, H. E. (1980). "And the bush was not consumed": The evolving systems approach to creativity (pp. 269–299). In S. Modgil & C. Modgil (Eds.), *Toward a theory of psychological development*. Windsor, UK: NFER Publishers.

Gruber, H. E. (1989). The evolving systems approach to creative work (pp. 3–24). In D. B. Wallace & H. E. Gruber (Eds.), *Creative people at work*. New York: Oxford University Press.

Kaplan, B. (1986). Value presuppositions in theories of human development. In L. Cirillo & S. Wapner (Eds.), *Value presuppositions in theories of human development* (pp. 89–103). Hillsdale, NJ: Lawrence Erlbaum Associates.

Kessen, W. (1991, Fall). Directions: Where do we turn now? *Newsletter of the Society for Research in Child Development*.

Kvale, S. (1983). The qualitative research interview: A phenomenological and hermeneutical mode of understanding. *Journal of Phenomenological Psychology, 14*, 171–196.

Louise Fishman, paintings 1987/1989. New York: Lennon, Weinberg.

Mishler, E. (1986). *Research interviewing: Context and narrative*. Cambridge, MA: Harvard University Press.

Pepper, S. (1957). *World hypotheses*. Berkeley: University of California Press. (Original work published 1942)

Polkinghorne, D. E. (1991). Narrative and self-concept. *Journal of Narrative and Life History*, *1*, 135–154.

Ricoeur, P. (1981). The narrative function (pp. 274–296). In P. Ricoeur, *Hermeneutics and the human sciences* (J. B. Thompson, Ed. & Trans.). Cambridge, UK: Cambridge University Press.

Shorr, H. (1990). *The artist's eye.* New York: Watson-Guptil.

Steir, P. (1986). *Pat Steir paintings.* New York: Harry Abrams.

Susan Crile paintings (1984). Cleveland, OH: Cleveland Center for Contemporary Art.

Wallace, D. B. (1989). Studying the individual: The case study method (pp. 25–43). In D. B. Wallace & H. E. Gruber (Eds.), *Creative people at work.* New York: Oxford University Press.

Watkins, M. (1986). *Invisible guests.* New York: The Analytic Press.

Werner, H. (1978). *Developmental processes: Heinz Werner's selected writings* (Vol. I & II; S. S. Barten & M. B. Franklin, Eds.). New York: International University Press.

Werner, H., & Kaplan, B. (1984). *Symbol formation.* Hillsdale, NJ: Lawrence Erlbaum Associates. (Original work published 1963)

IV

On Development in the History of Art

Concurrent Conceptual Revolutions in Art and Science

Sidney J. Blatt
Yale University
New Haven, CT

Art and science both express the fundamental *Weltanschauung* of a culture—its interests and predominant modes of thought. Although art and science each involve unique media and use different notational systems, structurally they are synchronous expressions of a culture's predominant representational mode or form of symbolic construction (Panofsky, 1924/1925). These representational modes develop in the history of civilization in a basically linear fashion toward increasing differentiation, articulation, and integration. Development occurs when prior cognitive structures are revised and extended in an attempt to resolve anomalies, ambiguities, and contradictions that were experienced with prior cognitive structures. These revisions are epigenetic in that they refine, enrich, and extend prior modes rather than replace them. The developmental progression of cognitive structures in art and science is driven by perturbations experienced with prior modes of representation rather than an inexorable march toward a telos or any concept of perfection. Subsequent cognitive structures are no better or worse than earlier ones; they are just more comprehensive. They also increase the range of the repertoire of modes of representation (Wolf, this volume).

Based on the development of the representation of the form of objects and of space, this chapter explores some of the synchronous structural similarities between concepts of space in art and science, as well as aspects of their coordinated diachronic development. Utilizing structural concepts derived primarily from cognitive developmental psychology and secondarily from developmental psychoanalytic theory, I consider the hypothesis that change in the modes of representing space and the form of objects in art and science across major epochs of Western civilization (Ancient pre-Greek, Classical Greco–Roman, Medieval, Renaissance, Baroque, Impressionism, Cubism, and Modern) follow a fundamental developmental sequence. This structural analysis is based on the assumption of Piaget and Werner that the basic principles of their developmental psychology define a genetic epistemology—a fundamental theory of how knowledge is acquired and organized in multiple cognitive endeavors.

A model of cognitive development defined external to cultural history, a theory derived from an independent series of observations, can provide a heuristic model that increases our sensitivity to important diachronic and synchronic dimensions of cultural development. An independently validated theoretical model of the development of the capacity to represent the form of objects and of space can provide the "vocabulary of form," the "system of schemata" (Gombrich, 1960), or the "semantics of the visual arts" (Janson, 1961) that many art historians believe is an essential theoretical matrix for art-historical analysis.

Structuralists, especially the genetic epistemologists Jean Piaget and Heinz Werner, have delineated major dimensions in the development of the concept of the object and of space. Piaget and Werner observed these processes in the developmental unfolding of children, but they assumed that there is a fundamental parallel between the development of thought in the individual and cognitive development as it occurs in culture. Thus, their assumption does not imply a commitment to a conceptualization of ontogeny recapitulating phylogeny but rather that there is a "formal parallelism" (Brunswik, 1959) among the development of all cognitive processes, whether they occur in individual psychological development or in various endeavors of a culture.

As summarized in Table 10.1, concepts from developmental theory can be integrated to define a basic process that unfolds from an initial mode of representation based primarily on the extension of action sequences and concerns about pleasure–pain and life–death (a *sensorimotor* mode), to a beginning intuitive coordination of a few dimensions (a *preoperational-intuitive* mode), to a systematic coordination and integration of different dimensions of the external manifest form of objects (a *concrete operational* mode), to the coordination and integration of more abstract dimensions of internal form and structure (a *formal operational* mode).

In terms of concepts of space, this basic developmental sequence also involves a progression from an emphasis on the surface, boundary, or contour of a single object (*topological* concepts of space) to representations of the relationships among different parts of a single object or among different objects in space. These relations are initially specified qualita-

TABLE 10.1
Development of Concepts of the Object and of Space

Concepts of the Object	Concepts of Space	Concepts of Scaling

I. Sensorimotor-
   Preoperational
	I. Topological
	   Concepts of Space
		I. Nominal
		   (Classificatory) Scale

II. Intuitive (Perceptual)	II. Projective-Euclidean
	   Concepts of Space
		II. Ordinal
		   (Ranking) Scale

III. Concrete Operational		III. Interval Scale
IV. Formal Operational	III. Riemannian Concepts of Space	IV. Ratio Scale

Note. From Blatt and Blatt (1984). Adapted by permission.

tively and intuitively and later expressed in increasingly precise quantitative terms (*projective-Euclidean* concepts of space; Laurendeau & Pinard, 1970; Piaget & Inhelder, 1948/1967); and finally to representations of space not as a fixed system defined around an arbitrary reference point, but defined in reference to the location and movement of a participant–observer (*Riemannian* concepts of space; Blatt & Blatt, 1984).

This developmental sequence is also expressed in increasingly complex mathematical concepts and scales (Stevens, 1951) proceeding from a *nominal* scale in which observations are placed in discrete, mutually exclusive categories; to an *ordinal* scale in which observations are qualitative and comparative, based on dyadic comparisons and contrasts; to an *interval* scale in which relationships among observations are defined by a common, but arbitrary, quantitative metric system; to a *ratio* scale in which observations about the relationships among a series of objects are specified by a precisely defined metric system based on an experientially relevant reference point and scale values.

It is important to stress that these formulations of the development of cognitive processes in the individual or in culture do not assume a progression toward a fixed, predetermined, ideal goal or telos but rather describe a natural, unending, developmental unfolding. This fundamental developmental process does not lead to any conclusion about the importance or value of earlier or later levels of development; it only assumes that different modes of representation occur in different phases of the developmental process, and that later modes are epigenetically built on earlier accomplishments and achievements. Earlier stages are not abandoned or replaced but are enriched, extended, and integrated in subsequent stages. Also, individual and cultural development can proceed systematically toward increasingly differentiated, articulated, and integrated levels of representation but without necessarily following a fixed, monotonic, linear sequence that has no variation, reversions, or sudden surges of progress.

Utilizing this conceptual model of cognitive development, this chapter, in a brief overview using very broad strokes, examines relationships among aspects of the structural development of concepts of space in art and in science during major epochs in Western civilization.

Representation in *Ancient art* employed topological concepts of space that emphasized the boundary or contour of an individual object in isolation. A single object is presented without regard for the surrounding field or the relation of the object to other objects in the field. Ancient art represented an object in isolation, in two dimensions, without depth or perspective. Frontal and profile views, without foreshortening, were presented simultaneously in a concrete literal representation of only the most essential details. As details were added within the contour of a single object, the most significant features (usually parts of the sensory-perceptual apparatus) were portrayed without regard for consistency of visual appearance. Figure 10.1, the *Hall of Bulls at Lascaux*, illustrates the life-size depiction of familiar animals (horses, bison, and wild boar) in outline form and vivid colors. Each object is clearly separate from, and independent of, any other object, and there is no concern with overall composition.

This mode of representation not only utilized developmentally early, topological concepts of space that emphasized the surface, boundary, or contour of an object in isolation, but it was also based on a sensorimotor-preoperational action schema. Ancient art primarily had a magical function—it was used in religious ceremonies and rituals in an attempt to conserve life and ward off the omnipresent danger of death and disintegration (Modell, 1968). The themes of Ancient art reflect a basic sensorimotor concern about survival and preserving and sustaining life (Rochlin, 1965). Even as art changed from the depiction of a life-sized

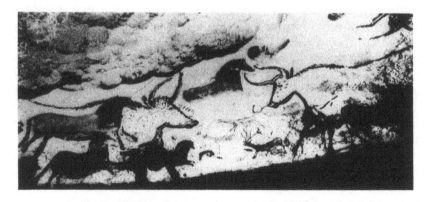

FIG. 10.1. *Hall of Bulls at Lascaux* (Early Magdalenian, c. 15,000–10,000 B.C.). Dordogne, France.

animal in isolation to diminutive representations of aggregates of people and animals, the themes still expressed predominant concerns about issues of life and death (see Fig. 10.2).

An unchanging, formal, static mode of artistic representation persisted throughout the 3,000 years of *Egyptian civilization*. Although Egyptian art remained fundamentally two dimensional, there was a beginning organization and spatial direction. Objects and figures were presented as a coherent group, precisely located and aligned on a ground line. Sharply drawn outlines of individual figures were presented basically in profile view, with the relationship between objects defined primarily by their relative size. This rigid, static mode of representation was consistent with the rigidity of Egyptian philosophy and social order. Figure 10.2 is an early (Old Kingdom) Egyptian "two-dimensional" representation of figures depicting essential profile and frontal details without foreshortening and perspective. Figures are organized in a single sequence along a defining baseline, and the size of figures within a coherent composition is determined by their rank and relative importance. But naturalism, emotional expression, and spatial illusion are not included.

This fixed Egyptian mode of representation continued for about 3,000 years but was interrupted briefly during the New Kingdom in Egypt, especially during the Armana revolution of Akhenaton in the 14th century B.C. (1379–1362 B.C.). In the Armana revolution, a more conceptual and humanistic monotheistic religion briefly replaced the basic anthropomorphic Egyptian religion (Freud, 1939/1964), and at the same time there was a new freedom of expression and a remarkable interest in naturalism and realism in art. With less emphasis on the boundary of an object in isolation, figures became softer, more corporeal and sensuous, with increased emphasis on interpersonal relationships. In Fig. 10.3, the *Cairo Stela*, figures are in more intricate arrangements of interacting and overlapping small groups. Greater naturalism and realism is expressed in more dynamic, sensuous figures in the intimacy of family life.

It is noteworthy that the naturalistic representation and the depiction of figures in intimate interaction seen briefly in Armana art emerges much later once again at two very particular times in the history of Western civilization—in Periclean Athens and again in the Renaissance—periods also characterized by a renewed interest in humanism and a revitalized emphasis on the dignity of man.

After the brief Armana revolution, Egyptian mortuary art returned to its long 3,000-year tradition of rigid, static, flattened forms defined primarily by contour and boundary, lacking depth and perspective and expressing predominant concerns about life and death.

All ancient pre-Greek art lacked objective size and depth relations, space was without continuity and meaning, and there was no concept of

FIG. 10.2. *Hippopotamus Hunt* (c. 2,500 B.C.). Tomb of Ti at Saggara.

FIG. 10.3. The Cairo Stela. *The Solar Disc of Aton Blessing the Royal Family of Akhenaton, Nefertiti and Their Three Daughters* (14th century, B.C.) Tel-el Armana, Cairo Museum.

infinity. Concepts were preoperational and space was fragmented and uncoordinated. The primary emphasis was upon the surface, boundary, or contour of individual objects presented in isolation, and the content and function of art reflected a basic preoccupation with preserving and sustaining life. In terms of developmental psychological principles, the content and structure of ancient art is at a sensorimotor-preoperational level, utilizing primarily topological concepts of space.

As in art, the earliest concepts of space in cosmology and science were based on a set of immediate, concrete, affect-laden experiences rather than objective measures. The ancient terms used for denoting universal space, for example, were filled with elements of fear and terror—terms such as *chaos*, or *yawning*, or *gaping* (Jammer, 1954/1969). One of the first steps toward a development of a systematic cosmology was the Egyptian theories of the sun and moon as being carried systematically across the sea of the heavens by the gods in their boats. Early ancient animistic concepts of space were replaced by Egyptian anthropomorphic sensori-motor concepts of planets as systematic wanderers across the heavens. This development marked a move from animistic conceptions of natural forces to the prediction of the appearance of heavenly bodies—the time and location of the daily rising and setting of the sun and the somewhat less regular change in the size, shape, and location of the moon. Egyptian cosmological conceptions were no longer based solely on immediate perception and sensory experience but on astronomical phenomena, first studied in relation to the seasons and motivated by curiosity as well as the need to produce food and to anticipate nature to survive.

Thus, the conception of space in ancient art and science was initially sensorimotor and preoperational and based on a nominal classification or scale in which isolated objects were assigned to mutually exclusive groups or categories without qualitative or quantitative order. Egyptian art and science, however, began to utilize comparative qualifications based on ordinal distinctions.

Changes in art from the Ancient period to the *Classical Antiquity* of Greek art involved a major transformation from the depiction of isolated objects as they exist concretely in nature to a depiction of the way objects are experienced visually. The content of art changed from the concrete, literal depiction of an object to a realistic and naturalistic portrayal of a general, universal, stable object in perfect form and proportion as it appears to an observer. The purpose of art also changed from a ritual function dealing with issues of life and death to a narrative recording of historical events. Figure 10.4, an early (8th century) Greek Attic Geometric Krater, illustrates the initial Greek representation of figures in isolation in frontal or profile silhouette according to a fixed geometric pattern.

In Fig. 10.5, a late (4th century) Apulia Krater, individual figures and objects are represented with depth and volume. Foreshortening and intuitive attempts to represent volume, depth, and perspective in architectural features and individual objects have only limited success because of a lack of a consistent spatial orientation and organization. The illusion of depth is achieved by irregular ground lines that create different levels, but without consistent variation of the size of the figures at different distances from the foreground.

The representation in Greek art of the manifest features of a consistent, stable, universal object as it appears from a particular vantage point involved the introduction of beginning phases of projective-Euclidean concepts of space. This shift to a representation of objects and of space from a subjective vantage point involved the development of fore-shortening, the use of shadows, and the development of intuitive (visual)

FIG. 10.4. Attic Geometric Krater, *Lamentation and Procession of Chariots* (middle to late 8th century BC). National Museum, Athens.

principles of perspective. But these early forms of projective space were still supplemented by topological concepts of space emphasizing the outline and contour of individual objects. Although there is much debate about the matter (e.g., Ivins, 1946; Richter, 1970; White, 1967/1972), it seems most probable that, whereas Greek artists were interested in naturalistic representation, they achieved only an intuitive or empirical (visual) conception of perspective that was based on the visual appearance

FIG. 10.5. Apulia Krater, *Iphigeneia and Orestes in the Land of Taurians* (4th century, B.C.). National Museum, Naples. Alinari/Art Resource, New York.

of an individual object without a unified and integrated (or operational) conception of space. More advanced concepts of projective space, including the development of linear perspective with a central vanishing point that systematically coordinates all objects within a precisely defined and quantitatively organized context, did not develop until the Renaissance.

The bold innovation in Greek art of depicting objects as they are experienced visually occurred simultaneously with other basic changes in Greek culture, philosophy, and science. All these developments in art, science, and philosophy were expressions of the increased emphasis on individualism and the dignity of man in Greek society. Greek artists beginning around the late 6th century B.C., for example, for the first time in the history of Western civilization began to sign their works (Kris & Kurz, 1934/1979).

As in art, Greek cosmology had no unified conception of the relations among objects. In Greek science, the conception of the universe was a system of 55 bounded, separate, independent, nested orbs. The transition from the Egyptian anthropomorphic conception of the universe to the Greek conception of a system of independent nested orbs was an elaboration of a cosmology based upon the experience and perception of an unmoving earth around which all other celestial bodies revolve. Although this rational naturalism of Classic Greece emerged from magical and mythical views, it rejected the animism and anthropomorphism of earlier cosmological conceptions and developed a consistent theory of planetary and stellar movement in terms of observable natural phenomena. But the Greek conception of the universe was still geocentric. Aristotle did not have an organized and coordinated concept of space but rather emphasized the boundary or container of separate individual bodies contained in independent crystalline orbs, organized primarily along a polarized vertical directionality from the earth (Woodbridge, 1965). Aristotle was not concerned about a unified conception of space but about properties inherent to each body and its specific and independent orb.

Based on a preoperational mode and utilizing essentially topological concepts of space, Aristotle was able to account for the gross structure of his geocentric universe—the relative dispositions of earth, planets, and stars, located in successively larger crystalline orbs each more distant from the earth, as well as everyday observations such as rocks (and apples) falling, smoke rising, clay eventually falling to the bottom of a once turbid mixture, and so forth. In Greek cosmology, space and time do not exist independent of bodies; according to Woodbridge (1965), space for Aristotle was "only the fixation of the boundaries of the bodies" (p. 57). The universe was conceived of as an object somehow bounded, contained, and existent only in contrast to an undefined chaos or void beyond the outermost shell. Thus, Egyptian cosmology and later Aristotle's concept of place, like the representation of objects in art, emphasize the boundary or surface of objects in isolation and the demarcation between individual bodies or between body and nonbody.

Aristotle's worldview, like the predominant mode of artistic representation, was essentially qualitative and descriptive and lacked a quantified, organized metric system. Whereas concepts of space in Greek art and science were based on objects in isolation without a unified conception of space, objects were compared and contrasted, one to another in a comparative, qualitative order. Thus, the basic mathematical structure in Greek science and art was an elaboration and extension of the ordinal scaling that emerged in Egyptian civilization.

The limited unity of individual forms qualitatively represented in an embedding context of space that was achieved intuitively in Antiquity was partially lost, however, in the *Middle Ages*. Representations returned to a primary emphasis on the contour and boundaries of isolated flattened forms. As indicated in Fig. 10.6, individual features are differentiated to some degree, in tall and slender Byzantine figures with powerful expressive grandeur. But basically the isolated individual figures have a fixed, stereotyped, solemn frontal image with uniformly defined bodies and faces. A sense of time and space is excluded to emphasize regal, divine, eternal qualities. Art in the Middle Ages lacked an interest in the representation of depth and perspective, and waves of iconoclasm demanded the destruction of human forms that violated the biblical commandment against graven images. Thus, some art historians view the Middle Ages as a regressive period in which the realistic representation of idealized forms within a general context of space achieved in Classical art was replaced by highly stylized representations with primarily religious connotations. Progress was considered to have begun once again only when there was a revival of the classical forms of Antiquity in the late Middle Ages. Byzantine art throughout the Middle Ages occasionally retained a number of the characteristics and concepts of Antiquity, including the residuals of stage space. Also, throughout the Middle Ages there were periods of recurrent interest in the naturalistic representation of the human form when the prohibitions of the Second Commandment were relaxed. Thus, although the human form was often

FIG. 10.6. San Vitale Mosaics, *Justinian and Twelve Members of His Court* (6th century). Ravenna, Italy. Alinari/Art Resource, New York.

represented as flat and in isolation, there were notable exceptions when the human forms were represented as substantial, corporeal, and realistic. The lack of interest in the representation of spatial depth and perspective in the Middle Ages, in fact, may have facilitated the fuller development of the representation of the human figure. It is even argued by some art historians (e.g., Bunim, 1940; Panofsky, 1924/1925) that the process in the Middle Ages of reducing the optical stage space of Antiquity to a flat, homogeneous surface that had a common unity with the figures was, in fact, an essential step in relinquishing the more limited, intuitive understanding of perspective achieved around the representation of each object in isolation during Antiquity. These art historians argue that the radical renunciation of all spatial illusion and perspective in the Middle Ages may have actually facilitated the discovery of the more comprehensive concepts of linear perspective that was applicable to all objects within a spatial context. The rediscovery of elements of classical stage space during the various renaissances from the 9th to the 14th century and the various revivals of interest in representing the human form during the Middle Ages made it possible to discover that the same visual laws could be applied to the representation of figures as well as to the space that contained the figures. This was the groundwork necessary for the development of a conception of space as homogeneous, continuous, isotropic, and infinite—the basis for the discovery of the rules of linear perspective. Giotto, early in the 14th century, expressed this new conception of space in naturalistic representations of interacting figures that are solid, substantial, and dimensional (see Fig. 10.7). Figures have an inherent volume as do the architectural structures that extend in space and enclose the human figures. The general relationship established between distance and relative size creates a sense that one is observing a segment of nature and an actual scene (Blatt, in press).

The Renaissance introduced a major extension of the Greek intuitive and comparative (ordinal) representation of distance in space by establishing a new and precise mathematical specification for the organization of space (an operational mode of representation). With the development of concepts of linear perspective, objects were placed in relation to one another within an enclosing spatial context, organized around a unifying reference point. The development of linear perspective marked a shift from an intuitive qualitative mode of representation based on visual experience and theory, to a precise, quantitative mode of representation based on the mathematical specification of the organization of space and how it should be represented on a two-dimensional surface. In both Classical Antiquity and the Renaissance, artists attempted to present objects as they appeared to the viewer. In Antiquity this was done intuitively, based on the visual experience of how each object appeared to a viewer as a separate entity in finite,

FIG. 10.7. Giotto, *Meeting of Joachim and Anna* (c. 1305). Arena Chapel, Padua. Alinari/Art Resource, New York.

nonhomogeneous space. But in the Renaissance, perspective was based on a comprehensive geometric system; all objects were systematically represented in relation to one another, organized around a defined, unifying reference point in infinite, continuous, homogeneous, and isotropic space. Linear perspective initially occurred primarily in symmetrical, pyramidal compositions. Leonardo's *Last Supper* (Fig. 10.8) is a fully integrated composition that utilizes linear perspective with a common vanishing point for both the figures and the background. This pyramidal composition places Christ at the vanishing point, with a horizontal, frontally oriented table and background wall supporting the centrality of Christ and creating a symmetrically balanced, harmonious composition. Light is from a single source, bright and uniform through the entire foreground.

Preoccupation with the development of linear perspective continued throughout the Renaissance. The development of linear perspective reached a culmination in art in the late 15th and early 16th centuries. Further investigation of the principles of perspective, however, continued in art into the 16th and 17th centuries, and in mathematics and geometry even into the 18th and 19th centuries. It was a long and complicated process to develop fully the principles of linear perspective with an

FIG. 10.8. Leonardo da Vinci, *Last Supper* (c. 1495–1498). Santa Maria delle Grazei, Milan. Alinari/Art Resource, New York.

identity of structure and reciprocal relations among all points, directions, and distances in infinite, homogeneous space.

In developmental psychological terms, the mode of representation in Renaissance art involved a progression from a preoperational, perceptual, intuitive mode to the beginning phases of an operational mode of representation. The new quantitative coordination of dimensions in linear perspective allowed for systematic transformation, reversibility, and conservation within a system of mathematical operations. Objects could be represented in different ways and at different points in space and still maintain their basic identity. At this operational level there is an understanding of the interrelationships among all parts within a basic unity. Each part can maintain its uniqueness and still be part of a complex, integrated totality. This quantitative conception of space that allowed for variations and transformations within a basic unity expressed the Renaissance ideals of harmony, order, and regularity.

The development of an operational mode of representation in the Renaissance, however, marks only the beginning of conceptual or operational modes of representation in art. Renaissance representations are operational or symbolic (Panofsky, 1924/1925) because they involve the coordination of several dimensions with the potential for transformation, reversibility, and conservation. They are only the beginning of an operational or symbolic mode of representation, however, because they deal primarily with transformation of the external manifest form and features of objects. Thus, in terms of developmental psychological principles, they are at the level of concrete operations.

The discovery of the central vanishing point for the representation of recession in depth and for constructing integrated and coherent compositions in art coincided with controversies in natural philosophy about the earth as the center of the solar system and the debates about the infinity of the universe. Developments in Renaissance and Baroque science and cosmology, like the development of linear perspective in art, was part of an evolving new conception of space as homogeneous, isotropic, and infinite (Ivins, 1946; Panofsky, 1924/1925).

The Renaissance, beginning with Alberti in art (1435) and Cusanus in theology (1433) marked the beginning of a new mathematical mode of artistic and scientific thought. The structure of measurement and scaling in Renaissance art and science moved from an intuitive, comparative, qualitative, ordinal ranking of objects to a quantitative interval scale in which there was an equivalence of scale values and of all points and directions in space, organized around a unifying reference point. The geometric rules for linear perspective involved issues identical in structure to the debate about the conception of infinite space in natural science and the development of the mathematics of a spatial coordinate system (Blatt & Blatt, 1984). The transition from an Aristotelian–Ptolemaic to a Copernican cosmology, like the development of linear perspective, depended on utilizing abstract mathematical principles to demonstrate the superiority of the conception of heliocentric orbits around the sun over the direct, sensory, geocentric experiences of an immobile earth. With subsequent elaboration of the Copernican system by Tycho Brahe, Kepler, Galileo, and Newton, cosmological concepts became less concrete and literal and increasingly began to utilize more mathematical, conceptual, and symbolic analyses (Butterfield, 1957). The development of linear perspective and the Copernican revolution were both part of a major shift in conceptual structure to an operational, coordinated, quantitative mode based on interval scaling (Stevens, 1951) that reached its culmination in the mathematical formulations of René Descartes and Isaac Newton.

Mannerism and the Baroque were periods of art that experimented with the precise balance and organization of space that had been achieved in the Renaissance. Artists sought to find new and expanded ways for representing volume and depth. Perspective was expressed in Renaissance art primarily in symmetrical, pyramidal compositions with the vanishing point located on the horizon in the center of the canvas (see Fig. 10.8). Beginning in Mannerism and the Baroque, however, concepts of linear perspective were extended to diagonal compositions (Arnheim, 1954/ 1974). The shift of the vanishing point from the center to the side of a composition allowed for a fuller representation of recession into deep space. The use of the diagonal, according to developmental psychological theory and research, is an important aspect of advanced concepts of projective space (Dolle, Bataillard, & Lacroix, 1974–1975; Olson, 1970). Tintoretto's *Last Supper* (Fig. 10.9), in contrast to Leonardo's (Fig. 10.8), is full of depth and tension. The vanishing point has been shifted from the center to the side of the composition. The diagonal composition creates a dynamic sense of depth and excitement that is enhanced by differentiated use of deep contrasts of light and dark. The diagonal composition and the dramatic use of light and shading create a sense of infinite depth and excitement.

Another indication of advances in the development of projective concepts of space in Mannerism and the Baroque was the ability to relinquish topological concepts of space that stress the boundary and contour of objects. The blurring of the boundary between figure and ground (Leonardo's *sfumato*), as well as the development of the diagonal composition and the use of variations of light and dark (*chiaroscuro*), allowed artists in Mannerism and the Baroque to achieve a more open, painterly integration of various parts of the composition (Wölfflin, 1915/1932) and a fuller representation of volume and depth in near as

FIG. 10.9. Tintoretto, *Last Supper* (1592–1594). S. Gieorgio Maggiore, Venice. Alinari/Art Resource, New York.

well as distant space. These new dimensions in art (diagonal compositions, the use of *sfumato*, and the contrasts of light and dark in *chiaroscuro*)
not only allowed for a fuller recession into space, but they also enabled
artists to create a sense of tension (Arnheim, 1954/1974) and achieve a
highly dramatic effect. At first, intense, focused, oblique rays of light
enhanced the representation of volume and depth and created an
emotional excitement. Later, nuances of light and shadow added to this
emotional intensity. Rembrandt, like Caravaggio, increasingly used light
to create a dramatic intensity and excitement about an event of
extraordinary importance. Rembrandt used chiaroscuro in increasingly
subtle ways to represent affective experiences and feeling tones that gave
his work an emotional intensity. Chiaroscuro enabled Rembrandt to create
powerful emotional expression of particular individuals at very specific
moments that stood in marked contrast to the posed attitudes of idealized
and universal classical figures in Renaissance painting (see Fig. 10.10).

In both Greco–Roman intuitive perspective and Renaissance linear
perspective, the role of the individual spectator was paramount. The
development of concepts of perspective in each of these epochs was
congruent with the basic humanism that pervaded these societies. The
decline in emphasis on topological concepts of space in Baroque art with
the increased merging of parts and the use of spatial voids and advanced
concepts of projective space are further evidence, according to Meyer

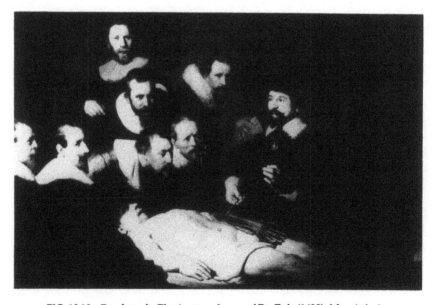

FIG. 10.10. Rembrandt, *The Anatomy Lesson of Dr. Tulp* (1632). Mauritshuis,
The Hague.

Schapiro (1953), of the increased role of the knowing, self-reflective subject (Jacobson, 1964; Schafer, 1968) as a major constituting factor in the perception and representation of Baroque art (Alpers, 1983).

The representation of subjective experiences that began in Classical and Renaissance art was extended in Baroque art, not only in the representation of depth in near, distant, and infinite space but also in the representation of subtle emotional experiences. Mannerist and Baroque art no longer represented idealized, universal figures in perfect harmony and balance as had been done in Classical Antiquity and the Renaissance but rather represented unique individuals in particular situations, at special moments, under specific conditions. These changes in the mode of representation in Baroque art were based on an increased appreciation of the individual in understanding nature. The individual defines a unique position, a stable reference point for organizing personal experiences (Blatt, 1983). The appreciation of the pivotal role of the individual was not only essential for the development of linear perspective but also for appreciating the important role of personal experiences (including meaning, emotion, and feelings) for understanding nature.

The simultaneous interest in the representation of an integrated conception of space and of subtle and profound subjective, inner experiences in Baroque art had its parallel in Baroque science and philosophy. As Lovejoy (1936/1964) pointed out, the Copernican formulation of a heliocentric rather than a geocentric universe elevated the conception of man—individuals on earth were no longer in a lowly debased position at the bottom of the universe but rather occupied a position equivalent to any other location in space. Thus, it is probably no coincidence that Descartes, the inventor of coordinate geometry built around a single, unifying reference point, was also preoccupied with a search for a fixed, immovable "Archimedean point," his hope to "discover the one thing that is certain and indubitable." And Descartes goes on directly, of course, to establish his own existence and personal experiences as that certain, indubitable reference point.

Like the increased fascination with inner form and experiences in Baroque art, Baroque science was also interested in powerful inner processes and structure that determine outer form and action, such as magnetism, electricity, heat, optics, light, color, the composition and structure of matter, the dynamics of motion, and the elasticity of air in the interaction of temperature, pressure, and volume. These early attempts to understand inner processes and structures in Baroque science were the prologue for the later development of molecular theory (Hall, 1954/1966). The extensive elaboration of subjective, inner experiences of affect and emotion in Baroque art and the understanding of inner processes in Baroque science indicate a move beyond the concrete operational mode for representing external manifest form to an emerging interest in representing more internal, abstract, formal dimensions.

Impressionism was an extension of the representation of subjective experiences and inner form developed in Baroque art. Impressionist artists subordinated an interest in the manifest external form of objects and concentrated instead on representing the basic constituents of visual experience. In this way they attempted to capture the inner form of nature in subtle and detailed nuances of visual experiences of light and color. The impressionists were able to relinquish a concern with manifest form and the overall configuration of an object because of the constancy, reversibility, and conservation that had been achieved in the representation of manifest form in linear perspective during the Renaissance and the Baroque. By overcoming the pull toward representing concrete manifest form, Impressionism made a major step in the search for representing more abstract inner dimensions. The form of objects and of space were dissected into individual flecks of light and color—into the constituent elements of visual experience, independent of the meaning of objects and their context. Objects were no longer represented by their manifest external form but now in terms of fundamental subjective visual experiences at a very particular moment.

The *Postimpressionists* continued the search for ways of representing inner form and structure. In addition to concentrating on dissected elements of light and color, the Postimpressionists sought to represent the intrinsic structural properties of objects as they are expressed in fundamental geometric forms. Cézanne, for example, considered geometric forms the essence of nature and believed that principles of linear perspective had to be violated to some degree to capture this basic inherent structure. Color was considered independent of the object and became an autonomous value in its own right, and objects were transformed into complex combinations of fundamental geometric forms. It is important to note that Cézanne's interest in basic geometric patterns was accomplished with minimal emphasis on the contour or boundary of objects. Objects tended to merge and there was continuity between objects and the surrounding space. Cézanne emphasized geometric structure and tectonics, supplemented by a "modulation" of color to achieve volume and a substantiality of form. He was actively concerned with the geometric structure of space and tried to reduce forms to their basic geometric elements—the cylinder, cone, and sphere. Recession into deep space was often closed off and the canons of linear perspective violated to some degree. To emphasize basic geometric forms, a table was partially rotated on its axis and appears to slope toward the observer, with the objects about to fall to the floor (see Fig. 10.11). Cézanne's representation of inherent, basic, natural, geometric forms provided the

FIG. 10.11. Cézanne, *The Basket of Apples*, oil on canvas, 65.5 × 81.3 cm (1895). The Art Institute of Chicago, Helen Birch Bartlett Memorial Collection. Photograph © 1993, The Art Institute of Chicago. All rights reserved.

basis for Cubism and the subsequent interest in the geometric and the abstract in modern art.

The emphasis in art on inner structure, beginning in the Baroque and more fully expressed in Impressionism and Postimpressionism, was structurally similar to changes occurring at that time in science in a shift from macro to micromechanical models. More manifest features of systems, such as pressure, volume, and temperature that had been articulated in 17th-century Baroque science, began to be defined as functions of internal invisible constructs such as particle number and speed. Chemical and physical properties became a function of an internal *quantitative* measure—atomic weight. Thus, both art and science became increasingly free of the manifest, concrete features of nature that had been central in art with the development of linear perspective and in the scientific concepts of Newtonian mechanics. Both art and science began to explore more fully aspects of inner structure that underlay manifest form.

In the late 19th century, some of the Postimpressionists relinquished a commitment to the techniques of linear perspective and Euclidean concepts of space and began to experiment with new modes of representation that were similar in conceptual structure to the non-Euclidean forms of geometry that had been developing in mathematics since about

1840. Van Gogh was interested in intrinsic geometric form as the internal structure of nature. He was especially concerned about perspective and recession into space and often used exaggerated orthogonals and a steeply inclined foreground plane to create a recession into deep space. Heelan (1972) commented that van Gogh's forms and his unusual perspective system are not constructed according to Euclidean rules but rather are based on a non-Euclidean hyperbolic geometry deriving from a strictly binocular visual representation of depth and distance. Heelan's analysis of van Gogh's *Bedroom at Arles* indicates that the apparent nonsystematic representation of perspective is actually a unified representation based on a systematic hyperbolic non-Euclidean geometry. Van Gogh experimented with representations based on hyperbolic, curvilinear concepts of space (Heelan, 1972) in which near space protrudes in a convex bulge toward the observer; distant space becomes concave and the differentiation of depth gradually diminishes with distance (see Fig. 10.12). This new mode of representation based on non-Euclidean, hyperbolic spatial concepts has been interpreted by Heelan (1972) as an expression of "lived space" in which qualitative and quantitative spatial distinctions are different from the equal intervals of rectilinear Euclidean space in linear perspective. In hyperbolic space the observer becomes an even more integral part of the spatial field than the arbitrary point selected as the fixed perspectival reference point. The representation of space is defined in reference to location, movement, and experiences of a participant–observer. Thus, the shift from rectilinear Euclidean to hyperbolic concepts of space not only involves a fundamental change in the basic structure of space but also a fundamental change in the concept of scaling and measurement. The representation of space is no longer based on the equal intervals of a coordinate geometry established from an arbitrarily selected and defined fixed reference point (interval scaling) but is now based on experientially and numerically relevant reference points and scale values (ratio scaling).

The emphasis on inner form and basic geometric structure in postimpressionist art was critical for the subsequent development of modern art, most immediately evident in the development of Cubism. *Cubism* continued the independence from the constraints of the manifest form of objects and extended the search for representing inner form and geometric structure. Cézanne's emphasis on geometric forms and van Gogh's unique form of perspective encouraged Braque and Picasso to represent an object from multiple perspectives to achieve a more comprehensive conception of nature. Cubist artists sought to represent simultaneously aspects of the manifest features as well as the abstract, intrinsic, geometric forms of an object. This provided a way to penetrate even further the seemingly closed manifest form of objects to represent more fully their internal structure (see Fig. 10.13). Cubism replaced linear perspective with a new method

FIG. 10.12.   Van Gogh, *Bedroom at Arles* (1888). National Museum, Amsterdam.

internal structure (see Fig. 10.13). Cubism replaced linear perspective with a new method of pictorial representation that enabled artists to integrate what they knew about an object with what they saw. Painting was no longer bound to a realistic representation from an arbitrarily selected, single, fixed perspective, and objects were no longer defined by the surface and boundaries of closed forms. The representation of multiple perspectives in Cubism was a natural extension of linear perspective that represented objects from a unitary, fixed conception of reality.

The Cubists emphasized that experiences are multifaceted and multidimensional, and that one must identify the basic structure of nature beneath surface appearance. Cubism was another expression of the new, emerging conception of space that recognized that a single, arbitrary view of nature is limited and that nature has to be considered from multiple perspectives. In this process, Cubists became increasingly aware of the individual's role in constructing definitions of nature, and they introduced into art a fuller self-reflective awareness about the act of painting. Thus, in many ways Cubism involved a further transition to a more symbolic or formal mode of representation—from an art of perception and mimesis to an art of conception and abstraction. Cubism, beginning in 1908, shortly after Einstein's initial contributions to physics in 1905 and Minkowski's 1908

FIG. 10.13. Braque, *Fishing Boats* (1909). The Museum of Fine Arts, Houston, John A. & Audrey Jones Beck Collection.

discussion of the space–time continuum, opened the Modern Epoch in art by relinquishing linear perspective and seeking instead to represent both the external form and inner structure of objects and space from equally relevant multiple perspectives. The attempt to represent multiple perspectives in art was structurally similar to the attempts in relativity theory to define a unified field theory equally valid for all frames of reference.

Postimpressionism and Cubism extended the topological and projective-Euclidean concepts of space utilized in prior periods to include the emerging, non-Euclidean, Riemannian concepts of space. Subsequent to Cubism, artists sought to go beyond representations based on the three Euclidean–Cartesian spatial coordinates and rectilinear concepts of space by including a temporal dimension and establishing artistic representations within a relativistic spatiotemporal field. Various attempts have been made in art to represent a fourfold spatiotemporal field. By constructing a series of successive images over time or by creating conditions in which the experiencing of the work of art is partly a function of the position and movement of the observer, artists have tried to extend the simultaneous representation of multiple perspectives of Cubism by introducing concepts of the space–time field and the principles of uncertainty and indeterminacy into the representational process in art. Duchamp, for example, used the multiple facets of Cubism to try to capture the sequential stages of action as a figure progresses through a succession of evolving movements. Duchamp, through a coordinated series of transformations of an object in motion, sought to introduce a temporal dimension into painting (see Fig. 10.14). Agam, in his optic and kinetic art, introduced temporal elements of sequence, progression, and continuity into painting by demanding that the observer view the painting by moving through a series of different positions. By a complex coordination of abstract geometric forms with color, Agam created a spatiotemporal field whereby the painting is experienced sequentially from an infinite array of equally valid perspectives. The viewer is an integral part of the spatiotemporal field; the painting can be defined only in relation to the observer and his or her movement around the work. The activity of the spectator, in interaction with the object, creates a sense of time and an unending series of actual and potential transformations. The picture space is extended to include the viewer, thereby creating a relativistic, indeterminate, infinite, spatiotemporal field (see Fig. 10.15).

The interest of art and science in inner form and structure, in the use of non-Euclidean concepts of space, and the appreciation of a relativistic spatiotemporal field are all expressions of a transition from a concrete operational mode of representation to a more formal, abstract, operational level. This transition involves not only greater abstraction but also a shift from an interest in a system of relationships to a consideration of the relations among systems of relationships (Piaget & Inhelder, 1948/1967). These changes in art and science also involved a transition from a system of measurement based on an arbitrary reference point (an interval scale) to a quantitative system of measurement and scaling based on experientially and numerically relevant reference points that create an equality of ratios in addition to an equality of intervals (a ratio scale).

Future directions in art will probably include further attempts to create a relativistic, spatiotemporal field in which there is a complex transaction

FIG. 10.14. Duchamp, *Nude Descending a Staircase, No. 2* (1912). Philadelphia Museum of Art, The Louise & Walter Arensberg Collection.

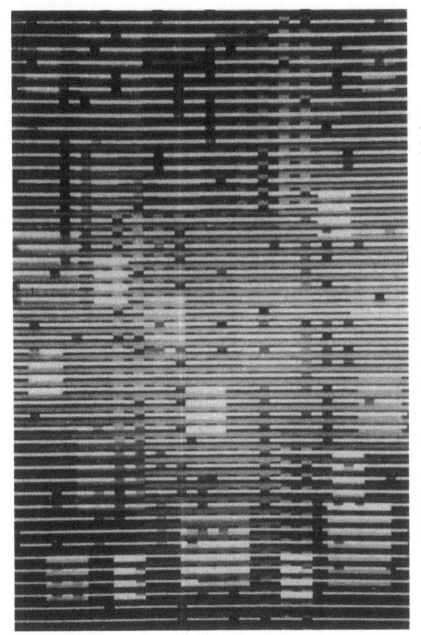

FIG. 10.15. Agam, *Transparent Rhythms II* (1967–1968). Hirshhorn Museum and Sculpture Garden, Smithsonian Institution, gift of Joseph H. Hirshhorn, 1972. Photograph by Lee Stalsworth.

221

will probably also involve integrating the formal, abstract mode of representation of inner form and structure with earlier modes of representations, such as the representation of manifest form, which could serve to enrich artistic representations and diminish the dehumanization (Ortega y Gasset, 1925/1972) inherent in the more purely abstract, formal mode of representation. But it is difficult to appreciate accurately historical trends within one's contemporary culture. We can understand our culture only in terms of available concepts, and it is difficult to anticipate subsequent development of new modes of representation beyond those currently available within our cultural heritage. We can only be certain that future generations, as in prior centuries, will continue a basic developmental progression in art as well as in science toward increasing differentiation, articulation, and integration.

No development in art and science can be regarded as final—art and science are open, unfinished, always alterable, developmental processes (Hauser, 1953/1959). Changes in modes of representation in art and in science will continue to be interrelated because they are both expressions of revisions in the basic cognitive structure with which we understand our universe. Art and science, as well as other disciplines, are parallel and interrelated expressions of the cognitive structure predominant in the particular cultural epoch. New cognitive constructs will evolve in our culture, and they will be expressed simultaneously in the multiple cognitive endeavors of the society, including art and science.

In summary, an analysis of the development of the modes of representing the form of objects and of space in the history of art and science indicates that the developmental theories of Piaget and Werner define a fundamental genetic epistemology that provides valuable guidelines for understanding both diachronic and synchronic dimensions of cultural development. In the past decade there have been a number of attempts to examine the philosophical assumptions of Piaget's genetic epistemology (e.g., Kitchener, 1986) and to apply these concepts in diverse areas such as the history of art (e.g., Blatt & Blatt, 1984; Edgerton, 1975; Gablik, 1976) and the history of science (e.g., Blatt & Blatt, 1984; Gruber, 1981; Holton, 1973, 1978; Miller, 1984/1986), to developments in psychological research and theory (e.g., Altman & Rogoff, 1987; Pepper, 1942/1961), to the study of moral development in medieval European legal and social institutions (Radding, 1986), to the study of music (Serafin, 1988), and to the development of modes of perception and communication across a wide range of cultural epochs (Lowe, 1982). These various investigations indicate that the assumptions of Piaget's genetic epistemology are consistent with assumptions of contemporary philosophy of science (Kitchener, 1986), and that these concepts are useful in describing and evaluating synchronic and diachronic patterns of change in multiple facets of cultural development. Miller (1984/1986), for example, in a detailed study of 19th- and 20th-century science, concludes that the history of scientific thought can be viewed as a series of hierarchical levels defined by Piaget's genetic epistemology. Altman and Rogoff (1987) evaluate the development of psychological analysis as proceeding from the study of isolated traits, to the study of interactions, to the investigation of organismic integration and complex transactions. And I believe this type of analysis can be applied in other areas of cultural development such as sculpture and architecture, and with various other structural dimensions such as the development of concepts of time in music, poetry, and narration.

Whereas concepts of genetic epistemology have been helpful in describing progressions in many facets of cultural development, these concepts appear to be less useful in understanding the dynamic-causative factors that create the external conditions that allow for change in epistemological structures (e.g., Antal, 1953; Hauser, 1951/1960). Concepts of genetic epistemology are most useful for understanding the inherent or internal dimensions involved in the transformation of cultural epistemes, but these concepts provide relatively little insight into the ways in which socioeconomic and political factors create the conditions for cultural change.

It is important to recognize that concepts of genetic epistemology themselves undoubtedly also have their own developmental history. Our concepts of genetic epistemology reflect the cultural epistemes predominant in our own cultural tradition. Thus, although these concepts provide understanding of the transformation of cognitive structures in prior cultural epochs, we must be aware of the distortions that our current concepts place on our view of prior traditions as well as accept the limitations that our contemporary views place on our capacity to predict future transformations. We, like prior generations, can only be certain that our understanding of nature and of ourselves will continue to become increasingly differentiated, articulated, and integrated.

In discussing concepts of genetic epistemology, it is also important not to confuse the realms of discourse in the assessment of the predominant cognitive mode of a cultural epoch with evaluations of the functioning of given individuals within the culture's level of cognitive organization. The predominant epistemological structure indicates the conceptual tools that are available within a culture; thus they define the limits within which individuals can operate within that culture. The level of organization of the predominant epistemes defines where a culture is in terms of the vertical decalage of cultural development; individual functioning ranges horizontally across this level. Creative individuals operate at various points across this horizontal decalage, often contributing to further elaboration of the contemporary cultural episteme through the assimilation of new experiences and techniques into the predominant cognitive structures. But some exceptional individuals with extraordinary talent, under appropriate social, economic, and political conditions (Berger & Luckmann, 1966), sense anomalies and inconsistencies and demand significant revisions of the predominant cultural episteme (Kuhn, 1962/1970), forcing a major accommodation or revision of the predominant cognitive structure. This revision of the predominant cognitive structure marks the origination of a new developmental level in the vertical decalage of cultural epistemes. We then can become aware of the potential within each of us to comprehend nature and ourselves in an even more differentiated, articulated, integrated, and comprehensive fashion.

REFERENCES

Alpers, S. (1983). *The art of describing: Dutch art in the seventeenth century.* Chicago: University of Chicago Press.

Altman, I., & Rogoff, B. (1987). World views in psychology: Interactional, organismic and transactional perspectives. In D. Stokols & I. Altman (Eds.), *Handbook of environmental psychology* (pp. 1–40). New York: Wiley.

Antal, F. (1953). Reflections on classicism and romanticism. *Burlington Magazine, 96,* 159.

Arnheim, R. (1974). *Art and visual perception: A psychology of the creative eye.* Berkeley: University of California Press. (Original work published 1954)

Berger, P. L., & Luckmann, T. (1966). *The social construction of reality.* New York: Doubleday.

Blatt, S. J. (1983). Narcissism and egocentrism in concepts in individual and cultural development. *Psychoanalysis and Contemporary Thought, 6,* 291–303.

Blatt, S. J. (in press). A psychoanalytic appreciation of Giotto's mode of artistic representation and its implications for Renaissance art and science. *The Psychoanalytic Study of the Child.*

Blatt, S. J., & Blatt, E. S. (1984). *Continuity and change in art: The development of modes of representation.* Hillsdale, NJ: Lawrence Erlbaum Associates.

Brunswik, E. (1959). Ontogenetic and other developmental parallels to the history of science. In H. M. Evans (Ed.), *Men and moments in the history of science.* Seattle: University of Washington Press.

Bunim, M. (1940). *Space in medieval painting and forerunners of perspective.* New York: Columbia University Press.

Butterfield, H. (1957). *The origins of modern science: 1300–1800.* New York: Free Press.

Descartes, R. (1968). *Discourse on method and the mediations.* (F. E. Sutcliffe, Trans.). New York: Penguin.

Dolle, J. M., Bataillard, A., & Lacroix, F. (1974/1975). Apprentissage operatoire de la representation graphique d'une figure volumetrique [operative apprenticeship of the graphic representation of a volumetric figure]. *Bulletin de Psychologie, 78,* 956–964.

Edgerton, S. Y., Jr. (1975). *The Renaissance rediscovery of linear perspective.* New York: Basic.

Freud, S. (1964). Moses and Monotheism. *Standard edition, 23.* London: Hogarth. (Original work published 1939)

Gablik, S. (1976). *Progress in art.* London: Thames & Hudson.

Gombrich, E. H. (1960). *Art and illusion: A study in the psychology of pictorial representation.* New York: Pantheon.

Gruber, H. E. (1981). *Darwin on man.* Chicago: University of Chicago Press.

Hall, A. R. (1966). *Scientific revolution: 1500–1800.* New York: Beacon. (Original work published 1954)

Hauser, A. (1960). The social history of art (S. Goodman & A. Hauser, Trans.) (4 vols.). New York: Vintage. (Original work published 1951)

Hauser, A. (1959). *The philosophy of art history.* New York: Knopf. (Original work published 1953)

Heelan, P. A. (1972). Toward a new analysis of the pictorial space of Vincent Van Gogh. *The Art Bulletin, 54,* 478–492.

Holton, G. (1973). *Thematic origins of scientific thought: Kepler to Einstein.* Cambridge, MA: Harvard University Press.

Holton, G. (1978). Dyonesians, Apollonians, and the scientific imagination. In G. Holton (Ed.), *The scientific imagination: Case studies.* Cambridge, UK: Cambridge University Press.

Ivins, W. M. (1946). *Art and geometry: A study in space intuitions.* Cambridge, MA: Harvard University Press.

Jacobson, E. (1964). *The self and the object world.* New York: International Universities Press.

Jammer, M. (1969). *Concepts of space: The history of theories of space in physics.* Cambridge, MA: Harvard University Press. (Original work published 1954)

Janson, H. W. (1961). Introduction to R. Bernheimer, *The nature of representation: A phenomenological inquiry.* New York: New York University Press.

Kitchener, R. F. (1986). *Piaget's theory of knowledge: Genetic epistemology and scientific reason.* New Haven, CT: Yale University Press.

Kris, E., & Kurz, O. (1979). *Legend, myth and magic in the image of the artist: An historical experiment.* New Haven, CT: Yale University Press. (Original work published 1934)

Kuhn, T. (1970). *The structure of scientific revolutions* (Revised ed.). Chicago: University of Chicago Press. (Original work published 1962)

Laurendeau, M., & Pinard, A. (1970). *The development of the concept of space in the child.* New York: International Universities Press.

Lovejoy, A. O. (1964). *The great chain of being.* Cambridge, MA: Harvard University Press. (Original work published 1936)

Lowe, D. M. (1982). *History of bourgeois perception.* Chicago: University of Chicago Press.

Miller, A. I. (1984/1986). *Imagery in scientific thought.* Cambridge: MIT Press.

Modell, A. (1968). *Object love and reality: An introduction to a psychoanalytic theory of object relations.* New York: International Universities Press.

Olson, D. (1970). *Cognitive development: The child's acquisition of diagonality.* New York: Academic Press.

Ortega y Gasset, J. (1972). The dehumanization of art. In A. Brown (Trans.), *Velázquez, Goya, and the dehumanization of art.* New York: Norton. (Original work published 1925)

Panofsky, E. (1924/1925). Die perspektive als "symbolische form." *Vortrage der Bibliothek Warburg* (pp. 258–330). Leipzig & Berlin.

Pepper, S. C. (1961). *World hypotheses: A study in evidence.* Berkeley: University of California Press. (Original work published 1942)

Piaget, J., & Inhelder, B. (1967). *The child's conception of space* (F. J. Langdon & J. L. Lunzer, Trans.). New York: Norton.

Radding, C. (1986). *A world made by men: Cognition and society* (pp. 400–1200). Chapel Hill: University of North Carolina Press.

Richter, G. M. (1970). *Perspective in Greek and Roman art.* New York & London: Phaidon.

Rochlin, G. (1965). *Guilt and discontents: The forces of change.* Boston: Little, Brown.

Schafer, R. (1968). *Aspects of internalization.* New York: International Universities Press.

Schapiro, M. (1953). Style. In A. L. Kroeber (Ed.), *Anthropology today*. Chicago: University of Chicago Press.

Serafin, M. L. (1988). *Music as cognition: The development of thought in sound*. New York: Columbia University Press.

Stevens, S. S. (1951). Mathematics, measurements, and psychophysics. In S. Stevens (Ed.), *Handbook of experimental psychology* (pp. 1–49). New York: Wiley.

White, J. (1972). *The birth and rebirth of pictorial space*. New York: Harper & Row. (Original work published 1967)

Wölfflin, H. (1932). *Principles of art history: The problem of the development of style in later art* (M. D. Hottinger, Trans.). New York: Dover. (Original work published 1915)

Woodbridge, F. J. E. (1965). *Aristotle's vision of nature*. New York: Columbia University Press.

11

Is a Developmental History of Art Possible?

Marx Wartofsky
Bernard M. Baruch College and the Graduate Center
City University of New York

FOREWARNING

The title under which I was originally invited to write, before I received Professor Blatt's chapter, was "What are the applications of the concepts of development to the history of art?" To get under way, I was going to ask four questions: The first question was to be "*What* development?" the second, "Development of *what*?"; the third, "*What* histories of art?"; and the fourth question, "*What* art?" (In the spirit of the Passover Seder, the first one might have been "Why is this developmental history of art different from all other developmental histories of art?" But I blocked that temptation.) After reading Blatt's chapter, I decided to change the title of my chapter to "Is a Developmental History of Art Possible?" But I should disabuse the reader at the outset concerning the new title; it is not to be taken seriously, because the question it raises can be answered trivially: *Yes*. Not only is *a* developmental history of art possible, but any number of such histories is possible. The domain of art history is strewn with the bleached bones and fossil remains of different species of developmental histories of art. In fact, *historicism*—the general view that things can be understood or explained only in terms of one or another rational reconstruction of their historical development or in terms of one or another norm of historical development—has had perhaps its richest and most conceptually sophisticated (as well as its most outrageous and fatuous) expressions in theories of art history. And art history has been

227

characterized in large part by debates, both substantive and methodo-logical, about historicism.[1] Beginning with Vasari's *Lives of the Artists*, through Hegel's paradigmatically historicist *Aesthetics: Lectures on Fine Art*, to Hegel's critic, Burckhardt, and the long list, including Dilthey, Wölfflin, Riegl, Worringer, Dessoir, Dvorak, Warburg, Cassirer, Panofsky, Rafael, and Hauser, among others, there has been a lively and often bitter colloquy on the question of the possibility—or more critically, the validity—of one or another developmental history of art.[2] The appropriate question, therefore, ought *not* to be "Is a developmental history of art possible?" but rather "Is a developmental history of art necessary?"

In recent years, the question of whether such a history of art is to be reconstructed or understood in terms of stages or levels of *cognitive* development has been broached, in such works as Gombrich's (1960) *Art and Illusion* and Gablik's (1977) *Progress in Art* (both of these influenced by Popper's falsificationist model of the growth of knowledge—or better, of the elimination of ignorance—in science, by the method of conjectures and refutations).

Now we have Blatt's proposal, namely that the history of art may usefully be seen as a development of stages of cognitive growth on the model of Piaget's genetic epistemology. Major historical eras of art, or of styles in art, may be periodized in terms of Piagetian cognitive stages: *sensorimotor, intuitive-perceptual, concrete-operational, formal-operational,* and so on. On this view, genetic epistemology represents not only an account of the ontogenetic recapitulation of the cross-cultural phylogenetic sequences in the acquisition of cognitive structures. It serves also as a kind of template—heuristic only, we are cautioned—for the reconstruc-tion of stages of cultural evolution as well. Borrowing freely from developmental psychoanalytic theory, and from Cassirer's theory of symbolic forms, by way of Panofsky, Professor Blatt elaborates a bold, grand, systematic periodization of art historical stages insofar as they

---

[1]Pace Popper. Popper's attack on *Historicism* is an attack on the notion of necessary, overarching laws of history or of historical development, which he rejects in favor of a view of history as ultimately contingent, and of historical knowledge as fallible. I have a more general and more classical view of "historicism" in mind here, which leaves open the question of "laws of history" or of teleology in history, or of any transcendent or immanent ends that history is fated to realize. If Popper's critical use of the term *historicism* had prevailed, I would have had to coin some alternative usage (e.g., *historicalism*, which I once introduced for just this purpose some years ago). But Popper's use hasn't prevailed, and I will continue to take the term in the broad sense I give it here.

[2]For a good recent discussion of the "history of art history," especially on the relations between Panofsky and Wölfflin, Riegl, and Cassirer, among others, see Holly (1984), *Panofsky and the Foundations of Art History*. Blatt (1984) conscientiously recounts the art-historical background also. He also notes there were earlier attempts to interpret art history in terms of developmental theory (e.g., Blatt & Blatt, 1984, pp. 26–32).

bear on one main feature of pictorial representation—the representation of space and of objects. Blatt proposes to show that this developmental sequence of cognitive development in art parallels and is (culturally) concurrent with changes in the theoretical representations of space and of objects in science. And, as if this were not enough, he coordinates these developmental stages in modes of representation with the hierarchical sequence of scales of measurement in Stevens' (1951) canonical schema (nominal, ordinal, cardinal, and ratio).

My initial joy at the boldness of this schematic historicism is mitigated only by my despair over the details. My own penchant for global developmental-historical frameworks runs a close second to Blatt's (which runs a close second to Hegel's, or perhaps more closely to Spencer's, all of which puts me running a weak fourth, at best, to Hegel's lead). This makes me initially sympathetic, or at least open to Blatt's project. What's more, my own project of a historical epistemology (see Wartofsky, 1979, 1987) also proposes a historical (and more problematically, a developmental) thesis on changes in modes of cognition in relation to changes in modes of representation in the arts and sciences, in the context of changing forms of social, technological, and artistic praxis. The question, then, is what kind of developmental history of art may be viable, among the many possible ones that are not. And here, my initial sympathy turns to critique.

My comments here begin with some very brief, relatively abstract and schematic considerations of various concepts of development, from thin to thick. Next, I examine the working out of some of these concepts in Blatt's version of art history as cognitive development and raise some questions about two specific interpretations he offers of stages in this development.

THE VARIETIES OF "DEVELOPMENT"

To speak about "*The* concept of development" is already wildly abstractive. To decide a priori what *development really* means is to presume that there is one, essential, canonical sense of the term, which is then exemplified, like a Platonic form, in all specific cases of development (or of development *proper*, as we might say), other cases being degenerate or misapplied uses of the concept. There is a nagging Platonistic tendency in our use of abstract nouns, which suggests that the term development must have its appropriate definition, or its boundaries, or its semantic field. But it doesn't, as Bernard Kaplan likes to point out. It is what has been called an essentially contestable concept, if one takes it seriously. What we make of it gives form to the domain to which it is applied, picks out certain criterial parameters that we can then designate and say: "What we mean is the development of *that*."

Nevertheless, we can talk about development formally and abstractly, in a number of different ways, as an exercise in conceptual alternatives, recognizing that in each case the abstraction is derived, either tacitly or explicitly, from recognizable domains of its concrete interpretation or from the range of uses that the concept has in our language. Here, I intend no more than to make a few ground-clearing (or ground-cluttering?) distinctions.

In the thinnest sense of the term, we may talk about development simply as one damn thing after another, or as some kind of sequence. Here development means "standing in the relation *next*, or *successor* to something else." That's a degenerate and not very interesting use of the term, in relation to its other and richer uses, but it is common and marks off the weakest sense of the term. If we interpret this "nextness" in terms of time, development then means no more than chronicle, or temporal succession, which, as a notion of development, is still pretty thin. Or we can talk about development as some kind of *change with direction*. This introduces two degrees of complexity: first, that there is not simply one thing *after* or *next* to another, but that the "same thing" *changes*; second, that this change is *directional*, that is, it is not simply an alternation or reciprocation where there is a return from a changed state to the original state, but where each changed state is different from the ones that preceded it, so that a unique ordering is established. Such change with direction needn't be *teleological*, or have an end-state that retroactively orders the series; or even *teleonomic* (i.e., tend toward an end-state as a result of an immanent law-like process or mechanism of change). Change with direction may even be cyclical, in one variant, where the direction is from the beginning to the end of a cycle that then begins again (as in clockwise motion or rotation).

Similarly, any notions of what Aristotle might have called *generation* and *corruption*—coming into being and passing away—any kind of growth process—is directed change in this sense (though organic growth, or even crystal growth, has features that go beyond these characterizations). This way of talking about development is a little thicker than the first concept of mere nextness or succession but is still not very thick.

The notion of development begins to get thicker when development means the kind of directed change or growth in which later states are, as Blatt correctly says, *epigenetic*, that is to say, where changes are cumulatively based on, or result from what preceded, without there being a *telos* or an end toward which they *aim*. The connotations here are that what precedes, in this ordered or directed change, is a condition for what eventuates; the language here is already one of process, of causes or conditions. Indeed, there is, in the notion of cumulative effect, the suggestion of increasing complexity, and the hint of a hierarchical ordering, therefore, where later or "more developed" states "contain" or "incorporate" or "integrate" what preceded them.

It is at this *epigenetic* level of development that one can start speaking of *stages* rather than merely successive *states*, because states need have no connection with each other (external or internal) other than temporal sequence or spatial or qualitative contiguity, in classical Humean fashion, whereas stages connote some causal or conditional relation to each other, in that one results from, or is brought about by another, or is marked off from the other by asymmetrically ordered changes in quality or in comparative degrees of some quality. Here one may also speak of "laws" of development in terms of canonical or epigenetically ordered sequences of such stages, where such sequences are law-like in that they are taken as necessary and universal for all cases in the given domain.

Beyond this there are the still thicker notions of development: from *adaptive* development, as in the contexts of *teleonomy* in biology, to the more full-blown *teleological* notions of development, namely those changes that are defined as end-directed or purposive (whether foreordained consciously, or simply implicit or immanent). And one may suggest, within the epigenetic, adaptive, or teleological modes of development, some further characterization of the ordered changes (e.g., as developing in the direction of greater differentiation, or greater complexity, or of hierarchy, etc.). Indeed, one may introduce, perhaps at the limit, the characterization of development as "dialectical" with all the elaborateness of the Hegelian or Marxian or Piagetian interpretations of dialectical change (e.g., of "determinate negation" or *Aufhebung*; or of the transformation of activity into structure, in objectification; or of quantitative into qualitative changes; or in the notion of levels of integration, and the concomitant notions of the irreducibility of such levels, and of laws appropriate to each such level). At this thick (or fat?) end of the conceptual spectrum, *development* verges on concepts of *emergence* and *evolution*, or even *emergent evolution*. (The literature on this worried topic is so extensive and varied that I forego even a comment here.)

To the innocent eye, it appears that to talk about the application of concepts of development to the history of art we first have to answer the question "*What* development?" and to pick out one or another of these concepts as the appropriate one for that context. But this presumes that we already have some idea of what the subject of this development is (i.e., that there is a *history* of art, or at least a sequence of artworks, or of styles, or of aesthetic forms, or of representational modes), and that this history of sequence has certain features that are theoretically represented best or better by one rather than another concept of development. This presupposes in turn that the history or sequence is something we can "objectively" observe or note, apart from any preconception of its developmental character (i.e., that the history of art is an objective history, that is, that it exists independent of any construals or interpretations of it; that our knowledge of this history—or even of art as having a history—is not itself already "theory laden," i.e., that we haven't preempted our very knowledge of the subject of our interpretation by a tacit interpretive framework that selects just those features of the domain that answer to our questions).

Thus, even to raise the question "*What* development?," it seems we have to have answered the question "*What* history?." Furthermore, we have already surreptitiously raised the question "*What* art?" or "History of *what*?" in considering whether this history of art is a history of styles, or of representational modes, or of artworks, or of aesthetic principles; or of the unfolding of figurative verisimilitude, or of visual Truth, or of the *Kunstwollen* or of the *Weltgeist*; or whether (as in Blatt's case) it is the cognitive development of our understanding of space and of objects, and so on, and so on. In short, we are into the paradox of inquiry raised in Plato's *Meno* (although Socrates dismisses it there as a debater's trick); or, more benignly, into the question of theory-laden observation, which has wreaked so much havoc with traditional logical-empiricist epistemology in the philosophy of science.

If, on the other hand, we distinguish "the history of art *proper*" (i.e., as the objective history of art, what "actually happened") from "art history," as the linguistic reconstruction or narrative account of this "real history," then we may take this metalevel of the art-historical narrative ("art history") as itself our subject matter, critically assessing one such developmental narrative or story against others. Or, indeed, we may eschew any developmental or "historicist" thesis about the history of art as an intellectually redundant frill, or as empty speculation; and, by contrast, take the proper task of the art historian to be the reconstruction of an accurate *chronicle* of what happened in art, and what happened next; in short, to get the facts straight and to make of art history an account of what happened as it actually happened without any interpretation: *wie es eigentlich war*, the way it *really* happened, *an sich*, so to speak. At the other end of the spectrum lie the grander notions that the history of art is simply the outward phenomenon or *Schein* of an internal dialectic of *Geist*, or Spirit, or God's Will, or the Will to Art, or the Will to Power, or something like that; and that it (therefore) has a foreordained and even divine end to which the whole of its previous history leads. Once its telos is attained, then of course we have reached the millennium, and Art is at the end of its History; it has fully realized itself and gone on to do something else: Poetry, Philosophy, Whatever.

This last view (a parody of a Hegelian dialectical history of art) has been articulated most recently by that most unlikely historicist of art history, Arthur Danto (1986). If Danto, a born-again Hegelian, has finally accepted Hegel in these terms (albeit in a peculiar way), it should be even less surprising that Blatt has as well, because, despite Piaget's frequent protestations that his dialectic is not Hegel's, Piaget's schema of cognitive development is certainly compatible with and suspiciously analogous to Hegel's. And because Blatt's developmental history of art is explicitly Piagetian in inspiration, we may at least suggest that it smacks of Hegelianism. For Hegel, the history of art is nothing but the sequence of the increasing liberations of the Spirit from its messy, massy shell, from its encumbrance by matter, as it attains to the fully rational and mature (adult?) world view in which the Absolute Idea comes to complete self-knowledge. Neither Piaget nor Blatt presuppose this kind of preordained end as the limit of cognitive development. (Nor is it clear that Hegel did either, in quite these terms; but it is certainly part of the Hegel folklore that he did.) And Blatt doesn't conclude (as Danto does) that art history has ended, as art turns into philosophy, having reached its Hegelian limits. Nevertheless, there is in Blatt's narrative of art-historical development just that very, very optimistic and lovely developmental notion that the history of art is a march of cognitive progress, a stage-wise realization of human reason in coming to know the world the way it really is, at least in its spatial-objective configurations, or at least insofar as its representational modes come to conform to that most cherished and problematic of Piagetian norms of development, "the adult scientific world-view." The stages of this development in art history neatly fit the (epigenetic) stages of Piagetian cognitive development, from sensorimotor to preoperational to all the rest of it, in stunning coordination with Stevens' four measurement scales, now revealed in their own epigenetic sequence as stages (because each is successively richer in parameters than the previous one).

BLATT: ART HISTORY AS COGNITIVE DEVELOPMENT

Speaking analogously about understanding past social formations, Marx (Karl, remember him?) said, in the *Grundrisse*, that "Human anatomy contains a key to the anatomy of the ape. The intimations of higher development among the subordinate animal species, however, can be understood only after the higher development is already known" (1973, p. 205). That is to say, we can understand past history only from the point of view of the present. We couldn't have predicted this present development from the vantage point of the past. We can only reconstruct it retrospectively. But this suggests that all history (i.e., all narrative historical reconstruction of the past) is Whig history, colored by the interpretive standpoint of its own time and place. There is no privileged standpoint that is itself *outside* history; and worse yet, we are condemned to privilege our own standpoint, our "present," so to speak, because that's the one we have. There is no "view from nowhere," to use Thomas Nagel's striking phrase. The best we can do, perhaps, is to generate (or discover) alternative standpoints in the present as inducements to criticism and open-minded-ness, to the degree that this is possible.

So be it. But one of the problems of Whig history is its selective vision and, therefore, one of the problems with the application of concepts of development to the history of art is the problem of *critical choice* among alternative norms of what will be selected to count *as* art history; or more deeply, what the very idea of a history of art means, or what it would mean to talk about *alternative histories* of art. The presumption is that there is just *one* history of art (i.e., a canonical, linear, and inclusive history of art whose developmental scheme, being the unique one, yields the essential truth about the development of art). Alternatively, we could (and most often do) talk about the development of "Western" or "European" art (tracing this back to the caves at Lascaux, the banks of the Nile, the shores of the Aegean, and on and on, until the category "Western" or "European" is strained beyond limits). But we also talk of Pre-Columbian Art, Asian Art, African Art, and so forth, so that any simple notion of a canonical developmental scheme would depend on finding the *same* "stages" in a universal law of development that is cross- and transcultural. In any case, the kind of history of Western art of which Blatt has given us a *précis* here presents a problem of selection, of focus, of what will count, and of whether there is such a thing as "*the* history of art," or what exactly we mean by "the history of art."

One thing Blatt plainly means to argue is that the history of art is a matter of cognitive evolution: that what we didn't used to get straight we now know how to get straight; that what we didn't used to know how to represent the way it really looks, we now know how to represent the way it really looks, because we've simply gotten better at doing it, having solved the problems that our artistic predecessors hadn't yet solved. In effect, when Giotto is trying to resolve problems of perspectival representation, not yet having arrived at Brunelleschi's or Alberti's solution, he's getting a little closer to the "correct" linear perspective than we were before. When Alberti finally gets the geometry straight and when Brunelleschi and others develop the craft techniques for how to do it, when Leonardo da Vinci teaches us to "do it the way you would if you were working on a pane of glass or the way it looks in the mirror," we then have solved the problem of representing space and objects the way they really look.

What we have here is another historicist theory of art, reading its history as the cognitive evolution of our technological ability to represent the world properly (i.e., to achieve what Danto calls "an optical duplicate of it"). I don't mean to be cynical or disagreeable about all this. I think it is a very powerful idea. And, in fact that idea was the motor that drove the development of West European painting and drawing for several centuries and therefore I am not criticizing it as *having been* an idea of what the development of art should be. In fact, my thesis is that the *development of art took place precisely because this was the dominant idea of what the development of art should be*; and therefore, that the history of art is itself a product of what we conceive its historical direction to be, what we select as its telos. That is to say, a history of art results when the work of art is constructed (by the artist) or reconstructed (by its interpreters) historically, when a culture takes its art as a historical project in accordance with some world view or telos and then creates or understands its art in accordance with this self-conception. This act of historical self-conception creates history. There isn't any history otherwise. Now this is not to say that "history" is not "objective" or is merely a matter of our construal. Rather, it means that, objectively, human activity is historical because it takes itself as deriving from its past, recognized as its genesis, and as directed toward some future that is embodied in the norms of that activity. There isn't any history until our activity—whether in art, science, or politics or love—is constructed (and reconstructed) as historical by a historical consciousness of what we're doing. What I am proposing, then, is that this technical-cognitive evolution of art was in fact a historical project that a certain period—a very long period—of art set for itself. This *particular* project—the project of "optical duplication" of the visible world in painting and drawing (i.e., in two-dimensional representational artifacts)—was given up only when it was taken to be the case that this aim could now be achieved with the camera. Painting and drawing were now freed from their historical project because we had achieved an algorithmic, mechanical technique for doing it with camera lenses and the projection of visual images, photographically.

There is an interesting aside about the abandonment of this embodied theory of art history: The image that the camera forms is in accordance with the rules of linear perspective (and therefore taken to be veridical) because in the development of the camera lens it was required (by the artists using the *camera obscura* as an aid to verisimilitude) that the lens produce an image that would be in accordance with the laws of linear perspective. And it took 300 years to develop these lenses, to "get it right," so to speak. It is no surprise that photographic images look the way paintings did in the Renaissance, because photographic images were technologically evolved in accordance with the *norm* of Renaissance linear perspective. So it's a rather circular argument to say photographs "look real." They look as real as linear perspective looks and linear perspective looks real because it was accepted historically as the canon of what things really look like. Do they really look like that? That's where my own epistemological interest lies, but I do not pursue that here. I go into all this only to make a point about the historicity of our norms of progress or development in art, and therefore, *a fortiori*, about the norm of cognitive development in art, which underlies Blatt's historicist account of art history.

Another historicist theory of art, similar to this one, proposes that the history of art is really a history of problem solving. This, I believe, is also very close to Blatt's thesis. I think it's a very fruitful thesis. It's a kind of Deweyan–Piagetian–Gombrichian (and also, obviously, a Popperian) thesis. Still another way of looking at this is to say that the history of art is a history of the evolution of style. Here, we would take *styles* in art not simply as fashions or fads that happen to come one after the other, willy-nilly, simply on grounds of leaps of faith (or leaps of taste!) or as a result of the internal sociology of the professional community, but rather where we take style itself to be a kind of matrix of problems and solutions, research programs, if you like, which identify a certain community of artistic workers, craftsmen, or practitioners by the questions they ask themselves and the kind of answers to these questions they find acceptable. The *history* of style then becomes a history of problems posed and solved, new problems deriving from the solution of old ones. Apart from such notions of cognitive progress, in terms of problems and solutions, there is a peculiarly retrospective way of constructing the history of art as a history of styles phenomenologically, which reveals a great deal about the historicity of our own cultural consciousness. This is the phenomenological fact of how *dated* certain things look to us. If someone were to do a painting today *in the style of the 17th century*, we would say it looks like a 17th-century painting. It looks dated. We play on this dated look deliberately, when we "revive" a past style, for example, in fashion or in music or in literature. So too, in our futuristic visions, in science fiction, we populate the future with unmistakable hallmarks of our own present, anomalously. I think of the 1940 World's Fair *Futurama*, General Motors' contribution to imagining the future of cities and transportation. When I remember it *now*, from my childhood, what was regarded as futuristic *then* bears the clearly dated imprint of the 1940s imagination. Danto offers a very nice example of this, in talking about science fiction visions of the future that were proposed in the late 19th century. One such vision is of a futuristic restaurant in the sky, to which people would come by airships. But the restaurant itself is pictured as a fin de siècle institution, the waiters wear the aprons of that time, the ladies wear bustles, and so on.

The history of art may be reconstructed, then, on a variety of grounds, depending on the choice we make of a standpoint in the present from which we view the past. We may choose to view it from the standpoint of some schema of cognitive development, or of a sequence of problems and solutions, or of a history of styles, or in terms of our phenomenological consciousness of the pastness of the past, which is itself the product of the historicity of our cultural perception. But each of these presents us with an epistemological problem concerning the constitution of our knowledge claims: Is there *a* history of art, or are there alternative histories of art? To what degree do we impose a schema on the facts, and how tendentious is our reconstruction? How Procrustean are the efforts we make to fit the details into the schema? What empirical constraints are there on our theory construction, if the very facts we choose to account for are themselves theory- or schema-laden? And how would one criticize one schematism, if the grounds for critique inevitably entail an alternative schema? Here are some of the problems I have in attempting to assess Blatt's proposal, and also in finding some basis for my own criticisms. Without attempting to resolve these questions, let me proceed with some particular questions about Blatt's account.

The first concerns Blatt's view that Magdalenian art, in the cave paintings at Lascaux, Font de Gaume, and elsewhere, represents the sensorimotor stage in the art-historical analogy to cognitive development, and also the nominal scale of measurement, in which objects are represented by self-enclosed contours and remain isolated and unrelated to each other.

I must say that it never looked quite that way to me. For one thing, what seems to me a clear intimation of the ritual or practical functions of the paintings, as well as the very location of the paintings, deep in the caves, suggests a conceptually complex intentionality and therefore a network of relations in the cultural matrix in which the paintings had their significance. "Isolated" and "unrelated" may be criteria imposed from our later conception of a *framed* painting, where the related objects must be inside the frame. In religious painting and in Church art, the relations among objects in the paintings are often dependent on the placement of paintings in relation to each other, the different objects being related by this placement rather than within the same framed work. "One" painting, therefore, may include an ensemble of individual works in certain relations, and some of these relations may come to be understood only within the framework of a given religious culture or an iconographic tradition. Moreover, some of the cave paintings (e.g., the paintings of mammoths at Roussillon) portray not only "isolated" figures (in this now suspect sense) but herds or long processions of animals, and some of them fighting with each other.

Apparently, it also doesn't look the way Blatt interprets it to one of the deepest students of these paintings, Leroi-Gourhan (1965).[3] What he has discovered is that the paintings are not accidentally situated in isolation from each other. Leroi-Gourhan argues very persuasively that there is a complex cavewide pattern here, although we don't yet understand what it means. It turns out, on analysis, that only certain animals are represented in certain parts of the cave and other animals in other parts of the cave, and they occupy different parts of the cave in a very formal and strict arrangement. It required both thorough statistical analysis and sustained observation in many of the caves for Leroi-Gourhan to begin to see that there was some kind of deliberate pattern here. Now, we don't know what the significance of the pattern is because we don't know the form of life well enough yet. But I would not exclude the possibility that we may come to understand it if we ask the right questions. For then, either new evidence might be forthcoming, in response to newly framed inquiry, or presently available data may become relevant as evidence in a new framework. As tentative as all this is, it is enough to raise questions about Blatt's characterization of this early art and, therefore, to suggest that the more general schema may have some difficulties in the details.

I also raise a question about how "early" this art is, especially because Blatt locates it as a stage in a scheme of cognitive development. Cave paintings are, needless to say, earlier than what came later. That's tautological. But in terms of some schema of the cognitive development of modes of representation, I wouldn't call the cave paintings "early." I would think that they are rather late. That is to say, the Lascaux paintings, or any of the other cave paintings of the Magdalenian era, had very likely been preceded by perhaps 100,000 years of earlier attempts at representation (given how long even small changes in style and technique take in our record of prehistoric artifacts). Lascaux represents a highly developed level of sophisticated, really exceptional drawing. In elegance of line and in the extraordinary sensibility to the vitality of the animals' motions, I don't think there has been anything to beat it since in the way of animal drawings. In this respect, I don't think one can speak of progress in the drawing of animals. It is true that they are side views only. But whether this represents a *cognitive* limitation, rather than a choice of what it was relevant to portray, or what was a matter of stylistic convention, we cannot say. What we can say is that this level of sophistication in draftsmanship, representational skill, and observation is obviously the

---

[3]See especially Vol. II, p. 218ff; also Leroi-Gourhan, 1964–1965.

result of a very long history of artistic practice and cultural development. Therefore, it seems implausible to propose, as Blatt does, that in that period of time what was attained was no more than the sensorimotor preoperational stage. It underestimates the subtlety and conceptual complexity of the art of our nearer forebears. They were a very sophisticated bunch of painters. This, therefore, is one problem I have with the developmental model that Blatt proposes, even if only heuristically.

There is a second case of such interpretive difficulty in the details of Blatt's schema, and that concerns the relative cognitive achievement represented by the development of linear perspective in the representation of space and objects. This presents a striking case, because so much of Western and Eastern painting has not only failed to use perspective but has deliberately eschewed it even when it was available as an option, technically. In fact, much of Asian and Western representational painting and drawing has used *reverse* perspective, that is, where the foreshortening is "the other way around," so to speak: Lines designating parallel edges of objects tend to diverge rather than to converge, with distance. Boxes and houses are wider at the ends further away from us than they are up front, so they look *to us* like trapezoidal figures instead of rectangles. (I'll explain why I italicized "to us" shortly.) We know that this "looks wrong" because we can just look and "see" that it looks wrong. And, of course, if we look at the world "out there," we can just "see" (and also *know*, by unconscious inference, as Helmholtz described it) that the world looks the way correct paintings look (i.e., the way it is correctly represented by the use of linear perspective).

One afternoon, driving up FDR Drive North at about 34th Street, south of the UN building, I had this visual epiphany: The UN building—a cleanly rectangular solid—appeared to me in reverse perspective! It gave all the appearances of having been built wrong, because the side of it that was further away from me diverged instead of converging. I said to myself: "Come on, you've been writing too much stuff about this and you're beginning to convince yourself that you're right even though what you've been saying is obviously false." I urged myself to take another look! Well, I have looked at a lot of buildings since then. And the fact is they look like they diverge in the distance instead of converging. Then again, they sometimes look like they converge, the way they are supposed to. Of course, the parallel lines don't diverge, but neither do they converge. They just *look that way* perspectively. Perhaps because they are parallel, and I expect them to converge perspectively with distance, I may be overcompensating for their "known" parallelism, and thus they "appear" to diverge. Or perhaps my vision is being affected by looking at a lot of Chinese and Persian and Byzantine paintings using reverse perspective. But shouldn't there be a way they look, independently of how one or another stylistic convention represents them?

What I think about this (and have argued for elsewhere) is that there is no way things look apart from the way in which we have gotten used to representing them and gotten used to seeing them (see Wartofsky, 1972, 1978, 1980). And if I, for one, have gotten used to seeing them two different ways, I'm going to get duck–rabbit effects in my perception of the visual world; that is, the visual world is perceptually underdetermined with respect to what it looks like, and the determination of it is very much a matter of the history of our culture and the history of our art and particularly of our representational art. But it seems to me that there is nothing in this that speaks to any scheme of cognitive development. Representation in accordance with the rules of linear perspective emerges historically in connection with a host of other developments in mathematics, in church architecture and in city planning, in physical science, in politics and theology, in technology and crafts (e.g., in connection with scenic design, and with floor mosaics, in ancient Greece; with false painted windows with outdoor scenes on them, in ancient Pompeii; in connection with Roger Bacon's theological notions of light and infinity; in connection with the use of the cartographic grid in Renaissance map making, and on and on, in one of the most richly researched moments in the history of art). Certainly, this representational mode is an achievement, and certainly it is the result of what preceded it. It is a development of human knowledge and skill, and of aesthetic possibilities. But cognitive development, if I understand it correctly, is a matter of supersession: of going beyond the limits of the previous stage to a more inclusive grasp of things, while preserving what was attained as the condition for the development. The higher stages are not only cumulative but normatively more fully developed. Cognitive growth is cognitive progress. Contrary to Blatt (and to Gablik and others), I think there is no progress in art of this kind. Just as Beethoven is not an improvement on Mozart, simply because his work is a development from that of Mozart, linear perspective is not a cognitive improvement on what preceded it. It is a different tune.

REFERENCES

Blatt, S. J., & Blatt, E. S. (1984). *Continuity and change in art: The development of modes of representation*. Hillsdale, NJ: Lawrence Erlbaum Associates.

Danto, A. (1986). *The philosophical disenfranchisement of art*. New York: Columbia University Press.

Gablik, S. (1977). *Progress in art*. New York: Rizzoli.

Gombrich, E. H. (1960). *Art and illusion: A study in the psychology of pictorial representation*. Princeton, NJ: Princeton University Press.

Holly, M. A. (1984). *Panofsky and the foundations of art history.* Ithaca & London: Cornell University Press.

Leroi-Gourhan, A. (1964–1965). *Préhistoire de l'art occidental* [The prehistory of western art]. Paris: Edition d'art L. Mazenod.

Leroi-Gourhan, A. (1965). *Le geste et la parole* [word and gesture]. Paris: Editions Albin Michel.

Marx, K. (1973). *Grundrisse* (M. Nicolaus, Trans.). New York: Vintage.

Popper, K. R. (1957). *The poverty of historicism.* Boston: Beacon.

Stevens, S. S. (1951). Mathematics, measurement, and psychophysics. In S. Stevens (Ed.), *Handbook of experimental psychology* (pp. 1–49). New York: Wiley.

Wartofsky, M. (1972). Pictures, representation and the understanding. In I. Scheffler & R. Rudner (Eds.), *Logic and art: Essays in honor of Nelson Goodman* (pp. 150–162). Indianapolis & New York: Bobbs-Merrill. Reprinted in M. Wartofsky (1979), *Models: Representation and the Scientific Understanding* (pp. 175–187). Dordrecht & Boston: Reidel.

Wartofsky, M. (1978). Rules and representations: The virtues of fidelity and constancy put in perspective. *Erkenntniss, XII,* 17–36.

Wartofsky, M. (1979). Perception, representation and the forms of action: Towards an historical epistemology. In M. Wartofsky, *Models: Representation and the scientific understanding* (pp. 188–210). Dordrecht & Boston: Reidel.

Wartofsky, M. (1980). Visual scenarios: The role of representation in visual perception. In M. Hagen (Ed.), *The perception of pictures* (Vol. II, pp. 131–152). New York & London: Academic Press.

Wartofsky, M. (1987). Epistemology historicized. In A. Shimony & D. Nails (Eds.), *Evolutionary epistemology* (pp. 357–377). Dordrecht & Boston: Reidel.

12

Response to Wartofsky

Sidney J. Blatt
Yale University
New Haven, CT

I want to thank Professor Wartofsky for his provocative and informative commentary on my chapter and our book, *Continuity and Change in Art: The Development of Modes of Representation* (Blatt & Blatt, 1984). His challenging comments and observations provide me an opportunity to clarify and elaborate some of the basic assumptions underlying my work assessing the development, in Western civilization, of the capacity to represent spatiotemporal dimensions on the two-dimensional surface of the picture plane. I respond neither as a philosopher of science nor as an art historian, but as a psychologist primarily interested in processes of mental representation in normal and disrupted psychological development and, as expressed in this work, in cultural development as well. As a psychologist, I view historical analyses as essentially retrospective narrative constructions of a particular topic, during a particular time, from a particular point of view. In this sense, there is no one history of any topic or of any period but a variety of histories, each constructed from a particular vantage point that describes, assesses, and evaluates aspects of prior events from a perspective somewhat different than the views that predominated when the events occurred. Any reconstruction, like any experience of a contemporary event, is always made from a particular orientation and, therefore, is limited by the particular orientation, vision, and assumptions of the observer.

Approaches to developmental processes, likewise, vary as a consequence of the assumptions of the observer. Every approach to reconstruct development and/or history is theory laden; therefore, it is not possible to have "a history of art *proper*—i.e., as the objective history of art, what 'actually happened.' " We are always working with developmental narratives and thus it is impossible to assume that any reconstruction will be *the* authentic chronicle—one that "get[s] the facts straight and . . . make[s] of art history an account of what . . . actually happened . . . without interpretation." The task in any reconstructive process (historical or developmental) is to make as explicit as possible the interpretative frame within which the work is conducted and to seek to evaluate, independent of the reconstructive analysis, the validity of the basic assumptions of that interpretative frame. The primary interpretative frame in my art-historical analysis derives in large part from Piaget, which Wartofsky links to Hegel and his assumptions that development is an expression of "increasing liberations of the Spirit . . . as it attains . . . the fully rational and mature . . . world view in which the Absolute Idea comes to complete self-knowledge." Although Wartofsfy acknowledges that I (and for that matter, Piaget) do not presuppose this preordained limit to cognitive development, Wartofsky views my model as having an implicit telos because he interprets my conception of cognitive development as assuming that human reason eventually will come "to know the world the way it really is . . . [in] the adult scientific world view." Quite to the contrary, I (and I think Piaget) assume that the understanding of the phases or stages in human cognitive development is an ever-evolving construction established at a particular moment from a particular vantage point. Although these constructions are probably correct to a substantial degree, they, by definition, remain open to subsequent revision as we learn more about development and as the human condition changes.

Wartofsky correctly describes my position as one that assumes that all historical reconstruction is "colored by the interpretative standpoint of its time and place." Wartofsfy, however, assumes that this leads to the necessity of making a "critical choice" among alternative histories of art. Quite to the contrary, I believe that we do not have to assume "that there is just *one* history of art, i.e., a canonical, linear, and inclusive history of art whose developmental scheme . . . yields the essential truth about the development of art." Rather, I assume that there are multiple histories of any phenomena including art, and, depending on the dimensions(s) considered in the analysis, there may be different configurations of change and different developmental sequences. Not all aspects of art-historical development will necessarily follow the same developmental pathways and the same developmental principles, and some processes may not have a developmental progression at all. In my work, I propose that one important dimension in art-historical development, namely the capacity for representing spatiotemporal dimensions on a two-dimensional surface, has certain fascinating parallels with the development of concepts of space and time through the life cycle and with concepts of scaling. Therefore, the cultural development of these dimensions seems to follow some basic cognitive developmental principles. I assume that other dimensions in art history might follow different developmental trajectories or not even be part of any developmental sequence. The task for subsequent art historians (or philosophers or even psychologists) is to seek possible integrations of different art-historical analyses, taken from different perspectives and based on different theoretical assumptions, and to consider how the development of these different dimensions of art might be interrelated. I believe that an important strand in such an integration would require acknowledging that one essential element in art-historical analyses is the cognitive evolution of the capacity to represent spatial–temporal dimensions in an increasingly differentiated, articulated, organized, and integrated fashion.

Wartofsky's concerns about establishing the precise and authoritative historical account of art, "one which gets the facts straight," influences his interpretation of art as seen in his seeming assumption that art reached an apparent ideal endpoint or telos with Brunelleschi and Alberti's development of linear perspective—when they "finally get(s) the geometry straight" and "solve(d) the problem of representing space and objects the way they really are." Wartofsky seems to assume that the development of linear perspective is the endpoint of a developmental sequence— the telos of "the dominant idea of what the development of art should be." Although I agree with Wartofsky that the capacity for "optical duplication" (Danto, 1986) dominated artistic style for approximately 5 centuries, it is not an ideal endpoint of a developmental sequence. The belief that linear perspective ("the representation of space and of objects in the way they really are") is a telos is as much an illusion as the belief that there exists an objective history of art that reports things as they really happened.

Consistent with Panofsky (1924/1925), I view linear perspective as another, albeit very important, step in the development of the capacity to represent aspects of space and time on a two-dimensional surface. But much of subsequent art, beginning with Mannerism and the Baroque and certainly Impressionism, Cubism, and aspects of Modern Art, has been an attempt to overcome the constraints of the compelling geometric solution of linear perspective in order to find methods for representing additional aspects of space and time on the picture plane. I agree with Wartofsky that linear perspective—what he and Danto call the optical duplication of nature—was a consequence of the dominant world view that began in the quatro and cinquecento. But it is important to stress that more recent artistic styles (e.g., Impressionism, Cubism, and Modern

Art) are also expressions of a dominant world view, one that occurred later, not only in art but in literature, science, and mathematics as well. I agree with Wartofsky's assumption that art, like most of a culture's intellectual activity, is a reflection of its dominant world view. But I disagree with Wartofsky's assumption that "the project of optical duplication . . . was given up only when [its] aim could now be achieved with the camera." Quite to the contrary, the move in art to modes of representation beyond optical duplication was an essential expression of a pervasive move throughout our culture from a Cartesian–Newton to an Einsteinian conception of nature. Much as the Einsteinian conception of the universe and of nature was an elaboration, extension, and revision of the Cartesian–Newtonian world view (a developmental progression, if you will), so too Impressionism, Cubism, and much of Modern Art were extensions of Renaissance linear perspective and the subsequent experimentations with and revisions of linear perspective that began primarily in Mannerist and Baroque art.

Linear perspective is a major nodal point in the development of modes of representing space and time on a two-dimensional surface, not so much because it creates the optical illusion of duplicating nature but because it is a quantitative method that coordinates, in an integrated and systematic fashion, the manifest dimensions of the scene being portrayed. The systematic quantitative integration of various aspects and dimensions in a coordinated portrayal of the scene is the essential quality that makes linear perspective such a remarkably important stage in the development of modes of artistic representation in Western civilization. And it is this extensive, systematic, quantitative coordination that creates the compelling optical duplication of nature. In the study of the development of modes of representing dimensions of time and space in other cultures such as in Eastern art, one would seek to identify such an integrative phase, one that may or may not have led to optical duplication as accomplished by linear perspective, but a phase in which various manifest features of the scene are presented in an extensive systematic, integrated, and coordinated fashion.

Progress in science and art does not occur as a function of seeking some ideal goal or telos but primarily as a function of reactions and responses to perceived inconsistencies and inadequacies of prior solutions and conceptualizations. We are clearly unable to define where we are going or we would already be there; but we can eventually recognize, acknowledge, and revise the inadequacies and insufficiencies in our current formulations and understanding and seek new conceptualizations that more fully account for the facts as we are currently aware of them. Progress in art as well as in science is the consequence of the identification of problems currently defined and solved, in which new solutions not only resolve some of the contradictions of past conceptualizations but also eventually provide the basis for others to identify some of our deficiencies and seek solutions that compensate for these deficiencies. In this regard, Wartofsky and I seem to be in agreement that progress occurs through resolution of inconsistencies and inadequacies of past solutions, although Wartofsky seems to reserve this view to a discussion of style and seems reluctant to view this model as the basis for considering the development of certain dimensions in art history. But the history of style in art is a history of art, and it is this process of different periods in art seeking solutions to the inadequacies of the representations of prior periods that gives art as well as science its developmental history. For example, one must assume that the epistemological dilemmas Wartofsky poses about our current attempts to evaluate aspects of art history will be partially resolved by subsequent generations of scholars who will identify inadequacies and insufficiencies in our contemporary formulations, but who will also be struggling with their concerns about their own epistemological dilemmas as they seek solutions to our insufficiencies.

In terms of Wartofsky's comments about the cave paintings in Magdalenian art, the figures in these paintings are in isolation not because the painting lacks a frame but because the figures were not portrayed in interaction. Although Leroi-Gourhan (1967) has demonstrated that the placement of these figures was not accidental and that certain animals are portrayed in clusters in special locations throughout the caves, each figure is portrayed in isolation with emphasis primarily on the contour of the isolated figure, without any systematic attempt to represent the depth of the figure or the context. Although the figures are extraordinary in their elegant simplicity of just a few lines to capture remarkable vitality, the figures lack a sense of dimensionality. Their systematic placement in the caves expresses the meanings assigned to each of the types of animals—their relative accessibility, value, and/or danger—but their systematic placement in various parts of the caves does not alter the fact that the figures express a relatively early mode of artistic representation because each of the figures lacks indication of any attempt to integrate and coordinate various spatial dimensions of the figure or the spatial dimensions of a field in which the figures could be in interaction. It was only somewhat later in cave paintings, in the Mesolithic period, that representations of animal and human forms were organized in coherent interacting groups around the shared activities of a hunt, battle, harvest, or ritual dance.

The essential point in evaluating the developmental level of the representation of space and time in the picture plane is not how the painting looks or its aesthetic appeal but its level of cognitive organization—its degree of differentiation, articulation, organization, and integration. Much as science has a developmental progression, so too the cognitive organization of painting. The representation of space and time in science, as well as in art, has progressed in a systematic fashion. Each succeeding level of representation is generally more differentiated, coordinated, and integrated because of prior achievements. To debate the relative value, beauty, or degree of improvement of earlier and later contributions is a distraction from recognizing and appreciating how later developments depend on and emerge from prior contributions. Later contributions are no better than earlier ones; later contributions are usually just more differentiated, articulated, organized, and integrated than earlier ones because they have been built on these prior contributions. The representation of dimensions of space and time in the picture plane provides vivid examples of how succeeding epochs depended on the remarkable contributions of earlier periods to achieve modes of representations that were more encompassing. Depending on aesthetic sensibilities, one might value different phases and different modes of artistic representation, but analyses of spatiotemporal dimensions clearly indicate how succeeding periods were established in response to perceived inadequacies and insufficiencies and were elaborations, extensions, and revisions of prior contributions. Whereas I agree with Wartofsky—my aesthetic sensibilities also prefer a Mozart quartet to a Beethoven symphony—I assume that the basic organization and temporal structure inherent in Beethoven's compositions are more articulated, differentiated, and integrated than those of Mozart, in large part because of Mozart's prior accomplishments. Likewise, whereas I enjoy much more fully the quiet serenity of Giotto's Scrovegni Chapel in Padua than I do the grandeur of Michelangelo's Sistine Ceiling in Rome, there is no question that the complexity, scope, and grandeur of Michelangelo's work is in large part due to Giotto's accomplishments some 2 centuries earlier (Blatt, in press). And in turn, Picasso's early 20th-century development of Cubism, with its attempts to represent multiple perspectives simultaneously, as well as aspects of the inner form and structure of objects, was built on the accomplishment of linear perspective that occurred in the Renaissance, from Giotto to Michelangelo. It is this process of elaboration, extension, and revision that gives aspects of art, like aspects of science, their developmental history. The basic question, however, is not whether there is developmental progression in the evolution of cognitive structures in art and science, but whether this developmental progression follows some fundamental developmental principles that can be defined independent of the developmental sequences observed in art and science. The basic point in my analysis of the development of the representation of space and time in the picture plane in the art of Western civilization is that these representations follow some fundamental developmental principles that have been observed in another process—in the cognitive development of the child. Following Wartofsky's contrast of Mozart and Beethoven, it would be a fascinating analysis to explore how and in what ways the child's development of a sense of time and the concept of number provides guidelines for understanding the development of the basic structural and temporal organization in musical compositions in the history of Western civilization. The fundamental assumption in this exploration, as in my explorations in the history of art, would be that there are fundamental processes involved in all cognitive development, whether this development is observed in the individual or in culture. The identification of dimensions of these fundamental principles in one domain may serve to increase our sensitivity to aspects of this development in other domains.

REFERENCES

Blatt, S. J. (in press). A psychoanalytic appreciation of Giotto's mode of artistic representation and its implications for Renaissance art and science. *Psychoanalytic Study of the Child.*

Blatt, S. J., & Blatt, E. S. (1984). *Continuity and change in art: The development of modes of representation.* Hillsdale, NJ: Lawrence Erlbaum Associates.

Danto, A. (1986). *The philosophical disenfranchisement of art.* New York: Columbia University Press.

Leroi-Gourhan, A. (1967). *Treasures of prehistoric art* (N. Guterman, Trans.). New York: Abrams.

Panofsky, E. (1924/1925). Die perspektive als "symbolische form." *Vortrage der Bibliothek Warburg,* 258–330. Leipzig and Berlin.

Author Index

Subject Index

255